The Myth of Fair and
Efficient Government

The Myth of Fair and Efficient Government

Why the Government You Want
Is Not the One You Get

Michael L. Marlow

 PRAEGER

AN IMPRINT OF ABC-CLIO, LLC
Santa Barbara, California • Denver, Colorado • Oxford, England

Library of Congress Cataloging-in-Publication Data

Marlow, Michael L.
　　The myth of fair and efficient government : why the government you want is not the one you get / Michael L. Marlow.
　　　p. cm.
　　Includes bibliographical references and index.
　　ISBN 978-0-313-39291-7 (hardcopy : alk. paper) — ISBN 978-0-313-39292-4 (ebook)
　1. Administrative agencies—United States—Management.　2. Fiscal policy—United States.
3. Taxation—United States.　I. Title.
　　JK421.M346　2011
　　351.73—dc22　　　　2011007608

ISBN: 978-0-313-39291-7
EISBN: 978-0-313-39292-4

15　14　13　12　　　　　　2　3　4　5

This book is also available on the World Wide Web as an eBook.
Visit www.abc-clio.com for details.

Praeger
An Imprint of ABC-CLIO, LLC

ABC-CLIO, LLC
130 Cremona Drive, P.O. Box 1911
Santa Barbara, California 93116-1911

This book is printed on acid-free paper ∞

Manufactured in the United States of America

Contents

Preface

This book is written for readers curious about why they are so disappointed with federal government. Readers are unlikely to ever look at government the same again, but will understand the necessary steps for true reform. My book explains that growing disappointment stems from citizens asking too much of government and politicians overpromising what they can deliver. This is a surefire recipe for an ever-expanding government that fails to meet expectations of citizens. The book concludes with a chapter on improving government. Eliminating ill-suited tasks and fixing fundamental structural flaws are the only effective means of achieving greater satisfaction.

Our disappointment owes much to mistaken promises that government so easily improves upon market outcomes. Markets are often mischaracterized in ways that overstate their failings. Mischaracterization is common because markets mostly work underneath the surface of everyday life. It is difficult to appreciate what is mostly unseen. Markets are imperfect, but they receive far too little credit for their ability to reach efficient and fair outcomes. Misplaced beliefs that markets are mostly to blame for economic problems offer a one-way ticket to disappointment.

Myths of efficient and fair government encourage many ill-suited tasks that, in effect, continually repeat government mistakes of the past. Blaming markets for the failures of government has become an all too common theme that often results in even more government. Recent dramatic growth of government comes with extraordinarily high expectations of performing amazing feats well beyond its capabilities. Government that takes on too many tasks is one destined for poor performance.

Ideas for this book come from over 30 years of both working in federal government and teaching at several universities. My five years at the U.S. Treasury during the 1980s offered a front-row seat to the practice of government. Those five years provided a lifetime of questions concerning the role of government in our lives that my research has attempted to answer. Many topics addressed in this book were introduced to me during my role as a government economist. I have been fortunate to have been able to use my research on government policy in the classroom. My courses emphasize the difference between theory and practice of government that is so often neglected in the academy.

Although this book is largely a personal statement, I have many people to thank. I have been lucky to have worked with numerous gifted coauthors over the years. These include, in alphabetical order, William T. Boyes, Gordon L. Brady, W. Mark Crain, Barrie M. Craven, John Dunham, David Joulfaian, Neela Manage, Angelo R. Mascaro, William Orzechowski, Alden F. Shiers, and George E. Wright. I am especially indebted to Alden F. Shiers, William Orzechowski, and Wayne Farel for many useful comments on early drafts of this book. I also want to thank Brian Romer, senior acquisitions editor at Praeger/ABC-CLIO, who has offered wonderful insights into improving my writing style.

My wife, Valerie Marlow, and our children, Emily and Graham, have graciously endured many months of my writing. The importance of their unwavering support, in both small and large ways, cannot be overstated.

ONE

Our Disappointment with Government

KEY POINTS IN THIS CHAPTER

- Government is called upon to correct failings of markets, but widespread misunderstanding of markets leads to programs that often make matters worse.

- Americans understand recent rapid growth of government is bad, but somehow it continues expanding even as our disappointment grows.

- Good intentions of government rarely match actual consequences. Government programs come with both benefits and costs.

- Thorough assessment of efficiency and equity of government programs requires full disclosure of both winners and losers.

- The key to raising satisfaction with government is to assign it appropriate tasks with the knowledge that both markets and government are imperfect.

Disappointment with government is an equal-opportunity emotion. Few are pleased with its performance as demonstrated by recent polls revealing that almost four out of five Americans distrust government.[1] Figure 1.1 shows just how bad the experience has become for most Americans: distrust rose from 23 percent in 1960 to today's 78 percent.

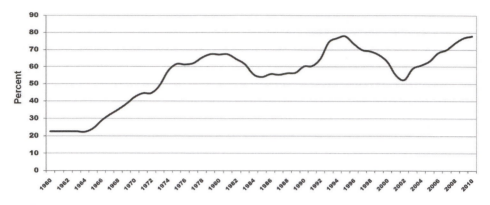

Figure 1.1 Percent Who Distrust Federal Government. (*Source:* Pew Research Center.)

The same poll also made clear just how poorly politicians are viewed when compared to other professions: from low to high trust were: Finance (22%), Congress (24%), Big Businesses (25%), National Media (31%), Unions (32%), Entertainment Industry (33%), White House (45%), Church (63%), Technology Firms (68%), and Small Businesses (71%). That trust of the Presidency (45%) was nearly double that of Congress (24%) suggests faint praise at best.

The following mishmash of ideas is often used to explain widespread disappointment with government:

- growing bickering between political parties,
- Internet bloggers spewing ideological venom,
- out-of-control costs of government programs,
- an unending spate of scandals involving politicians,
- growing influence of special interest groups,
- declining newspaper readership,
- the rich not paying their fair share of taxes, and
- growing influence of corporate lobbyists.

Perpetual repetition has a way of making these claims represent truth. But, these perennial complaints offer no new insights and merely reflect symptoms rather than causes of our disappointment. It is little wonder so many of us are so puzzled that government continually fails to meet expectations.

A critical but overlooked piece to the puzzle is that government exists because of our disappointment with markets. Markets—also known as free markets, capitalism, or private markets—determine production, prices, and income through the process of supply and demand. Complaints about markets center on two issues: efficiency and fairness of market outcomes. Government is thus offered as the remedy to our disappointment over efficiency and fairness of market outcomes. Proposed remedies are plentiful and have led to dramatic growth of government based on promises that remedies improve upon market outcomes.

Government policies or programs are general terms that describe these remedies. It is customary to measure government by its spending, although regulations, laws, taxation, employment, and debt should also be considered when measuring government's influence on our lives. A short list of proposed remedies includes:

- minimum wage laws for low-income workers,
- bailouts of bankrupt businesses,
- regulation of the financial industry,
- laws setting maximum rents landlords may charge residents,
- regulations establishing minimum gas mileage requirements,
- social security programs providing income to retirees,
- allowing mortgage interest to be deducted from taxable income,
- mandates establishing health insurance coverage,
- lending to college students, and
- subsidization of alternative energy sources.

Government arises from beliefs that it *should, can, and will* remedy our disappointment with market outcomes.

The rapid rise of federal government spending (in 2009 dollars and on a per capita basis) is displayed in Figure 1.2.[2] In 1900, per capita spending was $177 in 2009 dollars. By 2015, spending per capita is projected to rise to $12,337—a 6,870 percent increase! A recent poll found that a majority (56% vs. 34%) of American voters thinks the country is moving toward socialism.[3] But, less than one in five voters (18%) felt that moving away from markets was good for the country. Sixty-nine percent of voters believe moving toward socialism is bad for the country. Apparently American voters understand government expansion is bad, but somehow it continues expanding even as our disappointment grows.

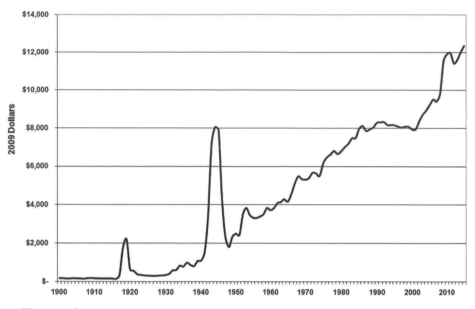

Figure 1.2 Per Capita Federal Spending, 1900–2015. (*Source:* Office of Management and Budget.)

The irony is that our disappointment arises because of mistaken promises that government so easily improves upon market outcomes. Recent rapid growth in government comes with extraordinarily high expectations of performing amazing feats well beyond its capabilities. One reason is that markets are often mischaracterized in ways that overstate their failings. Markets are imperfect, but they receive too little credit for their ability to reach efficient and fair outcomes. Myths of efficient and fair government also encourage government to undertake more ill-suited tasks that breed even more discontent with its performance. Both reasons go a long way toward explaining our growing disappointment with government.

Consider laws mandating minimum wages paid to low-income workers who are unable to command income sufficient to meet minimal standards of living. These laws are very popular with the public, despite the fact that such laws create fewer jobs because low-skill workers become costlier to hire. Markets set wages on the basis of supply and demand and not on the basis of what income workers "should" receive in order to meet minimal standards of living. In effect, minimum wage laws address symptoms—low wages—rather than causes—low demand for and high supply of such workers. It is easy to believe such laws magically raise wages without raising unemployment when we do not understand how markets promote efficient outcomes.

The following vicious cycle timeline follows enactment of a minimum wage hike.

- Step 1: A symptom—low wages—is identified by politicians as a problem stemming from markets.

- Step 2: Government action—minimum wage law—is proposed to remedy the low wage problem. No mention is made that these laws harm workers who lose their jobs.

- Step 3: Government statistics reveal unemployment rises for low-income workers. Politicians now attempt to remedy two problems—low wages and fewer jobs—without realizing their past action—minimum wage law—created fewer jobs.

- Step 4: Markets are blamed again. Another minimum wage hike is proposed to remedy worsening conditions of the poor. Again, there is no mention that these laws harm workers who lose their jobs.

- Step 5: Cycle keeps churning as government and disappointment grow in tandem.

Before the reader quits in despair, please understand my encouraging message: rethinking the joint cults of over-promising by politicians and over-demanding by citizens improves satisfaction with government. Simply put, citizens expect government to solve any problem they assign it and politicians over-promise what they can deliver. Disappointment is inevitable from this perspective and requires a strong dose of realism before we can become more satisfied. The essential question is: Which fails more at various tasks, markets or governments? This issue leads us to determine what role for government serves us best.

This book is written for readers curious about why the government they want is so often disconnected from the one they receive. My ultimate ambition is for readers to respond, "Duh! What do you expect?" when explaining to friends that disappointment stems from citizens asking too much and politicians over-promising. Eliminating ill-suited tasks and fixing fundamental structural flaws are the only effective means of achieving greater satisfaction. Government that takes on too many tasks will likely perform few of them well. The rest of this chapter introduces basic themes developed throughout this book that help us understand why commonly held views of markets and government are often incorrect and thus responsible for much of our misery.

INTENTIONS DO NOT GUARANTEE CONSEQUENCES

Understanding actual consequences of government requires caution, patience, humility, and willingness to peel back layers underneath good intentions. Government is based on good intentions since otherwise there would be no supporters. Passionate promises of improved lives are often based on the government *should, can, and will* mentality that apparently dulls interest in assessing how well consequences match intentions. Consequences are often unintended, opposite to intentions, and in evidence months or years following action. We would have solved our problems long ago if all it took were good intentions and there would be no need for this book.

Policies are often chosen solely on intentions simply because of their close match with short-term consequences. This close connection provides instant gratification that is very hard to resist. Rather like the immediate gratification that comes from eating pizza, ice cream, and chocolate. We feel great while eating these foods, but then we feel sick when we overindulge and then are also disappointed when we gain weight. The lure of immediate gratification associated with intended consequences tempts all of us.

Many find it troubling to doubt the importance of good intentions. "There ought to be a law" is a frequently uttered solution toward perceived injustices. But noble intentions rarely predict consequences perfectly. Consider monthly payments of $750 to the unemployed. At first glance this appears a perfect fit between consequence and good intentions since the jobless can buy more food, health care, and other necessities. However, payments lessen resolves to search for work thus rewarding behavior opposite to good intentions. Skills erode as well during bouts of unemployment that make job applicants less attractive to employers. Skeptics argue eliminating programs make recipients $750 poorer, and while this argument has some merit, it loses steam the longer workers remain unemployed. Surely, not all unemployed lessen job search, but short-term improvements need to be weighed against longer-term harm. The $750 also has to be taken away from other citizens, thus harming them. Intentions easily match consequences only when we ignore harm.

Grants for college students provide another example. Recent years have seen rapid tuition hikes that have been met with programs aimed at helping students attend college. Intended consequences—more college students—sync quickly with initial consequences. But, the story does not end here. Rising tuition rates are an unintended consequence because these programs raise demand for college.[4] Focusing on immediate benefits— enrollment gains—while ignoring longer-term harm—tuition hikes and higher taxes—promotes the vicious cycle of government expansion discussed above. Intentions do not so easily match consequences when we consider unintended harm.

Examples abound. The U.S. Department of Transportation may now fine airlines up to $27,500 per passenger for any tarmac delay lasting more than three hours. The new rule was applauded by all who have ever suffered through long delays on tarmacs. The rule took effect in April 2010 and was aimed at decreasing long flight delays as well as making passengers more comfortable by requiring airlines to provide food, drinking water, and working toilets. But, regulations usually have unintended consequences. One is that cancellations will increase since the rule does not apply to cancelled flights. Passengers who end up rebooking flights back at the terminal may not be amused. Also, rules don't apply to foreign airlines or international flights thus raising possibilities their passengers will sit on tarmacs for longer periods of time.

Policies that push us into fuel-saving automobiles are intended to reduce our dependence on oil and decrease air pollution, but they also encourage more driving due to better fuel economy. Policies that encourage more driving also promote traffic congestion. Regulations that make lighting more efficient will tend to increase energy use as consumers respond to lower prices.[5] Consumers will want more of it—more lighting fixtures and they will have less incentive to turn them off while not in use. Paper recycling policies decrease demand for new pulp, but tree planting also falls due to decreased demand for new pulp. Fire prevention efforts in forests promote future fires that are more frequent and costly as they foster buildup of more brush. Fire protection also encourages building of homes in wooded areas thus raising future public spending on firefighting. A vicious cycle erupts whereby more policy "fixes" are proposed even though current problems are partially caused by past actions—more stringent fuel standards, more efficient lighting, more recycling, and higher spending on firefighting.

Thirty states in the United States, as well as the District of Columbia, have banned cell phone texting while driving. Bans are designed to keep drivers' attention on driving rather than texting. But a recent study of four states with bans finds that more road crashes rather than fewer resulted from bans in three of those four states.[6] Apparently, drivers addicted to texting drive more recklessly because they attempt to hide the fact they are texting in order to avoid fines. Again, good intentions rarely indicate adverse consequences.

Unintended adverse consequences of policies often surface later thus fostering dissatisfaction after their introduction. This mismatch in timing makes it difficult to put two and two together and connect today's disappointment with yesterday's policies. Confusion is inevitable, especially when policy proponents promised immediate benefits while ignoring longer-term harm. It is easy to push for government expansion when today's problems are believed to be unrelated to past government "fixes." This provides a one-way ticket to growing dissatisfaction.

The focus on immediate gratification is fostered by the fact that successful politicians win elections by focusing on the next election. U.S. representatives are elected every two years, senators every six years, and presidents every four years. Politicians thus cater to immediate gratification preferences as long as voters either don't comprehend or care about longer-term harm from well-intentioned government programs. Skeptics might claim politicians serve the greater good and thus would never sacrifice longer-term harm for the sake of winning elections. But, why would politicians seeking reelection not cater to voter preferences for immediate gratification?

Let's play devil's advocate. Consider politicians who understand future harm is associated with policies offering immediate gratification. They would still cater to voter preferences if they want to win elections, especially when voters don't like hearing the bad news that policies offering immediate benefits come with longer-term harm. Politicians may ignore voter preferences, but they risk losing the next election as voters interpret their actions as admissions that they can't deliver on campaign promises. Meanwhile, enterprising competitors happily point out cases where incumbents failed to keep promises. Competitors are also likely to promise they can deliver immediate benefits without longer-term harm.

There is a delayed gratification problem. It is cute to see a young child spend every dollar they receive since they fail to see that saving yields greater future income. Mature individuals think longer term thus enabling them to stay in school and save for houses and retirement. But, citizens and politicians may find it hard to delay gratification for many reasons that include:

- immediate gratification is irresistible,
- inability to predict future harm from today's policies,

- a tax system makes us believe someone else pays,
- inability to connect today's problems with past government actions, and
- the assumption that most problems stem from markets.

Growing disappointment with an expanding government is unsurprising in this environment.

REALITY, NOT ROMANCE

Strong convictions that government *should, can, and will* improve our lives through its power, ingenuity, genuine compassion, and authority are often fueled by romantic visions of government. The romantic view is just as it sounds. It refers to beliefs that government exists simply to save us from market outcomes we don't like. It is also romantic to believe government remedies provide benefits with little or no harm.

Of course, romance is not always synonymous with reality. The fact that roughly 50 percent of marriages end in divorce indicates this cold reality. Most couples marry based on intentions of remaining together with great happiness. But, couples often face consequences out of sync with intentions. Many divorced people learn from bad experiences stemming from mistaken beliefs that romance always mirrors reality. Romantic views of government can also disappoint. Apparently, rising disappointment with government indicates that many citizens cling to romantic views of government, even as intentions and actual consequences dramatically collide.

Minimum wage law offers a clear example of believing a magic wand solves problems. Its intended consequence—higher wages for low-income workers—is noble and even the most unromantic of us finds it uncomfortable to point out it inflicts harm on workers who lose jobs. Fear of being viewed as unsympathetic toward the poor may also provide a strong incentive for many to refrain from pointing out basic economic principles. Reality is that wages are determined by supply and demand and not by what workers "should" earn. Romantics believe minimum wage hikes simply lead to higher wages and no lost jobs.

Consider the case of a new diet supplement advertised as a low-cost and effective method for losing weight. Tests of effectiveness should allow for different possibilities: weight loss, weight gain, no change in weight, or weight loss with some adverse side effects (e.g., nausea). Few of us would be content to simply believe its intended effect—losing weight—when it has not been proven. Some may be initially swayed by the romance of the moment since who does not want a low-cost effective treatment for weight loss? But, it pays to be suspicious when claims sound too good to be true. The same holds for government. We will be disappointed when we believe intended consequences—minimum wage laws unambiguously help the poor, for example—are true simply because we hope they are.

Realism versus romance also describes recent controversy about extending unemployment benefits. Harvard University economist Robert Barro calls the expansion of unemployment-insurance eligibility from 26 weeks to as much as 99 weeks in 2010 the "folly of subsidizing unemployment."[7] This extension has been motivated by compassion for those without jobs. However, it also raises unemployment because it subsidizes unemployment. Continued payments lessen incentives to search for jobs or to accept job offers. Barro's calculations suggest that unemployment would have been 6.8 percent by summer 2010, instead of 9.5 percent, if jobless benefits hadn't been extended to 99 weeks.

A realist accepts that designing effective government remedies is challenging, complex, and not guaranteed. Reality poses the need for careful thinking about both short-term and long-term consequences of government policies. Realism also encourages us to think long and hard before calling upon government to remedy problems that may have little to do with failings of markets. While unromantic, realism offers a better chance of being pleased with activities we demand our government engage in and that scaling back government should also be entertained as a solution to problems.

CONFUSING SYMPTOMS WITH CAUSES

Anyone who has dealt with a fever understands fevers represent symptoms rather than causes since otherwise we could just blame the rising liquid in the thermometer for our fevers. Most fevers resolve on their own, but more serious causes sometimes underlie unabated fevers. Prescribing analgesic medicines as the sole treatment for unabated fevers can be disastrous since they ignore causes as they focus on symptoms.

Confusing symptoms for causes holds true for our study of government. Our many problems—unemployment, poverty, obesity, illiteracy, homelessness, disease, poor health, and poor education, to name a few—are easy to spot and thus lead to many calls for government remedies. Symptoms, however, are much easier to spot than causes. Previous discussion of higher education grants, paper recycling, fuel standards, and forest fire prevention demonstrates unintended consequences from government actions unfolding over time that exert harm far outside intended consequences.

Our recent housing market crisis clearly fits this confusion. Everyone sees rising foreclosure rates, falling housing prices, and lost savings. These are symptoms, however, and not causes. Many policies—tax credits, government loan programs, community reinvestment mandates, regulation of financial institutions, government-sponsored enterprises such as Fannie Mae and Freddie Mac, subsidies for low-income and first-time borrowers, and low interest rate policies of the Federal Reserve, for example—have been introduced over many years. Policies addressed symptoms that included high mortgage payments and unequal access to financing. Government remedies were well intentioned and produced quick benefits. People that otherwise would not have purchased a home were able to do so. Many also purchased homes much larger than they would otherwise have chosen. So far, so good. Government was credited for much happiness among home owners.

Then the long-term unintended harm arrived. The eventual housing bubble was a rude awakening to those unable to make mortgage payments and those finding themselves "underwater" whereby home values were below what they owed. Some quickly assigned blame to markets as they pointed to symptoms such as falling housing prices, rising foreclosures, or the fact that high-risk borrowers had been given loans they were unlikely to afford. But, these symptoms arose after numerous government remedies aimed at "fixing" problems many believed solely stemmed from markets. These remedies were cheered by the public as their short-term benefits—more housing and rising prices—were enjoyed. But, eventually housing prices began to fall back toward earth as the longer-term harm phase from past government programs arrived.

The following framework orders questions in a way that provides clarity to the interrogative of whether markets or governments cause symptoms.

1. How do markets allocate resources in a world without government?
2. Are there problems with efficiency or fairness of market outcomes?
3. Can government improve upon efficiency or fairness of market outcomes?
4. What remedies might achieve desired improvements?
5. Do intended consequences match reality of programs?
6. If not, do we redesign remedies or ditch remedies and leave markets alone?

This ordering helps uncover answers to basic questions of whether markets or governments cause symptoms that breed discontent. The ordering is necessary because the real world consists of neither extreme—markets without government or government without markets. This sequence also avoids the vicious cycle that arises from common beliefs that most problems stem from markets.

THEORY IS NOT PRACTICE OF GOVERNMENT

This book presents the conventional theory of how government may promote efficient outcomes as taught in classrooms around the world. Interventions include providing public goods (e.g., national defense), controlling negative externalities (e.g., pollution), promoting positive externalities (e.g., vaccinations), policing competition in markets, conducting fiscal policy, and disseminating better information to consumers and producers. Markets may also be perceived to be unfair even when they achieve efficient outcomes. Efficiency and fairness are not synonymous and markets can only be expected to achieve the former. Promoting efficiency and fairness form the theoretical basis for the role of government in our economy.

A theoretical basis for government does not imply government intervention improves efficiency or fairness. Application of theory rarely coincides with expectations when placed in the context of reality. One high hurdle is that government lacks necessary information. It is easy to draw graphs in classrooms that clearly show efficient levels and what taxes, subsidies, spending programs, or regulations remedy market failings, but they are only perfect remedies within the classroom. Government—as an outside observer—of markets faces the Herculean task of gathering an immense amount of information that by its very nature no outside observer could ever imagine. Government is a very poor substitute for markets in these regards, no matter how wonderful motivations may be.

Also, government has veered far away from the theoretical basis for a limited role in our economy. Recent bailouts of failing businesses are prime examples where intervention is at odds with its mission of improving efficiency. It not surprising that businesses lobby for government protection, but this role is hardly compatible with the theory of government. Rather, these polices reflect "crony capitalism" whereby government chooses winners and losers rather than allowing markets to weed out inefficient businesses so that their resources may be more efficiently utilized by other businesses. Winners are owners and employees of "saved" businesses, but losers include owners, employees, and consumers of businesses receiving no protection and taxpayers footing the bailouts. The fact that bailouts create winners and losers demonstrates that their effects on fairness become debatable. Again, it is easy to become disappointed with government when any benefits it provides are believed to come with little or no cost.

Government also mostly redistributes income between citizens, though this fact is not commonly known. Politicians are happy to spend taxpayer dollars that serve their local constituents. Many recipients are not poor. Recent stimulus bills are "poster children" of pork barrel spending, despite promises that government spending reflects "investment" for all citizens. Senators Tom Coburn (R-OK) and John McCain (R-AZ) document a few of the more obvious pork barrel spending projects in the "stimulus" bill of $862 billion in 2009.[8] Their list includes:

- $554,763 for the Forest Service to replace windows in a closed visitor center (Mount St. Helens, WA),
- $1 million for new iPod Touches for high school students (Salt Lake City, UT),
- $1.9 million for international ant research (San Francisco, CA),
- $5 million for loans to liquor distilleries, breweries and wineries (CO),
- $521,005 for studying whether soda taxes can cure obesity (Chicago, IL), and
- $25,000 for the International Accordion Festival (San Antonio, TX).

Politicians used economic theory for "cover" when they argued that such programs would grow our economy. However, empirical evidence is clear that economies with growing governments are less efficient and thus grow slower than economies where government is kept in better check. Theory again does not match its practice. The above "stimulus" spending programs merely transfer income from one pocket to another. Taxpayer dollars are also less efficiently spent than when those same dollars are spent in markets. Again, a surefire recipe for disappointment with government is to believe programs yield benefits at little or no cost and to base government on theory rather than its practice.

FAIRNESS ASSESSMENT REQUIRES FULL DISCLOSURE

Government programs are frequently promoted on the basis of fairness. Fairness issues often focus on government's critical role in helping the truly needy among us. Citizens in ill health, the poorly educated, and those with very limited resources are clear examples. But, the very definition of fairness is usually given short shrift as if everyone understands its meaning. Unfortunately this is very far from reality and explains again why we are so often disappointed with the practice of government.

Recall our discussion of minimum wage laws. These laws are often believed to be fair because they remedy low wages for the poor. But, while these laws help those who keep their jobs, these laws also cause other workers to lose jobs. It now becomes more difficult to argue these laws are fair. These laws only meet an unambiguous test of fairness when we explicitly admit that those harmed matter less than those who gain. While some citizens may judge this trade-off to be true, it is doubtful all citizens agree. Clearly, the admission that those harmed matter less than those who gain makes for an uncomfortable discussion. But, the fairness discussion is incomplete without full disclosure of who gains and who loses.

Recent stimulus efforts aimed at pumping up sales of automobiles—"cash for clunkers"—offer another example. Government provided rebates from $3,500 to $4,500 to citizens purchasing new fuel-efficient cars in 2009. Nearly 700,000 cars were taken off our roads, costing taxpayers $3 billion.[9] A program that speeds up purchases today also lowers car purchases tomorrow thus shifting further down the road even larger problems for the auto industry. Monies could have been saved by those who were prodded into purchasing new cars, or used to pay down debt or spent on other products. Some taxpayers could surely think of better ways to use their tax dollars for themselves than subsidizing someone else's purchase of brand new cars.

It has been estimated that of the 700,000 cars purchased during this program, it "created" only 125,000 purchases. That is, 575,000 buyers didn't need prodding over the program timeline, but still enjoyed cash payments as high as $4,500. Given its $3 billion cost, this works out to $24,000 per purchase "created" based on 125,000 cars. This program also artificially raised used car prices by decreasing supply thus harming low-income buyers who typically can only afford used cars. One estimate is that used car prices rose an average of 10 percent, with a nearly 36 percent hike for used Cadillac Escalades.[10]

Skeptics might argue that destroying inefficient cars that pollute too much was the real reason behind the program. Of course, the program literally destroyed thousands of used cars in drivable condition. But, good intentions aside, it was an extremely expensive means of meeting those intentions. One estimate is that the cash for clunkers program paid at least 10 times more than conventional methods to reduce emissions of the greenhouse gas carbon dioxide.[11] Thus, the program could hardly be deemed efficient.

But another purpose of the cash for clunkers program was to shore up businesses that could no longer stand on their own feet. Government thus prevented resources from flowing to more efficient businesses and inflicted longer-term harm on their owners, customers, and workers that should be compared with shorter-term gains to failing businesses. Taxpayers also lost. Everyone will not judge the program to be fair unless everyone agrees winners deserve taxpayer subsidies that others do not. Despite promises that bailouts were "win-win" whereby all citizens gain, this is untrue.

The point is simply to argue that assessment of fairness requires full disclosure of both winners and losers. This requires that gains be compared against harm and that we are willing to accept that programs often exert unintended harm as well as benefits. Of course, gainers may prefer that public debate not delve too deeply into those harmed for fear their programs will be diminished or even shelved. Nonetheless, full disclosure is necessary before careful judgment may be made on whether programs pass tests of efficiency and fairness and is an essential ingredient toward receiving greater satisfaction from government.

OUR TAX SYSTEM IS A MAJOR PROBLEM

Much of the blame for why government is rarely efficient or fair can be placed on our tax system. Our tax system cannot possibly direct citizens to efficient choices over the government we want because tax bills of individual citizens bear no direct relation to values they place on the government they receive or costs of providing government. This critical point, however, requires understanding of the role that prices play in guiding markets toward efficient outcomes.

Consider income taxation where tax bills are determined without reference to either values or costs of government. Individual taxpayers are not charged more for services they value the most or are more costly to provide. Tax bills simply rise in sync with income. It takes no leap of faith to understand how taxation distorts choices of citizens. Anyone who has dined at a fixed-cost food buffet knows the outcome of not directly connecting costs with choices. Diners pile so much food on their trays that much ends up being thrown away. Diners behave like this because they are not personally responsible for funding their food choices.

The important lesson here is that our tax system has set into motion incentives that "bake into the cake" much of our disappointment with government. This book takes the view that incentives matter and changes in incentives are often the key to improving outcomes. Citizens have little ability to determine which programs are worth keeping and which should be shelved or reduced as long as they do not directly connect program costs with benefits from those same programs.

In our dining discussion, few of us would ever make the same choices if we understood we were personally responsible for paying for each additional serving. Our tax system thus promotes an inefficiently large government as its citizens operate under a cloudy connection between costs and benefits. In effect, many citizens believe benefits—additional food—come at little or no cost. Of course, someone pays whether or not our tax system makes this clear.

Disconnecting taxes from costs and values from programs also makes for rather fruitless public debates over tax fairness. Conventional thinking is that comparing tax bills with income somehow reveals whether citizens are treated fairly. This comparison however indicates little about fairness since it does not reveal how beneficial government programs are to individual taxpayers. Focusing on tax payments without any comparison to how beneficial government is to taxpayers suggests little about fairness.

Let's place this in the context of our food buffet example where diners are charged on the basis of their income. The fact that a poor person pays little bears no connection to whether they have piled more or less food on their plate than a rich person. Information on benefits never appears in assessment of fairness. This is how assessment of tax fairness proceeds since tax bills are never compared with benefits from government. It is also a mistake to believe government programs always shower benefits on the poor. Politicians direct programs to the politically powerful and the poor are often not members of this club.

Our tax system thus creates a multitude of invisible transfers of income without clear recognition by any citizen. Citizens predictably demand programs that benefit them with the hope that someone else picks up the tab. But what is beneficial for an individual is disastrous for society as more citizens push for government programs that they would never request if they were personally responsible for their costs. Meanwhile, government expands with little attention to who gains and who loses thus making assessment of fairness a most difficult, if not impossible, exercise as well.

It is predictable we are disappointed with government that can never be efficient and one that cannot even clearly assess fairness of its tax system. Fundamental reform of the tax system is an essential component of getting government back on a track where it earns respect and trust of its citizens. The fact that these concerns are rarely addressed is reason enough to keep on reading so that you too can respond, "Duh! What do you expect?" to questions about why we are so dissatisfied with government.

TWO

What Markets Do Well

```
┌─────────────────────────────────────────────────────────────┐
│                 KEY POINTS IN THIS CHAPTER                    │
│  • Prices are the language of markets guiding consumers and   │
│    producers toward efficient outcomes.                       │
│  • Markets achieve efficient outcomes only as long as they    │
│    are free to set prices.                                    │
│  • The creative destruction process weeds out businesses      │
│    customers like the least.                                  │
│  • Markets naturally "regulate" businesses. Mistakes happen,  │
│    but are eventually corrected.                              │
│  • "Crony capitalism" occurs when businesses receive          │
│    government favors such as liability caps, entry barriers,   │
│    tax preferences, and bailouts.                             │
│  • Markets cannot be efficient when some businesses are       │
│    insulated from creative destruction.                       │
└─────────────────────────────────────────────────────────────┘
```

Study of markets begins with examining a world without government. This uncluttered world guides subsequent questions regarding whether government improves upon markets. Markets are guided by natural reflexes that are easily missed thus leading many to undervalue how well prices guide us toward smart choices. Adam Smith was the first to marvel at how markets promote the greater social purpose as if guided by an "invisible hand."[1] The mass of knowledge brought to markets defies easy comprehension, but nonetheless consumers and producers unwittingly provide it to markets. Smith's keen observation leads to questions of whether the very "visible hand" of government could ever outperform the "invisible hand" of markets.

Prices are the language of markets that enable smart decisions by consumers and producers. Smart choices require no advanced training with experience often the best education. Consumers choose houses, restaurants, and between different brands of soap by comparing prices with values connected to purchases. We snatch "good deals" and run from "bad deals." Prices also guide producers. Wages are prices and, along with land prices and capital prices, guide decisions on employment, where to locate businesses, and how many machines to purchase.

Further, prices guide consumers to reach "highest valued uses" of their limited incomes. This is just a fancy way of saying smart choices are efficient. Consider, for instance, a food court with many eateries. Diners may go immediately to the pizza or sandwich stands or meander around gathering information. Prices allow diners to differentiate between "good buys" and "bad buys." We prefer to pay $3 rather than $4 for a hamburger. Tastes are also important. Some of us love pepperoni pizza, others are vegetarians who love meatless pizza, and others dislike all pizza. Many choose between brands of soda simply on which has the lowest price, but others believe no substitutes exist for their drink of choice. Incomes also matter. These commonsense statements are so ingrained in us that few of us ever ponder them.

Producers choose what to produce, but consumers ultimately determine which products represent good values. Businesses track opinion polls as they understand that consumers "regulate" them. YouGov PLC is one survey company that tracks opinions for corporations such as BP and Toyota.[2] It sends out surveys to one million U.S. adults in order to monitor at least 5,000 completed surveys per day on 1,100 brands. Businesses bear the risk of failure as long as consumers remain free to make their own choices within markets filled with alternatives. Profit is the other side of the coin.

Resource prices and technology guide labor, land, and capital decisions of business owners. Grocery stores using self-checkouts allow them to compete more favorably on price. One employee supervises multiple checkouts thus reducing labor costs. The following questions are relevant to the issues confronting owners deciding whether to invest in self-checkouts.

- Will they raise profits?
- Which machine is the best buy?
- Should I delay purchasing?
- Should I purchase an extended warranty?
- Will my competitors invest in them?
- How will my employees react?
- Will customers like them?
- Will I lose more to theft?

Bad decisions lower profit and can even break businesses. Little wonder most of us prefer to collect a steady paycheck rather than run our own businesses.

Behind the scenes, owners struggle over messy details. They adjust to ever-changing prices on labor, land, and capital as well as technological change, tax laws, regulation, and threats of competitors. Learning from mistakes through trial and error and accepting risk yield specialized knowledge that cannot be easily transferred to outside observers. Of course, outsiders might be tempted to observe: "They were stupid to replace workers with self-checkouts," or "They should not have raised prices on their baked goods," or more simply, "I can do better."

Our economy is littered with businesses that failed to provide products consumers want at prices that allow them to remain in business. According to the Small Business Administration, there were 670,710 new businesses created in 2005–2006.[3] But, 599,333 closed during the same period. The net change is 71,377 more businesses. Reasons vary for closures and include new competition, increases in rent and insurance, difficulties meeting debt obligations, loss of major clients, failure to collect payments owed by customers, tax and regulatory problems, personal troubles such as divorce or ill health, and retirement. Despite claims of up to 55 percent, the percentage of personal business bankruptcies stemming from medical problems is 17 percent.[4]

Restaurants often fail with some reports indicating over half failing within a few years of opening. Conventional wisdom has restaurants failing at rates as high as 90 percent in the first year. But a recent study found a 59 percent failure rate over a three-year period.[5] The highest rate was 26 percent during the first year, followed by 19 percent in the second year, and 14 percent in the third year. Franchised chain restaurants failed at a 57 percent rate and independents failed at 61 percent over a three-year period.

The point is that successful businesses provide products consumers want at prices that allow them to remain in business. These prices are products of market knowledge of owners and consumers. The invisible hand that guides these decisions reflects a wealth of information borne out by millions of consumers and producers guiding market outcomes underneath the surface of everyday life.

EFFICIENT PRICES EMERGE

Prices don't just magically appear but rather emerge through an equilibrium process that ends when prices no longer rise or fall. Prices set too high result in excess inventories since consumers are unwilling to fully accept quantities offered by sellers. Department stores, for instance, hold "sales" in hopes of unloading excess inventory. Price reductions would not arise otherwise since owners would prefer to sell sweaters at $40 each rather than $30. But, if consumers won't buy all at $40, they must reduce prices until equilibrium emerges where supply equals demand.

Shortages signal that prices are set too low. For instance, a price of $10 might have 200 shoppers wanting "great buys" but, because sellers can't profitably sell 200 sweaters at $10, only 50 sweaters are offered. A shortage of 150 sweaters is the symptom of this mismatch. Consumers, of course, complain and producers provide more sweaters, but at higher prices. Prices stop rising when supply equals demand at equilibrium.

Despite common misperceptions that price hikes always reflect "greed," two reasons underlie the adage "to produce more, it costs more." First, more land, labor, and capital entail higher costs—it costs more to hire three workers than two workers. The second reason is known as the "law of diminishing returns" whereby additional resources are of lower quality since otherwise businesses would have employed them first. Anyone who has compared land in the desert to that on the fertile plain understands resources are of unequal quality.

Another common misunderstanding is that costs fall with higher production. Examples of falling computer prices excite us into believing the "to produce more, it costs more" adage has been overturned. But, price reductions are driven by technological innovation over time and thus reflect two different production eras. Many products—especially those connected to rapidly changing technology like computers and health care equipment—often have falling prices over time. Within each era of technology, however, costs rise with higher production since they remain stuck to that era's technology. To produce more today, and not with tomorrow's technology, requires costs to rise and hence owners must raise prices to remain in business.

PRICE SYSTEM ENABLES HIGHER-VALUED USES

Reconsider our sweater example and suppose 50 sweaters are offered at $10 each. Consumers do not value sweaters equally. Some rate them as "great buys" at $10, but not at higher prices. Others who value them more than $10 may find no sweaters left. Customers grabbing "great buys" are ecstatic, but holding prices at $10 is inefficient because sweaters are not directed to highest-valued users. Shortages thus are symptoms of inefficient outcomes. The solution is simply to allow prices to rise as this directs sweaters to those valuing them the most and to be rejected by those now viewing them as "bad deals." Again, consumers require no special training to decide whether prices reflect good or bad buys.

Protests of "price gouging" often accompany severe weather events such as hurricanes and major snowstorms. Newspapers publish editorials claiming businesses take advantage of consumers when prices of everyday necessities—flashlights, water, and food—rise dramatically. This provides another example of blaming symptoms—rising prices—rather than causes. Rising demand and shrinking supply cause rising prices. Suppliers miss deliveries that shrink inventories of necessities. Consumers rush to stores to purchase whatever remains on shelves "just in case." Meanwhile, sympathy for owners is in short supply as owners are believed to be taking advantage of consumers.

Remember an efficient outcome requires that prices direct products to highest-valued users. Some owners fear customer backlash so much they do not raise prices. Of course, this strategy means frantic customers are unhappy when unchanged prices mean empty shelves. Freezing prices might be a rational strategy for a business owner, but it is not efficient for society since lower-valued users may end up with products that higher-valued users can no longer purchase. Price increases eliminate shortages enabling efficient outcomes and should be applauded rather than booed if efficiency is the goal. Prices direct products to highest-valued users rather than on the basis of first in line, luck, age, gender, education, political affiliation, or ethnicity. Critics assert price increases are unfair, but it remains unclear which factors better reflect value than prices consumers are willing to pay.

The following example provides more clarity for why it is inefficient to hold the line on prices of all products during a severe weather event.

Consider a flashlight that normally goes for $5. Bill is willing to pay $8 for it while Mary is unwilling to pay more than $5. If prices are kept at $5, Mary might luck out and purchase the last one before Bill enters the store. Bill, however, placed a higher value of $8 on that flashlight than Mary. The remaining flashlight thus does not go to the highest-valued user. Pure luck explains why Mary got the last flashlight that has nothing to do with the fact that Bill valued it more than she did.

Consider how the price system could allocate airline seats in the event of overbooking. Suppose there are 200 ticket holders on a flight that can only service 190 passengers. One solution would be to simply bump those last in line. This is inefficient when bumped ticket holders value seats more than those lucky enough to get seats. Holding auctions whereby ticket holders compete for future travel vouchers if they agree to take later flights is more efficient. The airline starts bidding at say $200 and raises values until the first 10 vouchers are awarded. These 10 ticket holders value seats less than those not accepting vouchers. The price system cleanly allocates to highest-valued users. Government may mandate specific dollar amounts to those involuntarily bumped, but there is no reason to believe all bumped ticket holders value seats identically thus making vouchers good values to some and bad values to others. Regulation lacks the price system's finesse that allows consumers to determine when dollar amounts are worth their seat.

This discussion demonstrates two important points about markets. One, markets achieve efficient outcomes only as long as they are free to set prices. This represents the proverbial "free market." Shortages and surpluses are symptoms of inefficiency that can only be removed through raising or lowering prices. The second point is that outside observers cannot replicate this process because they do not possess the massive amounts of information brought to markets by consumers and producers. They can not possibly match supply with demand better than markets thus leading them to allocate on the basis of something other than price such as first in line, age, gender, income, location, political affiliation, or a lottery.

MARKETS REGULATE BUSINESSES

Joseph Schumpeter (1880–1950) wrote of the "creative destruction" process whereby businesses who fail to innovate are "standing on ground that is crumbling beneath their feet."[6] He understood the importance of competition in guiding markets toward efficient outcomes. There were 600,000 different stories lurking behind the business failures of 2005–2006 with the only constant being the businesses were not nimble enough to supply products at prices that allowed them to remain in business. Businesses unwilling to switch from VCR to DVD technology in past years were clearly on the road to failure. Restaurants that resist updating menus in line with customer tastes or employ servers that treat customers poorly may find themselves destroyed by competition.

Creative destruction weeds out businesses customers like the least. Where else would business owners target their innovations if not at customers for whom they believe they can provide better values? While some factors lie outside control of owners—state of economy, taxes, and regulations, for instance—businesses fail mostly because they could not efficiently use resources while catering to consumer preferences. Many of us have witnessed businesses becoming more shopper friendly only in response to heightened competition. More smiling and helpful employees magically appear almost overnight in reaction to new competitors.

Well-known examples demonstrate that dominance today does not guarantee future dominance. Polaroid introduced its first instant camera in 1947, but no longer dominates as competitors were better cost-cutters and developed cameras for the digital age. Xerox was so successful with its first plain paper photocopier in 1950 that "xerox" is still synonymous with copying. Many other businesses came along that eroded Xerox's initial dominance. Other businesses that enjoyed great success, but were unable to remain dominant, include Montgomery Ward, Sears, and Circuit City. An average of 24 firms dropped out of the Fortune 500 list every year over the period 1956–1981.[7] In 1982–2006, that number rose to 40 suggesting that forces of creative destruction have become stronger.

History is not on the side of those who believe that today's large businesses such as Wal-Mart will remain dominant. Wal-Mart succeeded in creatively destroying many smaller competitors with its innovations in inventory management, employee training, and marketing. Their dominance also makes them the target of businesses hoping to win over their customers with better products at lower prices. Customers will not remain loyal if Wal-Mart's competitors offer better values. Likewise, despite Microsoft's many successes, computer users are more than willing to purchase software products offering better values.

Hollywood Video and Blockbuster, Inc.'s bankruptcies in 2010 are recent examples of a business model—video rental—creatively destroyed by new technology in the form of cable on-demand, automated DVD-rental kiosks such as Redbox, and Internet-streaming Netflix. The owner of a 22-year-old video rental business put it succinctly: "People like things being given to them. We don't see as many warm bodies."[8] According to U.S. Census Bureau data, video-rental stores declined from 23,036 in 1997 to 16,237 in 2007. Few consumers miss the old days where they had to visit storefronts to rent their films.

Today's thriving businesses are often ones that destroyed older businesses. Employees lost jobs that sometimes threatened local economies that relied on these inefficient businesses. Workers were often forced to relocate, retrain, and/or find employment in another industry. Sometimes their lives improved and sometimes not. But, other pieces of this story are more positive. Creative destruction frees resources—labor, land, and capital—for new and existing businesses thus opening up new opportunities for workers and consumers. Creative destruction offers a "carrot" for new ideas as suggested by the saying "build a better mousetrap and the world will build a path to your door."

The following challenge places these important issues in context. Suppose you receive a $1 million inheritance with the only stipulation that you must invest the entire sum in stock of one company and cannot sell for 20 years. Would you feel comfortable investing $1 million in Wal-Mart, Microsoft, or Google? These businesses are very powerful today, but today's dominance does not guarantee future dominance. Creative destruction makes this a difficult question. You would need to determine if dominating companies are nimble in the face of competitors seeking their customers. These problems, however, are good problems for society as they result in better products and values to customers as well as jobs in businesses that succeed.

The bottom line is that markets—consumers and producers—have a natural mechanism to "regulate" bad business practices. Creative destruction keeps businesses on their toes watching competitors and making sure customers don't believe competitors offer better values. Successful owners live this mantra every day by keeping competitors at bay while meeting needs of their customers. Stock markets regulate corporations as their survival chances are monitored by ups and downs of share prices. Creditors also regulate businesses by aligning interest rates on their loans with risk of business failure. Businesses do not enjoy this "regulation" but nonetheless this invisible hand of markets guides them toward efficiency.

Of course, nothing is perfect and markets make mistakes. Companies like Enron are often brought up as examples where markets failed to regulate a business that was neither efficient nor trustworthy. This is true from a short-run view, but its share price eventually fell to zero when it became clear Enron failed to operate efficiently or provide value to customers.

Unfortunately, workers lost jobs and shareholders lost many dollars but the market eventually "corrected" this problem company by shutting it down. Learning is an exercise sometimes best learned through mistakes and difficult episodes such as Enron.

BP's oil spill disaster in 2010 provides another example. But, a problem with this example is that government provided a liability cap of $75 million to oil drillers that shielded them from bearing full costs of mistakes that impose substantial losses on outside parties. Richard Epstein argues that $75 million is "chicken feed" and that:

> The legal system should never allow self-interested parties to keep for themselves all the gains from dangerous activities that unilaterally impose losses on others—which is why the most devout defender of laissez-faire must insist, not just concede, that tough medicine is needed in these cases.[9]

A tough liability system provides compensation for serious harm following disasters and encourages sound practices as determined by solid insurance underwriting of risk. Insurers regulate businesses by discouraging high-risk practices as long as they are liable for full costs associated with disasters. Government liability caps enable incomplete market regulation because insurers were only interested in protecting themselves from the $75 million liability. Thus, the visible hand of government discouraged the invisible hand of markets from fully regulating businesses.

WAL-MART AND CREATIVE DESTRUCTION

Wal-Mart's success deserves special discussion. Its success at weeding out inefficient businesses is demonstrated by the amount of effort incumbent businesses exert in attempting to stop Wal-Mart from taking root in their communities. A recent article discusses how a grocery chain of nine stores attempted to stop a proposed new 200,000-square-foot Wal-Mart Supercenter from invading its territory in Mundelein, Illinois.[10] The local grocery chain hired an experienced consulting group to fight Wal-Mart through noisy protests and lawsuits that made it appear the work of nearby home owners, unions, and local activists.

Such is the fate of Wal-Mart as it has become the largest grocery in the United States—roughly one-half of Wal-Mart's U.S. revenues of $258 billion are from groceries. While stopping Wal-Mart from opening is the ultimate goal, efforts are also designed to generate negative publicity and delay opening of new stores. The Mundelein case was estimated to have stalled development by three years and cost millions in local lost property and sales tax revenues. Consulting firms use mostly clandestine methods to mask that they are funded by existing businesses that obviously have large stakes in keeping large competitors out of their terrain. Major clients include Safeway, Giant Food Stores, and other national grocery chains all with the shared purpose of stopping Wal-Mart from taking root in their home turf. It is romantic to view the fight as simply that of local citizens pitted against huge corporations, but fights are mostly from existing businesses that prefer to not lower prices and provide better values to customers.

Consulting firms often deploy managers to at-risk communities under assumed names where they manage local opposition on several fronts. One involves flooding local politicians with phone calls, often with multiple phone lines in order to make it appear all calls are unique. Other tactics include hiring local lawyers to press lawsuits seeking to stall Wal-Mart from opening, training local union reps on how to speak at public hearings about the dangers of allowing Wal-Mart to enter communities, distributing mass mailings assailing Wal-Mart's business practices, funding activists who claim devastating environmental damages will arise from Wal-Mart's entry, altering zoning for proposed locations to forbid Wal-Mart's entry, and hiring traffic experts to fuel anxiety over congestion associated with Wal-Mart stores. Local politicians are also pressured to pass ordinances mandating maximum store sizes in hopes new businesses are uninterested in opening smaller stores.

Another tactic is to try to pass "living wage" laws that only apply to large retailers such as Wal-Mart. One example was a bill in Baltimore City that required large retailers—those that gross more than $10 million annually, or are part of a chain that does—to pay workers hourly wages of $10.59 rather than the minimum wage of $7.25.[11] Although defeated, it was clearly an attempt by smaller merchants to raise costs of big-box stores in hopes they would retreat from entering their turf. Apparently advocates lost credibility when there were no good reasons for why smaller merchants should be exempt from paying "living wages" to their workers.

Skeptics are bound to declare: "But Wal-Mart destroys the small business sector, along with high-paying jobs in these communities." Conventional wisdom is that huge discounters are plagues set upon small businesses leaving downtowns barren and empty. A recent study concluded these claims are based on faulty and misleading analysis.[12] Their research finds that Wal-Mart has had no significant impact on the overall size and growth of U.S. small business activity. While they find that Wal-Mart does cause some small businesses to fail, these failures are entirely compensated for by entry of new small businesses.

Study authors discuss the case of their hometown—Morgantown, West Virginia—as it experienced firsthand the creative destruction process unleashed by Wal-Mart.

Shortly after a new Wal-Mart store opened, Morgantown's popular downtown area was wrought with empty storefronts. However, after only a brief period of time, the once-empty storefronts filled with new small businesses. A former women's clothing shop transformed into a high-end restaurant. A former electronics store converted into an ice cream parlor. One by one, each of the vacant stores filled with new businesses, such as coffee shops, art galleries, and law firms.

The logic is that, as Wal-Mart causes prices to fall, consumers have more spending money that can support new businesses that take over locations of creatively destroyed businesses.

The creative destruction process only works well to "regulate" businesses as long as it is allowed to play out naturally. Lessening worry about competitors leads some business owners to become rather "fat and happy." Businesses are naturally interested in slowing down this process by raising entry barriers into home turfs. Enlisting government is often the weapon of choice. If these efforts fail, they must fight by providing better value to consumers—lowering prices by paring down costs and improving product quality. Of course, they may also lose this fight with competitors.

PROFIT MOTIVE IS CRITICAL

Critics of markets often declare greed drives markets and is at the root of most problems. Collapse of Enron and the recent oil spill by BP are commonly believed products of greed. Proponents of minimum wage laws claim workers earn too little because owners are greedy. But, greed defies definition thus making it one of those "I know it when I see it" phenomena. However, the greed argument affords its proponents wide latitude when criticizing markets without being held to any clear meaning to what greedy behavior looks like or to point to any economic system that doesn't run on greed. Apparently, greed is believed synonymous with "unreasonable" profits, again never having to clearly define what "reasonable" profits look like.

Of course, behavior that defies clear definition provides little guidance on how to control or regulate it. It should also be understood that markets already correct for "high" profit levels because nothing attracts competitors faster than businesses earning "high" profits. The creative destruction process keeps profits in check. It is also true that today's "high" profits do not always predict future "high" profits as clearly demonstrated by Enron, BP, Montgomery Ward, and Circuit City.

"High" profits are also critical carrots for innovation. In an obvious play on words, economist Richard McKenzie has likened the importance of market power to that of "creative production."[13] Technology would not evolve as rapidly if inventors were forbidden to temporarily capture "high" profits when consumers flock to them. Inventors focus their attention to "high" profit areas through adding value to consumers and at lower costs than previously available. It is romantic to believe life-saving drugs are invented by high-minded caring individuals, but we would have far fewer innovations if "high" profits were never a possibility. Moreover, new products often fail to pass the test of markets thus requiring higher profits on those products that win. Famous product disasters include the Ford Edsel in 1958, the Apple Lisa computer of the early 1980s, McDonald's McLean burger in 1991, and New Coke in 1985.

Finally, it should be remembered that "high" profits can simply reflect businesses that succeed in providing valuable products to consumers. It takes patience to understand that creative destruction keeps business owners in check over time rather than instantaneously. Remember the invisible hand of markets guides us toward efficient outcomes, but it takes time and each step will rarely be perfect. But, history demonstrates that few businesses dominate for very long periods of time.

Adam Smith understood that pursuit of profit is socially valuable when he said:

It is not from the benevolence of the butcher, the brewer, or the baker, that we expect our dinner, but from their regard to their own interest.[14]

It makes no difference that owners mostly care about themselves when they provide products consumers enjoy at prices that allow them to remain in business. Adam Smith obviously suffered under few romantic illusions about motivations of business owners. But, he understood exchanges between consumers and producers are nonetheless mutually advantageous. Pursuit of profit is a vital ingredient in keeping profits in check since otherwise business owners would never fear outside competitors offering better products and prices. Rather than a bad thing, pursuit of profits is a good thing since otherwise markets could never be efficient if business owners never feared competitors attempting to drive them out of business.

A recent trend is for businesses to profess their "social responsibility" in mission statements under the theory that businesses hold responsibilities to society in general over and above those to owners. The underlying message is that unless businesses proclaim how they serve all members of society, they are likely to harm others in society. Milton Friedman, however, artfully argued businesses should only be concerned about providing value to owners and not attempting to right all wrongs in society.[15] Businesses are not charities and have no expertise in social work. Shareholders as owners of corporations are free to distribute their earnings however they please including worthy social causes. Remember too that businesses are regulated by markets and suffer financial harm when they harm society.

An unintended adverse consequence of spending time drafting and implementing social responsibility statements is when they distract businesses from pursuing profit opportunities.[16] Remember that such opportunities often stem from targeting bad business practices of competitors that may include excessive costs or inferior customer service. More time spent appeasing social responsibility advocates means less time uncovering ways to improve customer value and cost-cutting that lowers prices and strikes fear in their competitors. Ironically, the social responsibility movement may discourage business owners from achieving efficient outcomes.

Outsourcing is another example often used to demonstrate greed. Again, this view misunderstands what drives businesses to utilize resources in other countries. Profits are enhanced whenever costs can be lowered. Cost reductions stem from employing cheaper labor, but outsourcing is also triggered by high costs imposed by government. That U.S. corporations are taxed at 35 percent—versus the world average of 18 percent—explains how investing offshore increases returns to shareholders.[17] Burdensome regulations, lengthy permit processes, and growing scarcity of technical skills in the United States also explain outsourcing.

Another misconception is that one American worker loses their job for each job outsourced to another country. But, a recent study disputes this wisdom based on large-scale study of the hiring practices of 2,500 U.S.-based multinational companies.[18] Over 1991–2001, this study found that jobs at foreign subsidiaries of U.S. multinational corporations rose by 2.8 million jobs, but jobs at their parent firms in the United States rose by 5.5 million jobs—nearly two jobs created per one outsourced. Moreover, average pay of $56,667 for their American employees was 31 percent higher than their American competitors that did not outsource. Businesses that take advantage of outsourcing to raise profits are thus improving value of their businesses for their owners as well as salaries of their workers. Customers also gain from lower prices.

WHEN MARKETS ARE NOT FREE

We have so far mostly discussed markets that in theory have little to no government intervention. But, the visible hand of government is very busy intervening into markets. Government is a growing influence on our lives and it is illogical to solely blame markets when so many past problems have been addressed by government actions. Current problems may therefore be related to these past actions of government.

Recent years have seen a surge in "crony capitalism." This term describes an economy where some businesses receive government favors that include tax breaks, liability caps, entry barriers, government contracts, bailouts, and other advantages. Government thus influences who become winners and losers. Recent history demonstrates bailouts are a growing form of crony capitalism. For example, the U.S. Treasury has taken ownership positions in hundreds of large banks under the Troubled Assets Relief Program.

Government will not choose the same winners and losers that would be determined through creative destruction. There is simply no reason to believe government has the ability or interest to predict winners and losers resulting from creative destruction. Rather, government protects businesses from market "regulation" that caused them to become unprofitable or to fail. Government, in effect, stalls creative destruction by bailing out businesses. Bailouts "glue" resources to inefficient businesses thus discouraging their flow to businesses that could better utilize them for their customers.

Often bailouts are argued to be "investments" in free markets. A recent example is federal government "investment" of $14 million in the ZBB Energy battery factory in Menomonee Falls, Wisconsin.[19] This "investment" is part of the Department of Energy's $2.3 billion program to promote clean energy manufacturing. ZBB Energy was one of 183 recipients of the program. Research that went a bit beyond the claims of "investment" found that the business lost $4.9 million in fiscal year 2008, $5.5 million in fiscal year 2009, and had a "cumulative deficit" of $44.1 million.[20]

It is unlikely that propping up failing businesses makes them more efficient. Government "glues" resources to businesses that have not stood the market test. Even though bailouts lead proponents to claim success when their recipients show profits, their profitability required taxpayer help that other businesses did not receive. Taxpayers made them only appear successful on paper and it remains to be seen if they eventually become self-sufficient without further taxpayer support.

Bailouts also rearrange the risk-reward nature of markets because now successful business owners reap profits, but are subsidized by taxpayers when they fail. Owners suffer little downside because they remain in business in either case. Owners realize "heads they win and tails they win." Taxpayers, though, face very different odds. They have no claim on profits, but bail out businesses when they fail. Other losers include customers, workers, and owners of businesses that are not protected. This picture does not describe free markets and underscores the conclusion that markets can only be efficient when they must endure stresses associated with creative destruction. This requires government to stay out of the way by not bailing-out businesses that failed to meet the test of markets.

Government thus can either allow the market to "regulate" businesses or protect them from the discipline imposed by markets. Government can either encourage or discourage efficient outcomes. Government is thus the referee that can choose to allow the market process to proceed and weed out inefficient businesses or intervene and "pick and choose" winners and losers. This much-misunderstood lesson about the appropriate role of government is a critical one in light of the many recent bailouts of failing businesses.

THREE

Theory Is Not Practice of Government

KEY POINTS IN THIS CHAPTER

- Expanding government on the basis of theory rather than practice leads to disappointment.

- Government faces high hurdles—lack of information, motivation, and expertise—when it attempts to mimic how markets achieve efficiency.

- Despite popular notions of massive deregulation, regulation has been marching at a very rapid pace.

- Although externalities, public goods, imperfect competition, and information pose hurdles for markets, both markets and government fail to correct these problems.

- Government spending is rarely "investment" because it must be financed by higher taxes or more debt that "crowds out" more efficient spending in markets. Politicians also rarely spend dollars more efficiently than consumers.

- Using "nudges" to guide individuals toward efficient decisions as argued by "behavioral economists" makes more sense when offered by businesses than by government.

That markets are imperfect raises questions about what obstacles prevent perfection. It is commonly understood that externalities (e.g., pollution), public goods (e.g., national defense), imperfect competition, and imperfect information are hurdles preventing efficient outcomes. But, market imperfections cannot justify intervention simply on hopes that government *can, should, and will* promote efficiency. Claims that government can correct market imperfections must make the case that it somehow overcomes the same obstacles confronting markets. Government also faces many hurdles that do not confront markets.

Evidence also does not support popular notions of massive deregulation in recent years. The Federal Register lists all proposed and final federal rules and regulations and its number of pages is a frequently cited measure of regulation's scope.[1] Its trend indicates a dramatic rise in regulatory activity consistent with public spending expansion. Numbers of pages (per decade) are: 112,771 (1940s), 107,030 (1950s), 170,325 (1960s), 450,821 (1970s), 529,223 (1980s), 622,368 (1990s), and 730,176 (2000s estimate).[2] Regulation has been marching at a very rapid pace, despite many of us missing this trend.

Unfortunately, rising intervention has mostly left a bigger mess in its wake that enables the vicious cycle whereby past government failures lead to more interventions. Disappointment is inevitable due to how well government in theory or practice can improve upon efficiency in markets. More pages in the Federal Register or spending expansion will surely not raise satisfaction. This chapter carefully examines the case for intervention in both theory and practice and finds that government rarely enables outcomes that are more efficient than markets.

NEGATIVE EXTERNALITIES

Our lives are affected by actions of others with some factors clearly beyond our personal control. Time spent commuting to our jobs is affected by how many people decide to leave at the same time. Barking dogs disrupt our sleep. Markets can only be efficient when all benefits and costs are reflected in final outcomes. Air and water pollution are examples of "negative externalities" where not all costs are reflected in market outcomes.

Externalities arise because no one individual owns all resources and therefore no one has clear ownership rights over all resources. Chemical plants that do not pay for damaging air and water produce too much. Neighbors with noisy dogs produce too much noise when they do not compensate others for disruption of sleep. Efficiency requires property rights to resources since people rarely invest in protection of resources without benefit. Nobody washes a rental car, but individuals wash their own cars. Efficient market outcomes require ownership of all resources.

Government often uses taxes to remedy negative externalities. In theory, taxes equal to previously unaccounted costs are solutions that bring less production with higher prices. Higher prices enable efficient market outcomes. Regulation can also in theory guide markets to efficient outcomes. Regulations can require factories to utilize pollution control equipment or can mandate recycling as a remedy for externalities associated with garbage. Pollution permits are another remedy that allows businesses to decide how to meet mandates rather than imposing regulatory mandates. Permits are sold to highest bidders in an auction of transferable property rights to pollute up to allowable pollution levels.

Pollution is a favorite example of negative externalities as taught on blackboards in classrooms throughout the world. Professors draw diagrams showing efficient outcomes are smaller than market outcomes because producers do not pay for fouling air and water. Professors then reveal taxes that correct this inefficiency. For example, while 1,000 cans of paint might use $15,000 of resources, producers only pay $10,000. A tax of $5,000 on producers yields an efficient outcome by raising prices and decreasing production.

Now for some realism. The only time the $5,000 tax corrects the externality is within the classroom. Professors as outside observers of this market never have perfect knowledge of costs or benefits. This is like asking them to somehow equate demand with supply in markets—easy to do on a blackboard, but impossible in practice. They lack knowledge. It is wishful thinking to believe that guesses always improve matters because taxes may under-correct, overcorrect, or perfectly correct markets. Taxes set too high force markets to produce too little and taxes set too low result in too much. Again, both markets and government fail to perfectly correct externalities.

But, government faces additional hurdles. Political decisions are unlikely to be based solely on efficiency grounds, even if experts somehow knew correct tax levels. Voters often oppose taxes that eliminate jobs. Businesses push against taxes because they decrease jobs and profit. Politicians may find campaign funding more difficult to secure as both businesses and workers voice opposition. Environmental groups also enter this debate. Politicians carefully walk a tightrope with so many conflicting signals and it remains unlikely that, even if they somehow knew perfect tax corrections, those levels are chosen.[3]

The classroom exercise whereby correct tax solutions are determined has now morphed into something quite complicated. Ability to guide efficient outcomes is limited by motivation, knowledge, and expertise. It is naïve to believe perfect solutions always exist or are even followed when correctly identified. Even when doctors correctly identify ailments of patients, remedies may not exist to correct them. Patients might also disregard correct advice. Our realistic discussion demonstrates that theory of correcting externalities enables the myth that government always promotes efficient outcomes.

SODA TAXES CORRECT OBESITY?

Markets work well as long as consumers and producers base decisions on good information. But perfect information is impossible. Consumers may not fully understand risk associated with automobiles or behaviors such as cell phone usage, fast food purchases, smoking, or drinking alcoholic beverages. Producers may not fully understand costs or that better production techniques are cheaply available. Information imperfections yield inefficient market outcomes.

The theoretical remedy is for government to expand information to consumers and producers. Programs that disseminate previously unknown information build smarter consumers and producers. Heavier-handed remedies include regulation and outright bans of products or behaviors. These policies reflect a paternalistic role of government consistent with policies banning tobacco advertising on television and radio or forbidding drivers to talk on cell phones. Paternalism is clearly a contentious role for government that raises important questions about how much power government should be awarded when directing markets on the premise that it knows better than citizens they control through their policies.

Obesity provides an excellent example. Roughly one-third of U.S. adults are classified as obese, as defined by a BMI (body mass index) of 30 or higher. Various factors are believed to promote rising obesity rates, but the hypothesized relationship between sugar-sweetened beverages and obesity has increasingly become the focus of attention. Many public health advocates believe soda should be subject to higher taxes to correct what they view is a market that produces too many obese people.[4] They argue for taxes on three grounds: soda causes obesity, consumers lack adequate information and beverage choices, and soda drinkers impose health costs on others—negative externalities—through higher medical costs.

Three reasons explain why soda taxes are unlikely to correct for problems related to our nation's obesity rate.[5] First, an obvious correlation between soda consumption and obesity rates does not imply soda causes obesity. Empirical studies simply demonstrate that heavier people tend to drink more soda. Correlation is not necessarily causation. Even if soda causes obesity, soda is not a lone causal factor behind obesity since lack of exercise, age, genetics, and consumption of other foods and beverages are obviously contributing factors.

Second, it is difficult to argue that markets fail to meet consumer preferences for healthy foods and drinks. There are 40,000 food products in the typical U.S. supermarket and the U.S. Department of Agriculture concludes this array of products does not ignore consumer preferences for healthy choices.[6] It found that 35,272 new food products labeled "low fat" or "no fat" were introduced between 1987 and 2004 thus concluding that unhealthy food consumption patterns don't stem from a market failing to provide healthy food and beverage choices. Moreover, diet soda sales have been growing rapidly leading some forecasters to predict they will eventually overtake regular soda sales. An active market exists in providing healthy choices.

Third, taxes cannot correct a nonexistent externality. Public health advocates argue that negative externalities exist because consumers who become obese do not fully pick up their higher medical costs and thus taxes should raise soda prices to levels consistent with efficient consumption levels. Their argument ignores that, even if obesity raises health care costs of the obese, this externality should be corrected by raising insurance premiums. Few criticize surcharges imposed by auto insurance firms on drivers with drunk driving records, so why not correct for higher costs associated with obesity through insurance premiums? The appropriate corollary here would be to impose a car tax on all car owners to somehow correct for drunk driving. Taxing all car owners to deal with costs of drunk drivers is a remedy that few of us would accept.

A soda tax also encourages unintended adverse consequences. Many soda drinkers are not obese and a soda tax cannot differentiate between consumers by their weight. What logic suggests taxing consumers without weight problems? Recent studies also indicate taxes exert different effects on light versus heavy demanders with the likely result that taxes mostly cut consumption of those drinking few sodas.[7] Taxes don't decrease drinking much for those who truly love their sodas. Government may also makes it appear that the "eat less, exercise more" adage is no longer an effective course for controlling weight.

Intervention also crowds out market-based policies that are more likely to be effective than government in reducing obesity. Effective policies are ones where individuals personally bear costs and benefits of choices they make. Obese individuals are known to have higher medical expenses[8] and earn less income.[9] Incentives already exist for employers to reward workers who effectively control their weight and, unlike government actions, they are directly targeted at obese workers. It has been estimated that one-third of U.S. companies offer or are planning financial incentives for employees to lose weight.[10] At least one Internet site gets corporate sponsors to give cash rewards to obese individuals who significantly lower their BMI.[11]

POSITIVE EXTERNALITIES

Positive externalities arise when markets fail to account for all benefits. Immunization against communicable diseases is a common example since inoculated individuals benefit those who do not receive inoculations. Individuals who may transmit diseases are now fewer in number. Markets do not consider all benefits and thus too few inoculations occur. Lawn care is another example. When the Smiths keep a tidy lawn, neighbors do not compensate them for their higher property values. The Smiths would only consider benefits bestowed on neighbors when they collected payments from neighbors. Positive externalities thus result in too little production.

Subsidies equal to unaccounted benefits are the preferred theoretical correction. Government may reduce costs of inoculations, or provide them "free" to all. Home owners can be offered tax subsidies for purchases of lawn care products. Regulatory proposals might require everyone to be vaccinated or all home owners to keep tidy lawns.

Education is a favorite example based on the argument that education helps society when its citizens can read, write, and do basic math. Markets only cater to those paying for education and thus will provide too little from the viewpoint of society. This thinking motivates many people to routinely argue "the more the better" when it comes to public education spending.

But, correction of this problem is not so simple. First, there are limits to the argument that education has positive externalities. It is true for basic teaching of rudimentary topics, but advanced topics such as higher mathematics, philosophy, and literature criticism mostly confer benefits to those receiving instruction in the form of higher income and quality of life. Second, it is unclear how benefits and costs associated with education can be tallied thus making its efficient level a mystery to outside observers. The real world is likely to be quite different than efficient levels drawn on blackboards.

Despite these complications, conventional wisdom is that public education spending should be increased. Newspapers run countless articles and editorials lamenting lack of spending, but rarely are counterhypotheses—we spend the correct amount or too much—aired. Assessment of what constitutes an efficient level of education is rarely discussed probably because conclusions are consistent with claims that positive externalities always result in too little education. Only the most optimistic of us would look for efficiency in this environment.

PUBLIC GOODS

Government provides "public goods" such as national defense, roads, museums, and parks because their benefits are shared by all citizens. All activities provided by government are often called "public goods," but this is incorrect and unfortunately leads to much confusion. Public goods are "nonrival in consumption," which simply means benefits of others are not diminished when additional citizens consume them. Benefits from having a strong military are not diminished with arrival of new citizens.

"Private goods" are "rival in consumption" meaning the act of consuming them necessarily means benefits of others are diminished or eliminated. When Alice eats a pizza, no one else can consume that pizza. Buying 20 gallons of gasoline means no one else uses that gasoline. Private goods thus provide benefits only to purchasers, but benefits of public goods are equally available to all consumers.

Costs are effectively zero of providing public goods to additional citizens. It costs nothing to protect one more citizen within our defense program. In contrast, it costs more to provide more pizza. It is also virtually impossible to exclude benefits to other individuals enjoying public goods such as national defense. Excluding individuals from private goods is simpler. The cable TV industry excludes nonpaying individuals when it scrambles signals and grocery stores prosecute shoplifters.

The "free rider problem" causes markets to inefficiently provide public goods. If citizens can enjoy benefits without payment, many would choose to pay nothing. Free riders happily choose to let others pay. Markets are inefficient because suppliers do not care about benefits enjoyed by free riders and thus provide too little from the point of view of society. Producers do not cater to nonpaying customers.

Two policies correct inefficient market outcomes in theory. One is to subsidize sellers for providing public goods to free riders. Subsidies to movie theaters, museums, swimming pools, roads, parades, and firework displays are examples. The other is for government to take over provision and provide benefits to all. National defense and public museums are prominent examples. Correction thus focuses on subsidies or taking over production and providing public goods at efficient levels.

Again, corrections appear amazingly easy. A little reflection reveals little reason to believe government is very good at promoting efficient levels. One reason is that government mostly produces private goods, not public goods. Only one retiree can spend money from a monthly Social Security check. Only one person at a time reads a public library book. Only one person at a time benefits from Medicare. It is incorrect to view these programs within the lens of public goods theory.

Another common fallacy is to believe that defense spending is entirely consistent with public goods theory. Defense spending is often on private goods. The 2011 budget of the U.S. Department of Defense was $708 billion. Defense spending is notorious for often having little to do with national security as it constitutes "favors" to constituents of politicians. Such spending is often "pork barrel" reflecting "taking home the bacon" by politicians to their constituents. It is problematic to separate public goods spending from that of pork.

When spending promotes national security—and thus represents a public good—it is unlikely to be efficiently provided. Stories of Pentagon purchases of hammers for $434 and $600 for toilet seats are well known. A new weapons lab or naval ship may promote national security, but are unlikely to be built at lowest cost. Politicians compete for spending in their home districts and it is naïve to believe winners are always low-cost bidders. Secretary of Defense Robert Gates admitted one of his problems is attempting to kill "weapons programs" that the country did not need was that members of Congress object too strongly because restructuring the military means lost jobs in their districts.[12]

Efficient spending levels are also unknown by outside observers. They are not driven by the invisible hand of markets to arrive at efficient outcomes, but by the visible hand of government. High anxiety over national defense may also contribute to a culture where "more is better than less" simply because overspending is preferred to under-spending when it comes to protecting the country. This mentality has been described as "throwing mud on the wall and hoping some of it sticks." Again, government is not particularly good at spending efficiently other than in theory.

IMPERFECT COMPETITION

That customers are better off with competition requires little discussion. Owners that understand that each day in business may be their last strive to produce quality products at low prices. Monopoly is extreme lack of competition, but markets characterized by few competitors are inefficient as well. A city with few grocery stores would not be a market in which most of us would want to shop. Solutions include taxation, regulation, and breaking large businesses into smaller ones that compete against each other.

Government's record at promoting competition is very poor. That government is called upon by businesses for protection from competitors was discussed in the previous chapter. Businesses have two ways to deal with competitive pressures: provide better values to customers or lobby government to stall competitors. Politicians suppress competition in many ways. Limiting numbers of new bars or restaurants protects existing businesses. Zoning laws can restrict big-box stores such as Wal-Mart from entering communities. Laws forbidding Internet sales of prescription drugs and alcohol limit competitive pressures. Suppressing competition is at odds with stated goals of protecting citizens from lack of competition.

Oddly enough, government itself is either a monopolist or highly protected from competition in most areas it is involved. Government is a monopolist in areas that include national defense, Social Security, the post office, motor vehicle registration, air traffic control, airport security, highways, and prisons. But, there is no compelling reason to decry lack of competition only as long it characterizes markets. The unspoken, but incorrect, assumption is that government somehow never acts as a "monopolist" in the sense of placing itself before interests of citizens.

Public education exemplifies the belief that government monopoly is good. Parents are assigned to specific schools thus creating "exclusive territories" that force parents to undertake costly relocation when they prefer other schools. This arrangement is like assigning one grocery store per family based on location alone. Although a community has many grocery stores, each family may only shop at the one assigned to them. Few of us need to reflect long on how this arrangement would affect our shopping experience. Owners would understand their captive audience has no alternatives. But, this is exactly how public education has been provided with few citizens understanding that this is a government monopoly.

Private schools prove to be weak competitors because parents who opt for private schools must in effect pay twice for education. They pay private tuition and also support public schools whether or not they opt for private education. Private schools therefore experience a huge price disadvantage that undoubtedly contributes to their small fraction of overall education. Continuing the grocery store analogy, this would be the same as requiring all families to pay for expenses of the assigned grocery store whether or not they purchased at other grocery stores as well. Few would pay twice no matter how much better the quality of other stores.

Milton Friedman argued it is much better to give dollars to customers than to schools.[13] Parents would then pick among competing schools that now have greater incentives to perform well. Voucher programs work in this manner and are highly contentious because they fundamentally alter leverage between demanders and suppliers in education. The National Education Association (NEA), which is the largest teachers' organization with 2.7 million members, is vehemently against these reforms arguing that public schools simply lack funding, not motivation to perform well.[14] Proponents of expanded competition argue schools have never before feared closure for poor performance and enjoy the quiet life of monopoly.

Critics might believe this discussion unfairly blames teachers and administrators for the woes of public education. This conclusion is incorrect. The point here is that it is the institutional structure of monopoly that is the major problem. Even the best and most dedicated teachers and administrators in the world would find it a daunting task to provide quality education within a system that lacks competition and has little fear of being closed down.

GOVERNMENT SPENDING IS RARELY "INVESTMENT"

Government spending is often labeled "investment" when it is believed to enrich our future. The investment argument traces its routes back to John Maynard Keynes (1883–1946), the father of macroeconomics. One of his ideas was that government spending exerted a multiplied effect on economies suffering bouts of high unemployment. That is, economic growth as measured by Gross Domestic Product (GDP) rises by a multiple of spending. A multiplier of two, for example, would mean GDP rises by $2 for every $1 spent by government. The multiplier is the backbone of today's fiscal policy used to justify the huge government spending "stimulus" as a means of growing our economy.

There are two main problems with this argument. One is that politicians rarely spend dollars more efficiently than consumers. The previous chapter demonstrated the invisible hand of markets guides consumers and producers toward efficient outcomes that could never be replicated by the visible hand of government. Claims of large multiplier effects from public spending are seductive and have encouraged billions of dollars in new spending. Meanwhile, spending mostly funds local communities with little regard to how that spending enriches the nation as a whole.

Senators Tom Coburn (R-OK) and John McCain (R-AZ) document a few of the more obvious pork barrel spending projects in the recent "stimulus" bill of 2009.[15] In the forward to their "Summertime Blues: 100 Stimulus Projects that Give Taxpayers the Blues," they write:

> When Congress passed the $862 billion American Recovery and Reinvestment Act in 2009, otherwise known as the stimulus bill, it passed with assurances that it would stem the loss of American jobs and keep the economy from floundering. As most can see, it hasn't.

Their list includes:

- $762,372 to create "Dance Draw" interactive dance software (Charlotte, NC),
- $62 million for a tunnel to nowhere (Pittsburgh, PA),
- $450,000 to dredge a marina to restore waterfront location of a restaurant (Lancaster, VA),
- $253,123 for museum with 44 annual visitors to fund bug storage (Raleigh, NC),
- $1.8 million for a road project that is threatening a pastor's home (Newark, OH),
- $89,298 to replace a new sidewalk that leads to a ditch (Boynton, OK),
- $3.8 million for a "streetscaping" project (Normandy Park, WA),
- $200,000 to help Siberian communities lobby Russian policy makers (San Francisco, CA),
- $39.7 million to upgrade the statehouse and political offices (Topeka, Kansas),
- $700,000 to study why monkeys respond negatively to inequity (Winston-Salem, NC),
- $193,956 to study voter perceptions of the economic stimulus (Dallas and Houston, TX), and
- $363,760 to help the National Institutes of Heath (NIH) promote the positive impacts of stimulus projects (Silver Spring, MD).

An interesting side story to recent spending stimulus efforts is the estimated $20 million that has been spent placing signs across America that state: "Putting America to Work. Project Funded by the American Recovery and Reinvestment Act."[16] Some politicians believe there are better uses of stimulus funds than "tributes to politicians who have done nothing more than appropriate money furnished by their long-suffering constituents."[17] While placement and purchasing of such signs require workers, those dollars could better be used to fund projects of more lasting value.

A second problem is that government spending must be financed by higher taxes or more federal debt. Government spending therefore "crowds out" spending in markets. This necessarily means less private spending by consumers and businesses and therefore the multiplier effect of government spending on GDP is mostly fictional. Recent empirical evidence spanning 50 years of government spending concludes that the current multiplier in the United States is between 0.4 and 0.7, which means government spending shrinks GDP.[18] Thus, every additional dollar of government spending leads to an increase of 40 cents to 70 cents in GDP. When government takes a dollar out of the private sector, it puts only 40 cents to 70 cents back in and so the economy shrinks.

One claim is that government spending raises economic growth by placing dollars in the hands of the poor and middle class where they will spend it faster than the rich. This argument assumes that redistributing dollars from the rich to the non-rich stimulates GDP. One problem with this logic is that the so-called rich do not have idle funding sitting around under their mattresses but place dollars in banks and other investments where they expand the economy. These dollars enable loans and jobs to the non-rich and there is no reason to believe they are any less stimulative than when placed in the hands of the poor.

Evidence that government spending shrinks the economy is entirely consistent with the first problem that government spends less efficiently than markets. Our economy pays a heavy price when government expands and markets contract. Studies of developed economies conclude that government spending crowds out both consumer spending and business investment.[19] A comprehensive evaluation of existing economic research concludes that wealthy countries display significant and negative relationships between government spending and economic growth—when spending increases by 10 percentage points, annual GDP growth decreases by 0.5 to 1 percent.[20]

The facts on recent auto bailouts demonstrate how ineffective government spending can be in promoting efficiency. Recent claims of up to 1 million jobs have been made that include jobs outside the auto industry, but only 55,000 auto workers had been rehired at that point.[21] These numbers included those at Ford Motor, which did not receive a bailout. It is instructive to place these estimated jobs in context. The average cost of providing new jobs ranges from \$84,800 (1 million jobs) to \$1,541,818 (55,000 jobs) per job. This is not an efficient public spending program by either measure.

True costs are much higher. Job rehires at Ford should not be included in new jobs created. Ford also would have experienced fewer layoffs itself if its competitors were not bailed out. Also, the \$84.8 billion in government spending made taxpayers that much poorer. Above evidence on crowding out indicates the bailout was a net job loser because more than one job was lost for every one "created" by government. Fewer jobs in retail, construction, health care, and other industries, along with taxpayers, are the forgotten citizens that pay a heavy price as government props up inefficient businesses. Research indicates that for every 100 new jobs the government creates, 114 jobs in the private sector were eliminated in Sweden.[22] Examination of developed economies reveals similar results and that crowding out of private sector jobs also leads to workers being unable to find work.[23] Finally, the auto industry bailout suppresses the creative destruction process thus slowing the rate at which more efficient businesses take over the less efficient. Again, government in practice acts opposite to the theory that it makes markets more efficient.

The vicious cycle of using past failures to justify more government is alive and well. Recent proponents of bailouts have argued they did not solve our economic problems because they were too small. Of course, this is the proverbial "the hair of the dog that bit you" approach that attempts to cure a hangover with more alcohol consumption. Lawrence Lindsey places the \$800 billion spending "stimulus" in perspective of the 8 million people who became unemployed since the beginning of the recession and August 2010.[24] Each one of these people could have been handed government checks for \$100,000, which would have "stimulated" their economic lives much better than the government stimulus package.

The point is that there is little reason to believe government spending programs are investments in anything other than those being subsidized—such as failing businesses, their workers, and local communities with powerful members in Congress. Common sense suggests that cutting government spending raises GDP growth by replacing inefficient government with more efficient markets. Recent research concludes that tax cuts spur economic growth by a multiple of roughly 3[25]: a \$100 billion tax cut would raise GDP by \$300 billion.

It is well known that seniority in Congress yields powerful politicians who can really bring "home the bacon." A recent study supports this observation with evidence on "earmark spending" over 1967–2008.[26] The authors found that chairing powerful Senate committees overseeing finance and appropriations brings 40 percent to 50 percent more spending to their constituents. Senior members of the House bring 20 percent more to their constituents. The same study, however, concludes that such earmarks "directly supplant private sector activity—they literally undertake projects the private sector was planning to do on its own."[27] Increased public spending is also shown to cause significant retrenchment of corporations headquartered in states of senior politicians thus again indicating that government spending crowds out private businesses and their jobs.

CAN "NUDGES" PROMOTE EFFICIENCY?

Using "nudges" to guide individuals toward efficient decisions has recently been argued by "behavioral economists." Leading advocates are Richard Thaler and Cass Sunstein, who published *Nudge: Improving Decisions About Health, Wealth, and Happiness* in 2008.[28] Because they "nudge" rather than strong-arm or explicitly prohibit inefficient behaviors, nudges are labeled "benevolent paternalism." Behavioral economists believe these labels allow them to escape negative connotations attached to paternalism—policies aimed at protecting individuals who are believed unable to protect themselves. In short, behavioral economists promise nudges make us healthy, wealthy, and wise.

A few choice quotes by Thaler and Sunstein convey their logic.

People often make poor choices—and look back at them with bafflement!

and

We do this because as human beings, we all are susceptible to a wide array of routine biases that can lead to an equally wide array of embarrassing blunders in education, personal finance, health care, mortgages and credit cards, happiness, and even the planet itself.

Behavioral economists are on a mission to help us fulfill our dreams as they correct our self-inflicted behaviors that cause us to exercise too little, eat too much, take on too much debt, smoke, drink too much alcohol, and save too little for retirement.

Behavioral economists argue individuals are often irrational, or inefficient, in their choices. Rearranging food placements in cafeterias is a nudge favored by behavioral economists, who believe diners have difficulties controlling impulses to eat unhealthy food. Research suggests placing healthy choices at the start of buffet lines nudges diners into choosing apples, low-fat entrees, and other healthier items. Grocery managers could nudge shoppers by replacing candy with healthier snacks near checkout stands since this location is known to spark impulse buying.

Nudges have been proposed to spur employees to sign up for pension savings upon employment. Delay is argued to stem from indecision over choosing from too many savings options by employees who then delay by thinking daily losses of interest income are too small to worry about. Meanwhile, many dollars of future pension income are lost. Individuals are also believed to lack foresight concerning future regret over too few dollars saved for retirement. An additional error arises when individuals don't take advantage of matches by employers—some employers match dollar-for-dollar savings of workers up to some maximum. Behavioral economists believe workers are foolish to reject "free" matching dollars.

Various nudges are believed appropriate to guide irrational employees. One is to decrease numbers of savings plans based on the argument that there is such a thing as having too many choices. Another nudge makes enrollment in employer-matching programs the default choice. Behavioral economists argue their prescriptions are benign because employees still retain freedom to opt out of employer-matching programs as well as simply refuse to save any income for retirement.

Why would behavioral economists place themselves in positions where they are given authority to guide, or correct, those who they believe need their nudges? Skeptics remember Henry David Thoreau's (1817–1862) famous statement in *Walden, or a Life in the Woods*.

> If I knew for a certainty that a man was coming to my house with the conscious design of doing me good, I should run for my life.

Thomas Sowell has written several important books in which he refers to the "Vision of the Anointed" that defines intellectuals.[29] His insight easily applies to behavioral economists since they apparently believe their better knowledge entitles them to guide us in our everyday lives. Sowell argues they don't even know as much as the rest of us. What they do possess, however, is better knowledge of the language spoken by other intellectuals. This knowledge is mostly inconsequential, meaning it matters little to most people. Intellectuals are argued to incorrectly believe what knowledge they do possess can be generalized to other areas. Sowell argues there is a world of difference between wielding mathematical equations versus farming, carpentry, parenting, and the many other activities individuals attend to each day. Simply put, intellectuals overstate their ability to improve upon markets.

It is also important to recognize differences between "nudging" by businesses versus governments. Profits motivate businesses and thus their nudges foster efficiencies since otherwise there would be no purpose. For example, rewards for staying in good health are nudges that are in line with raising profits. Government and behavioral economists operate under no such profit constraint and thus efficiency may have little to do with their motivation. Just as government cannot match supply with demand better than markets, behavioral economists are unlikely to know how to successfully nudge us toward greater efficiency even when they believe they have uncovered irrational behavior.

Finally, it is perhaps obvious, but "benign paternalists" place themselves in the role of fathers guiding actions of children. This role is appropriate when exercised by parents over children, but it remains questionable to award behavioral economists this same role over all citizens. Behavioral economists believe we should thank them for their nudges, but apparently don't expect thanks since otherwise we would know enough to refrain from behaviors from which they attempt to steer us away.

FOUR

Government: The Last Place to Look for Efficiency

KEY POINTS IN THIS CHAPTER

- Politicians promise efficiency but most lack business experience.
- Government lacks ability and motivation to mimic how markets promote efficient outcomes.
- Government is either a monopolist or highly protected from competition in most areas in which it engages.
- Government spending is often of the pork barrel variety that benefits few at the cost of many.
- Taxes cannot direct citizens to efficient choices over the government they desire because value is disconnected from costs.

Apparently, politicians believe themselves competent to run the largest enterprise in the country. A reality check about just how large our federal government has become is helpful at this point. Figure 4.1 compares federal spending with revenues of the five largest businesses in 2010.[1] Federal spending of $3,721,000,000,000 dwarfs revenues of the top five businesses:

- Wal-Mart ($408,000,000,000),
- Exxon Mobil ($285,000,000,000),

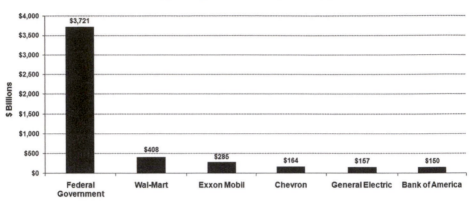

Figure 4.1 Federal Government vs. Five Largest Businesses. (*Source: Fortune* magazine and OMB.)

- Chevron ($164,000,000,000),
- General Electric ($157,000,000,000), and
- Bank of America ($150,000,000,000).

Combined revenues of these businesses are only 31 percent of federal spending.

This chapter argues that politicians lack ability and motivation to efficiently run such a huge enterprise. Five basic principles of government back the claim that government is the last place to look for efficiency. Unfortunately, overstating government's ability to guide efficient outcomes leads to the vicious cycle whereby failures of government lead to more programs based on the flawed premises that most problems stem from too little government and that government is more efficient than markets. Government is thus led to repeat its past mistakes.

PRINCIPLE 1: GOVERNMENT DOES NOT MIMIC MARKETS

Government is not called upon to mimic how markets work. It's illogical to call upon government to promote efficiency when markets do this already. Of course, politicians are never elected on promises they intend to make government inefficient. Examples from recent State of the Union (SOTU) addresses follow.

And finally, it [economic plan] seeks to earn the trust of the American people by paying for these plans first with cuts in Government waste and efficiency; second, with cuts, not gimmicks, in Government spending; and by fairness, for a change, in the way additional burdens are borne.

—William Jefferson Clinton, 1993 SOTU

Just as we trust Americans with their own money, we need to earn their trust by spending their tax dollars wisely. Next week, I'll send you a budget that terminates or substantially reduces 151 wasteful or bloated programs, totaling more than $18 billion. The budget that I will submit will keep America on track for a surplus in 2012.

—George W. Bush, 2008 SOTU

Starting in 2011, we are prepared to freeze government spending for three years. Spending related to our national security, Medicare, Medicaid, and Social Security will not be affected. But all other discretionary government programs will. Like any cash-strapped family, we will work within a budget to invest in what we need and sacrifice what we don't. And if I have to enforce this discipline by veto, I will. We will continue to go through the budget line by line to eliminate programs that we can't afford and don't work.

—Barack Obama, 2010 SOTU

The myth that government can be efficient often stems from mischaracterization of markets. Markets are driven by an invisible hand that matches demand with supply. The visible hand of government can never know how to better match demand with supply. Misunderstanding of how markets work apparently goes a long way toward believing politicians are better at guiding efficient outcomes than markets.

Recent bailouts demonstrate that government does not mimic markets. Businesses fail when they no longer provide good values to customers at prices that allow them to remain in business. Bailouts suppress the creative destruction process. While bailouts save jobs today, they also subsidize inefficient businesses. Automaker bailouts subsidize owners, workers, and local communities. Short-term benefits of helping these groups come at longer-term costs imposed on everyone else. Longer-term costs include "gluing" resources to inefficient businesses by slowing the rate at which resources flow to more efficient businesses. Owners, customers, and workers at more efficient businesses suffer harm as do taxpayers.

The "cash for clunkers" program of 2009 provides a case study in unintended consequences from bailing out failing automakers. The government used taxpayer funds to provide rebates from $3,500 to $4,500 when purchasing new, more fuel-efficient cars. The immediate effect was to drive sales up rapidly as consumers knew a good deal when they saw one. However, some buyers would have purchased cars without the rebates thus merely altering timing of purchase rather than decision to purchase. That is, rebates raised short-run sales at the cost of future auto sales. Rebates also led some consumers to purchase new cars rather than spending money on house repairs, used cars, paying off credit card debt, or saving for college expenses of children. Rebates themselves raised the attractiveness of buying new cars that had nothing to do with whether they reflected efficient purchase decisions.

The Federal Reserve—created in 1913 by the Congress to be the central bank of the United States—has joined the U.S. Treasury in rescuing failing businesses. Conventional wisdom is that the Federal Reserve only rescues private banks and other financial firms. However, recent disclosures reveal that the Federal Reserve's $3.3 trillion in emergency loans went to many businesses outside of Wall Street and to foreign-owned banks during 2008 and 2009.[2] Businesses included General Electric, Caterpillar, Verizon, Harley-Davidson, and Toyota. The Federal Reserve helped out Harley-Davidson 33 times by lending a total of $2.3 billion and General Electric 12 times by lending $16 billion. Federal Reserve officials argue these loans were necessary to stabilize the world economy.

There is no reason to believe the cash for clunkers program invigorates competitive spirits of the automakers as it suppresses the creative destruction process that other businesses confront on a daily basis. Investors send more dollars to protected industries simply because they now carry less risk. Of course, more efficient businesses without protection receive fewer dollars. Unfortunately, these programs have a way of becoming entitlements that guarantee continued protection by taxpayers.[3] Their adverse effects are therefore more permanent than commonly believed.

Markets would have allowed the process of creative destruction to selectively weed out the worst businesses one by one. Politics intervened and favored some businesses with the intention of stopping markets and their relentless drive toward efficiency. Recent events demonstrate how far the practice of government has veered away from the theory that government promotes efficiency.

Federal flood insurance provides another example where government does not mimic markets. A *Wall Street Journal* editorial described how, despite few readers knowing of a particular resident of New Orleans's Jefferson Parish, they had helped repair her home with federal flood insurance (NFIP) four times already.[4] Remarkably, previous residents of the same house had received similar help seven times. They argued that this was a symptom of a government insurance program that places unfunded liabilities onto taxpayers. Insurance premiums cover 60 percent of payments thus imposing shortfalls on taxpayers. NFIP had a $21 billion shortfall in 2006.

Some 120,000 properties received multiple taxpayer-subsidized flood insurance payments—at a cost of $7.25 billion—over 1978–2006. Some 26,000 properties received four or more flood payments. One property in Houston received sixteen payments totaling $807,000 in repairs that amounted to seven times its market value in what was described as: "The owner keeps rebuilding, mother nature keeps tearing it down, and hapless taxpayers keep footing the bill."[5] All in all, some 4,600 properties received payments exceeding their property values, which cost taxpayers $400 million.

Despite conventional thinking that property owners are the problem, the *Wall Street Journal* argues: "The real villain here is Congress for allowing this free lunch to continue."[6] Many payments go to wealthy owners of beachfront vacation properties. Dauphin Island off the coast of Alabama, for example, is an exclusive area of vacation homes inhabited by high-income citizens that received more than $21 million in payments. "Federal flood insurance, in short, is the equivalent of paying heart patients for smoking cigarettes and then also paying for their next triple bypass."[7]

Advocates claim that private insurers would charge unfairly high premiums and thus it is only fair that property owners receive lower-cost insurance through government. Of course, private insurers charge relatively high premiums because it is risky to insure homes in flood zones. Charging premiums that reflect high risk is an efficient pricing program that discourages overbuilding of high-risk homes on floodplains. Property owners of course prefer to receive subsidized insurance through government as an alternative to paying higher market-determined premiums.

Government flood insurance is a classic example of moral hazard whereby a program—flood insurance—that is supposed to protect citizens from risk—flooding—causes problems—flood damage—to become worse. Again, government does not attempt to mimic efficient outcomes of markets. Government charges lower insurance premiums than those available from private insurers and thus underfunds future payments from flood damage. Unfunded liabilities are shifted onto taxpayers.

But, flood damage is higher due to moral hazard because public flood insurance results in more properties and properties of higher value being built on floodplains. Again, government promotes inefficiency by subsidizing flood risks that then causes more property development in riskier areas and thus less development in lower-risk areas. Markets efficiently contain such risks, but again, government is rarely called upon to mimic the efficient ways of markets.

Proponents of public insurance programs often argue that government must supply insurance because of few private insurers. Ironically, government insurance itself "crowds out" private insurers who would more efficiently operate without taxpayer subsidy. Private insurance premiums would closely mirror risk thus resulting in far fewer insurance claims as fewer properties would be built on floodplains. Owners who purchased private insurance would also have incentives to reduce their risks—and control premiums—by choosing lower-risk locations and taking extra precautions to minimize damage in the case of floods.

It also remains difficult to argue that government flood insurance is fair unless the case can be made that it is appropriate that harm imposed on losers justifies gains of winners. Losers include taxpayers and those not receiving insurance subsidies and winners are those receiving subsidies.[8] A recent study concluded that winners are often wealthy when it argued:

> The current price of flood insurance both subsidizes new development in flood zones and subsidizes risk for those who already built in flood zones. These twin subsidies have left the NFIP with a gaping fiscal hole. The costs of the subsidies will likely be borne generally by taxpayers. But where there is a subsidy, there is a benefit. The benefits of the NFIP appear to accrue largely to wealthy households concentrated in a few highly-exposed states.[9]

PRINCIPLE 2: GOVERNMENT LACKS THE ABILITY TO MIMIC MARKETS

Government is unable to mimic how markets work. The visible hand of government is no match for the invisible hand of markets. Remember the invisible hand requires no outside observers orchestrating behaviors of consumers and producers. The process is so subtle that few ever ponder its existence. Government, however, is an outside observer of markets that must use its visible hand to intervene on the basis of limited knowledge and technical expertise. Correction cannot come naturally. This principle probably explains the strong temptation to focus on good intentions rather than actual consequences of government.

Markets are efficient because producers thirst for profits. This thirst is fundamental because it insures businesses keep costs low so that customers believe prices reflect good values. Cost-cutting is vital and owners ignore this function at their own peril. Successful owners require no special training to understand that profits rise with cost-savings. Disappointment must follow expectations that government is efficient because no invisible hand guides cost-cutting. Rather, government never fears creative destruction thus reinforcing the cold fact that little harm comes to the inefficient.

Critics of markets often claim cost-cutting associated with job layoffs is symptomatic of greed because it demonstrates owners care more about profits than people. Apparently this logic would dictate that businesses should not cut costs as technology rises or when demand falls. Demonizing cost-cutting is really arguing that businesses should be inefficient. Meanwhile, competitors here or abroad are happy to drop prices through cost-cutting. Cost-cutting is also critical to maintaining jobs since failed businesses can't employ anyone.

Government also operates under no such cost-cutting constraint because it is forbidden from earning profit. Citizens "own" government in some sense, but workers have few incentives to reap benefits from cost-cutting. Government workers surely understand cost-savings will not raise their income thus making incentives regarding efficiency vague at best. Workers might feel greater satisfaction from jobs well done or from winning special awards for cost-savings, but incentives pale in comparison to those in businesses.

Politicians display great interest in securing government jobs for their constituents as visible proof of helping their constituents. The "more government jobs the better" mentality enhances reelection prospects. What works well for a government that operates without a profit motive would be disastrous for competitive businesses where cost-costing is essential to success. Rather, job-padding will be the order of the day. Efforts to streamline government jobs would be met with opposition from those workers themselves as well as their elected representatives.

Milton Friedman described how this incentive for excessive government job creation played out in Asia in the 1960s. Upon visiting a government-run canal project he was struck by how many workers were hired to dig out the ground using shovels. He asked why no tractors or other heavy-duty equipment were used. His government escorts quickly responded that this was evidence of their effective government jobs program. Friedman responded with something like, "Then, why not give them spoons instead?" Unlike businesses who proudly tout cost-savings, government rarely mimics these successes as this case neatly demonstrates.

Friedman also explained inefficiency of government spending when he said, "Nobody spends somebody else's money as carefully as he spends his own." Politicians spend taxpayer money and there is little reason to believe they would ever spend it as carefully as their own. While perhaps ungracious to admit, many of us would rather receive gifts of money rather than fruitcakes, ties, or flowers. Why? Because we know best what we like. This observation explains much about the divide between markets and government since only in the former can consumers and producers spend their own dollars.

William Niskanen Jr. argued that forbidding profit pushes government workers to pursue "pay, power and prestige" instead.[10] Budget maximization is one symptom. Because large and lavishly furnished offices and non-essential trips add to amenities, government workers may maximize such amenities through maximizing budgets. Of course, they are no different from the rest of us in preferring high salaries. The unspoken goal of spending all budget monies by year's end is commonly seen as another symptom of behavior that pursues budget expansion at the expense of cost-saving. There are always justifications for additional government spending, but enhancing efficiency is unlikely as long as cost-cutting does not enhance "pay, power and prestige."

A recent paper by Chris Edwards examines pay received by the federal government's 2.1 million civilian workers and concludes they earn twice as much in wages and benefits as the average worker in the U.S. private sector: $119,982 versus $59,909 in 2008.[11] Figure 4.2 compares average compensation for both groups in 2008 dollars since 1990. Federal employees earned 50 percent more ($76,600 vs. $50,911) in 1990, but by 2008, they earned double ($119,982 vs. $59,909). Edwards doubts claims that differences reflect federal employees having skills and education well above private counterparts. Overpaying government workers is one method of redistributing income from taxpayers to government employees. Another advantage of federal employment is job security. One study states that private sector workers are five times more likely to get laid off than government workers.[12]

Another unspoken rule is "the last thing a government agency wants is to be effective." This insight makes sense when budget expansion is the goal. Effective programs thwart this pursuit because budget expansion is

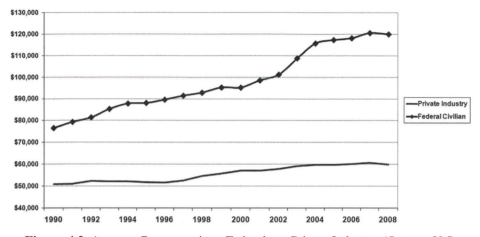

Figure 4.2 Average Compensation: Federal vs. Private Industry. (*Source:* U.S. Bureau of Economic Analysis.)

easier when poor performance can easily be blamed on "lack of funding." Most of us would laugh at businesses that publicly proclaim they can't be successful because they lack revenues from customers. Somehow, "lack of funding" become more credible when uttered by government.

Skeptics might argue that elected officials understand the importance of instilling efficiency incentives. Milton and Rose Friedman, however, argued that elected officials have more than met their match with unelected government workers.

> Bureaucrats in general have very long tenure. It is almost impossible to discharge them. The number of governmental employees discharged in the course of a year is trivial compared to the total number employed. The top bureaucrats were in place long before the current President was elected; they expect to remain in place long after the current President completes his term or terms in office. They have their fingers on the controls; they know where the bodies are buried. They can outwit the current President and the current legislature. Delay is an enormously effective instrument for this purpose and can be deftly exercised by bureaucrats.[13]

Government workers enjoy high levels of autonomy from elected politicians. Again, it remains doubtful elected politicians exhibit much interest in mimicking how markets work even if they believed they had such ability. Politicians interested in efficiency will also be at a severe disadvantage when monitoring performance of programs they watch over. Few to no market counterparts exist with which to gain comparable information. For example, it is difficult to contrast the efficiency by which welfare programs aimed at the poor operate when the only market counterparts are nonprofit charities. There are no good examples of private militaries either. Thus, monitoring government performance will be loose at best when we don't know how much it costs nongovernment entities to provide similar services.

PRINCIPLE 3: MONOPOLY GOVERNMENT CANNOT BE EFFICIENT

It is ironic that lack of competition in markets is viewed a problem, but an attribute in government. What is a problem in markets should also be a problem in government unless we believe government resists monopolistic urges to care little about keeping costs low and placing citizens first. Government is either a monopolist or highly protected from competition in areas that include national defense, Social Security, the post office, motor vehicle registration, air traffic control, airport security, highways, prisons, and education.[14] Lack of competition insures government provides all or most of these functions.

A common claim is that government monopolies are efficient because their large size allows huge economies of scale. After examining 50 studies of cost differences between government and market providers, Dennis Mueller argued: "The evidence that public provision of a service reduces the efficiency of its provision seems overwhelming."[15] In 40 studies (and controlling for quality, prices, and costs), government provision was found to be vastly more expensive than private provision and in only two cases was the opposite determined. Industries examined included airlines, cleaning services, bus services, fire departments, and debt collection.

Empirical studies merely confirm that monopoly governments have little ability or motivation to be efficient. How else to explain the U.S. Post Office? In 2010, the U.S. Post Office was the second-largest civilian employer of government with more branches than the sum of all McDonald's, Wal-Marts, and Starbucks.[16] The Government Accountability Office (GAO), the investigative arm of Congress, has declared the Post Office is not a viable business venture.[17] It lost $8 billion in 2010 alone and there is little hope it will become self-sustaining. Total compensation of the average postal employee was $83,000 a year in 2010, placing them among the highest-paid government employees.[18] Despite rapid increases in technology, compensation costs today are 80 percent of total costs. Recent pleas for higher fees for stamps and ending Saturday delivery are its latest proposals for solvency. Few expect these changes will make it efficient.

The growth of government inevitably slows down the pace at which government functions. An interesting fact is that the federal government constructed the Pentagon in only 18 months in the early 1940s. Michael Barone contrasts the high efficiency of government in World War II to the anticipated 42 months it will take to construct the Humpback Bridge over the Potomac River outside of Washington, D.C.[19] This bridge does not rise over 30 feet above the water and is only 244 feet long. Another example is building of the LaGuardia Airport in New York City in just 25 months. Barone argues government has somehow "unlearned" how to accomplish big projects. He argues: "Big government has become a big, waddling, sluggish beast, ever ready to boss you around, but not able to perform useful functions at anything but a plodding pace. It needs to be slimmed down and streamlined, so it can get useful things done fast."

One possibility for improving efficiency is to offer workers incentives to save dollars rather than waste them. John Steele Gordon recently wrote that the British Royal Navy under Admiral Lord Nelson (1758–1805) did just this.[20] The navy's job was to capture enemy warships and to stop enemy commerce. They succeeded because the Royal Navy awarded officers and crew the entire value of captured ships and their cargoes. Interestingly, the Royal Navy then purchased these warships, which explains why ships often carried French names. Modern-day workers might be given substantial incentives to save monies as well. For example, the Post Office might allow local branches to share in any savings they deliver over time. Of course, there would be monitoring problems and unintended consequences, but this strategy is still worth a thought. Another is to simply privatize it and force it to compete with market alternatives.

In 2009, President Obama called for "a process through which every government worker can submit their ideas for how their agency can save money and perform better."[21] The president's SAVE (Securing Americans' Value and Efficiency) Award enables workers to submit ideas for savings. The process was expanded in 2010 so that employees could both submit ideas and vote on ideas submitted by others. Hoping to capture enthusiasm associated with viewer-led voting on shows like American Idol, the American people rated the "final four" via online voting.

The first winner was a Department of Veterans Affairs employee from Colorado who proposed that VA medical centers permit patients to take home extra bandages and medication when they are discharged, for an estimated savings of $14.5 million over five years. The first winner yielded "peanuts" in savings when compared to federal spending of $3.7 trillion in 2010 alone. That did not include costs of administrating the SAVE program. It also remains unclear how much of the $14.5 million in savings will ever materialize. History does not suggest optimism.

Competition is also stifled when incumbent politicians have competitive advantages over challengers. The probability that an incumbent in the U.S. House of Representatives is reelected has risen dramatically.[22] Over 1990–2008, reelection rates averaged 95 percent for the House of Representative and 88 percent for the Senate.[23] One important advantage to being an incumbent politician is that they already have a support staff and public funds with which to fight challengers. Glenn Parker has argued that:

> The incumbent's advantage is clear: repeated exposure through trips to the district and mass mailings.... House incumbents have an assortment of resources for promoting their visibility within districts. The perquisites of office provide a member with funds to operate district offices and/or mobile vans that keep the incumbent's name prominent within the district and the local press; these incumbent "enterprises" are staffed and operated at public expense. In addition, House incumbents have use of the congressional frank that permits them to send mail to their constituents also free of charge.[24]

Politicians without fear of challengers are also less interested in pursuing efficiency in government.

Another edge to incumbent politicians is through gerrymandering political districts to favor their political party. Political jurisdictions are redrawn every 10 years and are determined in different ways. Gerrymandering reduces competition for political seats by diminishing the ability of voters to oust incumbents. The following forms are among those included in gerrymandering.

- *Packing* whereby many similar voters are placed within a district to minimize the number of elections they can influence.
- *Cracking* where similar voters are spread over many districts so they exert little influence over elections.
- *Hijacking* occurs when the district of an incumbent politician is purposively redrawn to minimize their chances at reelection.

North Carolina, in particular, has received much attention because of its liberal use of gerrymandering. For example, even though one of its districts stretched 190 miles, it was sometimes no wider than Interstate 85. It is hard to argue that politicians insulated from competition would have much interest or ability in running a government that is efficient.

PRINCIPLE 4: PORK BARREL SPENDING

The following example describes how parochial interests prevailed over general interests of the population.[25] In 1984, the late congressman Claude D. Pepper (D-FL) defeated a move that would withdraw $500 million from a $18 billion water project that funded new dams, canals, and bridges throughout the country. The $500 million project was to build a 110-mile canal across Florida. Even though the canal had been initially proposed to Congress in 1942 as a means of protecting shipping interests from Nazi U-boats, the $500 million project was authorized many years after the Nazi threat was long gone.

But, why would politicians support pork barrel spending serving parochial interests of a few voters? Vote-trading, or logrolling, explains how politicians trade votes amongst themselves that enable projects serving interests of minorities but approved by majorities. When opponents attempted to defeat the canal project they were informed by the chair of the Public Works and Transportation Committee that projects within the same spending bill that benefited their districts would be withdrawn. This tactic was effective since the project won approval. This behavior is also consistent with the widely known attitude that voters display toward Congress. Voters predominantly hold negative opinions of Congress, but are quite pleased with their own representative since they visibly "bring home the bacon" to them. The above reelection rates demonstrate this allegiance.

A few interesting pieces of political handiwork were described by the 2001 "Freedom to Manage Act" proposed by President George W. Bush.[26] The following examples demonstrate how legislation is written with specific aim toward narrow constituency interests of specific politicians.

- NASA was expressly prohibited from relocating aircraft based east of the Mississippi River to the Dryden Flight Research Center in California.
- The Defense Department was prohibited from outsourcing to the private sector more than 50 percent of major maintenance and repair of planes, tanks, and vehicles, regardless of cost-savings.
- The Department of Agriculture (USDA) was barred from closing or relocating even a single state Rural Development Office. Taxpayers are paying for 5,600 USDA county field offices (more than one per county), many located near one another.

These examples describe successful attempts at directing the benefits of government to very specific constituents at the cost of the general public.

The following "oinker" awards presented by the Citizens Against Government Waste for the 2010 Congress highlight some of the more obvious recent cases of pork.[27]

- "Dunder-Head Mifflin Award" to Senator Arlen Specter (D-PA) and Representative Paul Kanjorski (D-PA) for $200,000 for design and construction of a small business incubator and multipurpose center in Scranton, Pennsylvania.
- "Narcissist Award" to Senator Tom Harkin (D-IA) for $7,287,000 to continue the Harkin Grant program and to Senator Robert Byrd (D-WV) for $7,000,000 for the Robert C. Byrd Institute of Advanced Flexible Manufacturing Systems.
- "Steak Through the Heart of Taxpayers Award" to Senator Kay Bailey Hutchison (R-TX) and Representative Ciro Rodriguez (D-TX) for $693,000 for beef improvement research.
- "Jekyll and Hyde Award" to Representative Leonard Lance (R-NJ) for his ever-changing stance on earmarks; first signing a no-earmark pledge, then receiving $21 million in earmarks, then supporting the Republican earmark moratorium.
- "Kick in the Asp Award" to Delegate Madeleine Bordallo (D-Guam) for $500,000 for Brown Tree Snakes control and interdiction in Guam.
- "Plane Waste Award" to Senators Sam Brownback (R-KS) and Pat Roberts (R-KS) and Representative Todd Tiahrt (R-KS) for $3,500,000 for the National Institute for Aviation Research.
- "Do You Want Fries With That Award" for $2,573,000 in potato research in four states requested by five senators and five representatives.
- "Putting on the Pork Award" to Representative Maurice Hinchey (D-NY) for $400,000 for restoration and renovation of the historic Ritz Theater in Newburgh, New York.

Again, theory that government promotes efficiency clashes with its practice of pork barrel spending. Politicians and their constituents obviously know the difference, but theory of government apparently lags far behind.

Little public discussion is held on many of these projects. One study investigated the list of witnesses who provide input into congressional hearings.[28] A compilation before 14 hearings showed that of 1,060 witnesses, 1,014, or 96 percent, spoke in favor of programs (and usually higher spending); 39, or 3.7 percent, were neutral or mixed; and 7, or less than 1 percent, opposed programs or spending. As one example, 6 witnesses spoke before a committee on job training; all 6 were in favor and included, in addition to an economics professor, the Department of Labor official in charge of the program and officials of the private companies that operated its training facilities. Another hearing was on "Private Sector Initiatives to Feed America's Poor," and 8 of 11 witnesses were supporters of an expanded private sector role in antipoverty programs; however, many of the private sector programs were, in fact, federally funded programs and, of the 1 dissenter who provided testimony, he appeared at the end of the session when all the senators had left for the day and a staff member concluded the session. The same study found that a majority of congressional witnesses were federal administrators (47%), followed by lobbyists (33%), state and local government officials (10%), members of Congress (6%), and representatives of business firms and consultants (4%).

PRINCIPLE 5: TAXATION PROMOTES INEFFICIENT CHOICES

The fifth principle of government is that its funding system cannot possibly direct citizens to efficient choices over the government they desire. Equilibrium prices emerge from digesting an immense amount of information through the invisible hand of markets. Prices are higher (lower) for products consumers value more (less). Prices are higher (lower) for products that cost more (less) to produce.

Government has no such price guide. Taxes cannot guide citizens to make efficient choices since they ignore values and costs attached to products. Consider income taxation where individual tax bills are determined without direct reference to either values or costs of government. Individual taxpayers are not charged more for services they value more or that cost more to provide. Tax bills simply rise in sync with income.

The following example easily makes the point that our tax system leads to inefficient choices. Consider three citizens—Mary, Bill, and Emily—who are voting on whether government should provide a new swimming pool. Mary is a daily swimmer, Bill never swims, and Emily is an occasional swimmer. So, Mary values the pool the most, followed by Emily, and then Bill. Tax bills however contain no information on how these individuals value the new pool since government "prices" the pool on the basis of income. The person with the highest income is charged the most irrespective of how much they value the pool. Taxes thus do not guide voter decisions in any way remotely comparable to market prices.

Consider grocery shopping where we are used to being guided by individual prices attached to products—for example, milk at $3 per gallon, apples at $2 per pound, and pears at $3 per pound. Shoppers choose good values knowing that the more items placed in shopping carts the more their wallets are emptied. They pick and choose efficiently since otherwise they understand they are wasting their income. Mistakes, of course, are made but there are clearly incentives in place to learn and become better shoppers.

Now replace the market's price system with the income tax. Shoppers find many great values when they are no longer personally responsible for paying for every item placed in their carts. Shopping carts would probably be too small as shoppers are now smart enough to figure out that prudence or frugality reaps little individual reward. Many have experienced something similar, but on smaller scales, when paying a fixed price to eat at an all-you-can-eat buffet. We eat more and certainly waste more food than when we are personally charged for each and every item we place on our tray as we stroll the buffet. Our trays would hold fewer items if we had to pay for each and every item separately.

Our tax system also distorts choices because citizens are not separately charged for each government program. Programs are bundled together without separate statements detailing costs of each program thus making it impossible to compare costs with values attached to individual programs. Anne, for example, owes $7,500 in taxes for the sum of all programs, but is not given information showing that $1,233 funds national defense, $50 funds a new education program, $33 for a new park, and so on. Consider how grocery shoppers would respond if individual prices for apples, bananas, chicken, and bread were not visible as they went about their shopping. This describes the experience for citizens who take on the formidable task of thinking carefully about which government programs represent good values. The experience is unlikely to result in an efficient government simply because citizens have little incentive to scrutinize each and every program when they are bundled together into a huge blob labeled "government."

Divorcing payment from consumption creates only a fuzzy connection between tax bills and government that makes it impossible for even the most prudent citizens to wisely choose programs on the basis of benefits and costs to society. What goes on underneath the surface of markets is more subtle than the very visible hand of government thus making it difficult for us to understand how prices guide citizens to efficient choices in markets. It is predictable that lack of understanding of this most basic characteristic of markets makes it difficult to understand government cannot be efficient. Our income tax system discourages citizens from making efficient choices, but unfortunately it is easy to miss this fact.

FIVE

Government Rarely Promotes Fairness

KEY POINTS IN THIS CHAPTER

- Government rarely promotes fairness when policies are promoted on promises of benefits with little to no harm.

- Assessment of fairness often focuses on income inequality despite the fact that income varies for many reasons other than inequality of opportunity.

- Poverty rates overstate poverty thus making it difficult to recognize who is most deserving of government help.

- Employers and landlords respond to minimum wage and rent control laws in ways that adversely affect the poor and non-poor alike.

- Proponents of bailing out failing businesses and home owners rarely delineate winners from losers.

Efficiency and fairness are not synonymous and markets can only be expected to achieve the former. Government has spent more than $13 trillion fighting poverty since President Lyndon Johnson declared our "war on poverty" in 1964.[1] We now have 122 separate antipoverty programs that spent $591 billion in 2009. This figure translates into $14,849 for each person in poverty, which ironically is substantially larger than the poverty line of $10,830 in that year.

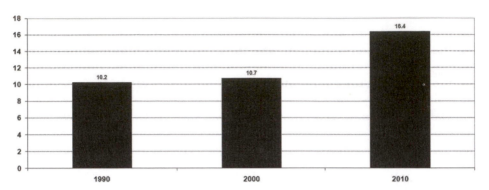

Figure 5.1 Government Payments to Individuals: Percent of GDP. (*Source:* Office of Management and Budget.)

Figure 5.1 shows the dramatic rise in government payments to individuals: from 10.2 percent in 1990 to 16.4 percent of GDP in 2010—an increase of 61 percent.[2] Payments in 2010 were $2,393 billion, or roughly $7,478 per citizen, for programs that include Social Security, unemployment benefits, medical care, housing, and food assistance.[3] Few believe fairness has grown in sync with the government's expanded role in promoting fairness.

This chapter argues that even if government at times promotes fairness, it won't do so efficiently—a predictable result given the inefficient nature of government. Laws mandating minimum wages and maximum rents are shown to often hurt those they attempt to benefit. Programs also often redistribute income to the non-poor. Bailouts of failing businesses and programs aimed at helping home owners often redistribute income to the non-poor. Previous chapters described how bailouts promote inefficient outcomes, but this chapter argues they rarely promote equity because they are based on promises of benefits with little to no costs. Meanwhile, citizens receive a one-way ticket to disappointment with an expanding government.

MISPLACED FOCUS ON INCOME EQUALIZATION

Income Differences Overemphasized

Income equality and equality of opportunity are not synonymous. Perfect income equality means all individuals receive equal incomes. Equality of opportunity means all individuals have equal opportunities to earn income. Of course, all individuals do not have identical opportunities.

Public schools that fail to provide adequate preparation limit income opportunities for students. Children may be disadvantaged when parents lack resources to purchase proper nutrition and health care.

There is no reason to expect equality of opportunity results in equal incomes. Differences in effort arise even when workers have identical education and abilities. One worker may prefer $45,000 and live in a small town with many weeks of vacation and another with equal ability and opportunity may prefer $75,000 in a large city with little vacation. Educational choices vary as well. We may envy high salaries of medical doctors, but choose not to invest in so much schooling. Natural ability varies as shown by professional athletes earning high salaries. Luck surely plays a role too as exemplified by lottery winners or those simply "in the right place at the right time." Americans understand that hard work and effort pay off. A recent poll indicates Americans mostly agree (85%) that, "While people may begin with different opportunities [in America], hard work and perseverance can usually overcome those disadvantages."[4]

Income differences do not clearly measure differences in consumption opportunities. Not all income is received in monetary payments as demonstrated by employer contributions to pensions, government transfers (e.g., food stamps and free medical care), and fringe benefits (e.g., free coffee and parking). Salaried workers may be willing to trade off more vacation time or shorter work weeks for less salary. Fringe benefits should be included in a comprehensive measure of income if we want to measure differences in opportunity to consume.

Consumption opportunities also vary by net worth. Changes in net worth often occur through changes in home values. If a house appreciates in value from $125,000 to $140,000, net worth rises by $15,000. A capital loss of −$15,000 occurs if its value falls to $110,000. However, only "realized" capital gains or losses are counted as income and so some individuals show little income even when they are "sitting" on great wealth. Income thus does not necessarily mirror net worth.

Income inequality can therefore present a distorted picture of consumption opportunities and what roles are played by effort, choice, ability, chance, and inequality of opportunity. Despite these many distortions, income inequality is the main assessment tool for fairness of market outcomes. This method of assessment is like a test that fails to fully assess the medical condition of an ill patient. The test might offer limited information but it is unwise to believe it explains all that ails the patient.

In theory income equalization focuses on "shaving" income off of higher-income individuals and transferring it to lower-income individuals. Our progressive income tax code is based on this "Robin Hood" agenda. But, in practice it opens up its own can of worms. One is that it damages incentives to earn income by those being "shaved" when they respond by hiding income and working less. Another is when those receiving income transfers work less. Both predictable responses work against good intentions.

Claims that redistributing income from high-income to low-income citizens stimulates the economy are also unfounded. Taking $200 from Paul to provide $200 to Mary leads to no additional spending. But, transferring income may encourage Paul to work less when he prefers not to support Mary. Mary may also find working less rewarding when she receives Paul's support and thus cuts back on working. Incentives matter and rewarding Mary for not working and penalizing Paul for working may shrink an economy. Again, predictable responses work against good intentions when income redistribution distorts behavior of citizens.

Falling average or median incomes are often used to prove the poor are losing at the expense of the rich. Again, this exercise does not clearly demonstrate this result. Table 5.1 shows incomes of five individuals in a hypothetical society with three alternative income distributions. All have average and median incomes of $51,000. Inspection indicates widely differing income distributions: $25,000–$79,000, $51,000–$51,000, and $3,000–$95,000. Thus median and average income can hide wide differences between income distributions. Efforts to equalize income based on assessments of average or median incomes can be quite disappointing.

Table 5.1   Hypothetical income distribution

Individual	Distribution		
	A	**B**	**C**
Mary	$25,000	$51,000	$3,000
Bill	$35,000	$51,000	$16,000
Anne	$51,000	$51,000	$51,000
Michael	$65,000	$51,000	$90,000
David	$79,000	$51,000	$95,000
	Summary Statistics		
Average	$51,000	$51,000	$51,000
Median	$51,000	$51,000	$51,000

Defining Poverty

Defining poverty is more art than science. The "poverty threshold" is used to define poverty. The statistic is assembled by adding up what a bare bones income would look like for families of various sizes.[5] Thresholds measure percentages of families in poverty. Its 2008 value of 10.3 percent is the same as its value in 1980, despite previous discussion that government payments to individuals increased 61 percent over 1990–2010.[6]

Problems arise with this measure of poverty. First, income is an imperfect gauge of opportunity and the ability to consume. Second, poverty rates have been raised by immigration of many lower-skilled workers in recent years. Three, data ignore food stamps, health insurance, housing and energy subsidies, and tax rebates for low-income earners. Research suggests their exclusion cuts out about half of real income. In addition, poverty measures ignore that over one-half of America's poorest one-fifth did not own a car in 1973, but 73 percent did by 2003.[7]

The "poor" versus "rich" is also an ever-changing mix. In the mid-1980s, one-third of all families moved each year from one quintile to another.[8] An income quintile represents one-fifth, or 20 percent, of the population. For the three lowest quintiles, roughly 18 percent of families moved to a higher quintile in the following year and, for the three highest quintiles, more than 20 percent of families moved to lower quintiles the following year. Growing income dispersion does not necessarily mean the "poor get poorer" and the "rich get richer."

Of course, these facts do not mean the poor no longer deserve help. But, determining how poverty has changed or even recognizing who is most deserving of government help remains elusive. It is not surprising so many are disappointed with government efforts to help the poor.

Transferring Income to the Politically Powerful

Citizens may earn income either through working in markets or receiving government payments or laws that benefit them financially. "Rent-seeking" is the act of extracting income through government by special interest groups that include farmers, retail shops, the Sierra Club, the United Auto Workers (UAW) Union, the National Education Association, and AARP. Conduits between special interest groups and favorable policies are politicians.

Gordon Tullock wrote about the Egg Marketing Board, which was awarded monopoly rights to distribution of all eggs in British Columbia in 1956.[9] The Egg Marketing Board was created by 200 egg producers who raised egg prices an average of 10 percent above free market prices. While costing an average family an additional $10 per year, sellers experienced average wealth gains of $300,000.

Why did this transfer of income occur? The Egg Marketing Board claimed it supported "family farms," but Tullock concluded it used politicians to increase their wealth:

> The individual who works hard and thinks carefully in order to make money in the market will also work hard and think carefully in order to use the government to increase his wealth. From the individual standpoint, the effort and ingenuity he puts into the project and the return he gets are the important variables, not whether he is using the government or the market for his income.[10]

Government confers substantial benefits on small groups while distributing costs widely over the population. Here, benefits were large ($300,000 per producer) and flowed to few (200 producers), but costs ($10 per family) were spread thinly across all consumers. Benefits and costs to supporting or fighting programs are vastly different. Gainers (200 egg producers) have strong incentives to lobby politicians for monopoly distribution rights. Losers—egg consumers—have little incentive to fight given the $10 per year they would gain by defeating the policy. Politicians respond to the powerful and concentrated signals of special interest groups and not the weak and dispersed signals of those harmed.

Rent-seeking theory also explains regulatory capture whereby regulators protect businesses they regulate. Businesses expend great energies making sure politicians protect their interests before interests of the general public. Government, for instance, took major stakes in failing automakers. The UAW Union is a very large special interest vying for political favors such as bailouts of their employers. Headquartered in Detroit, Michigan, the union has about 390,000 active members and more than 600,000 retired members.[11] Owners of automobile businesses also gain from taxpayer bailouts. Automakers captured politicians who recognized their supporters were more united in their efforts to receive bailouts than the many harmed.

As previously discussed, bailouts slow the ongoing onslaught of creative destruction that has dogged automakers since they were hammered by foreign imports during the 1960s. High labor costs that include underfunded pensions have also placed growing pressure. Lowering costs and building better products are the only viable means of staying in business unless they secure bailouts that buy more time without fundamentally restructuring businesses. Bailout costs are spread thinly over many taxpayers, unlike benefits awarded the industry. The U.S. Treasury has also taken ownership positions in hundreds of large banks under the Troubled Assets Relief Program in another display of taxpayer monies flowing to a particular industry.

The bottom line is that transfers often flow to the politically powerful. Recall discussion in the previous chapter of federal flood insurance. Subsidies were often awarded to high-income property owners including many owners of vacation properties. The myth that transfers only go to the poor often provides effective political cover for transferring income to the politically powerful. Meanwhile, the poor are rarely politically powerful despite the myth of fair government.

Payments to Non-needy

Three recent examples describe how wasteful programs aimed at helping the poor can be in reality. One is the Low-Income Home Energy Assistance Program that serves 8.3 million U.S. households.[12] Its well-intentioned goal is to provide payments for air-conditioning and heating. The Government Accounting Office (GAO) recently determined that $116 million went to applicants ineligible for the program that included individuals using 11,000 dead people's Social Security numbers, 725 individuals in prison, and 1,100 non-poor government workers. A postal worker earning $80,000 per year collected an $840 payment. The audit was only of seven states so these numbers underestimate fraud.

Another is GAO's estimate of fraud of between $600 million and $1.4 billion in disaster relief for Hurricanes Katrina and Rita through the Federal Emergency Management Agency (FEMA).[13] GAO found that FEMA paid $6,000 to a fictitious applicant who submitted a vacant lot as a damaged address. The following itemization uncovers other examples.

We also found that FEMA provided expedited and housing assistance to individuals who were not displaced. For example, millions of dollars in expedited and housing assistance payments went to registrations containing the names and social security numbers of individuals incarcerated in federal and state prisons during the hurricanes. In addition, FEMA improperly paid individuals twice for their lodging—paying their hotels and rental assistance at the same time. For example, at the same time that FEMA paid $8,000 for an individual to stay in California hotels, this individual also received three rental assistance payments for both hurricane disasters. Finally, we found that FEMA could not establish that 750 debit cards worth $1.5 million went to hurricane Katrina victims. We also found debit cards that were used for a Caribbean vacation, professional football tickets, and adult entertainment.

Public anger at President George W. Bush's response to Hurricane Katrina clearly enabled even more inefficiency as speed rather than caution became more important for disaster relief. Future crises will be even more inefficiently managed if speed continues to take a higher priority rather than caution.

A different GAO report found significant fraud in Head Start, a federal agency with a $9 billion budget that provides child care to roughly one million children in low-income families.[14] GAO concluded that about one-half of their undercover agents found that government workers underreported family income in order to allow payments to ineligible families. One example was a day care center in which two families with incomes in excess of $110,000 received payments.

This does not mean that no help is provided to the needy. Rather, it is unlikely programs will efficiently help the poor with many dollars wasted and other dollars flowing to the non-poor. Accounting measures such as Head Start spending thus overstate how much help is really provided the poor. Waste and misapplied funds go a long way toward explaining our dissatisfaction with government.

CONTROLS ON WAGES AND RENTS

Minimum Wage Laws

Minimum wage laws are enacted to protect low-skilled workers from unfair wages. The federal minimum wage as of July 24, 2009, is $7.25 per hour, though states may adopt minimums above the federal rate. These laws find broad support in polling because their intentions are noble. It is also commonly understood these laws only make life a bit easier because workers still have trouble making ends meet at the minimum wage. A full-time worker earns roughly $15,000 per year at the minimum wage.

These laws are a classic example of government not attempting to mimic markets. Markets move toward efficient outcomes and it would be redundant for government to pass laws requiring markets to do something they already do. Proponents characterize business owners as exploiting low-skilled workers with few opportunities. But, there is no conspiracy since both employers and job hunters determine wages. Equilibrium wages are where demand equals supply. Labor markets do not set wages above equilibrium because workers outnumber jobs available in what is commonly known as unemployment. Wages fall until workers equal jobs available.

Now let's impose a minimum wage above equilibrium on the promise that low-skilled workers receive an income boost. The law forbids markets from doing what they do so well—removing surpluses—unemployment in this example—by dropping wages. Minimum wage laws force markets to retain unemployment for the sake of fairness because job hunters permanently outnumber jobs available at wages set above equilibrium. Despite noble intentions, the law in effect creates unemployment, though this fact requires an understanding of how markets work.

Two types of unemployment are created. One arises because employers lay off workers as they become more costly because the law cannot raise their productivity. Layoffs are the result of harm reduction by businesses as they cut expenses. Unemployment also arises because the law acts as a carrot enticing people to look for work who previously did not want to work at lower wages. They now want to work at higher wages. A cruel irony is that there are no jobs for these workers.

Economists understand the basic principle that minimum wage laws create unemployment, but polling indicates roughly half of economists nonetheless support them.[15] Supporters believe those lucky enough to earn higher wages justify those who cannot find jobs. Some also believe few workers are laid off thus making the fact that it creates unemployment for an unlucky few a bit more palatable. A few economists even believe workers become more productive because they experience greater fears of being laid off—an idea lacking widespread support.

Unintended consequences are many and work against noble intentions. In addition to creating unemployment, marginally profitable businesses relying on low-skilled workers are harmed. About 7 in 10 workers earning the minimum wage in 2008 were employed in service occupations, mostly in food preparation and serving related jobs.[16] The service industry thus suffers much of the harm. While it is common to believe harm is entirely placed on owners, this is untrue. Workers suffer job loss, customers suffer higher prices, and some of these citizens are indeed poor. Taxpayers pick up higher tabs from heavier burdens placed on income support and public housing.

Workers with lowest skills are harmed the most because they are usually the least productive. They are the least experienced, often young, poorly educated, and more likely to live in inner cities. They are thrown into a Catch–22 situation where jobs require previous experience, but the law makes it more difficult to gain first-time experience as it creates fewer jobs.

The poor are often mischaracterized as doomed to lives working at the minimum wage, but over 60 percent of workers progressed beyond minimum wage work after one year with a typical wage gain of 20 percent.[17] Some workers struggle at minimum wage jobs for many years, but they are mostly in part-time jobs and did not complete high school.

Minimum wage laws make it unsurprising that teenagers and minorities experience the highest unemployment rates. Unemployment for everyone over age 16 was 9.3 percent in 2009, but was 24.3 percent for those ages 16 to 19; see Figure 5.2.[18] Broken down by race for everyone over 16, the unemployment rate was 8.5 percent for whites, 14.8 percent for blacks, and 12.1 percent for Hispanics. Other factors contribute to unemployment, but the minimum wage is a major factor causing it to be higher than otherwise for these groups.

Battles to improve wages often abruptly end with passage of increases in minimum wage rates. These laws create a false sense of security about how much good they have done since they lower employment prospects of these workers. Some benefit from higher wages, but others are thrown out of work or lured by false promises into looking for work that will not materialize. Minimum wage laws thus unambiguously promote fairness only as long as the harm imposed on individuals is somehow believed to justify the gains of other individuals. Meanwhile, less effort will be given

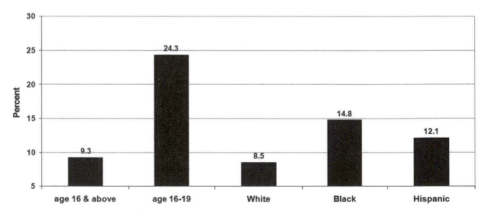

Figure 5.2 Unemployment Rates in 2009. (*Source:* Bureau of Labor Statistics.)

to policies such as improved educational opportunities that offer more promise to improving income opportunities of the poor.

Rent Control

Rent controls set rents hundreds of dollars below those of comparable units not subjected to controls. The underlying rationale is that market rents are unfair to those with limited incomes and paying less rent allows their very limited incomes to go farther. Similar policies are placed on gasoline, heating oil, and natural gas. Rent controls are opposite to minimum wages since they mandate ceilings below equilibrium rents rather than floors above equilibrium wages.

The law of unintended consequences is alive and well under rent control. Basic understanding of supply and demand reveals they cause shortages as more people want to rent than there are units available when rents are not allowed to reach equilibrium. Markets naturally eliminate shortages by raising rents to equilibrium, but rent control freezes rents below equilibrium. Shortages are so acute in New York City that native New Yorkers often contend the only way to get a rent-controlled apartment is to read the obituaries and be the first in line the following morning to apply for newly vacated units.

Favoritism or racial, gender, or ethnic discrimination are rationing devices when landlords choose applicants on characteristics they prefer in tenants. Landlords may also regain income losses by requiring that renters lease furniture or by soliciting bribes of money or gifts. Landlords often recoup losses by reducing maintenance expenditures. Lower-income individuals may be placed on permanent waiting lists. For every renter who complains, others on waiting lists stand ready to take their unit.

Landlords may convert rental units into condominiums and co-ops not subject to rent controls thus exacerbating shortages as conversions shrink supply of rental units. Potential investors in new apartment buildings are also dissuaded from investing thus further contributing to a decreasing supply of rental housing that raises rents of units without controls. These reactions also push the poor into units without controls thus raising rents for the poor and non-poor alike. Taxpayers pick up higher tabs from heavier burdens placed on income support and public housing.

Rent controls unambiguously promote fairness only as long as one doesn't delve very deeply into their consequences. Ironically, the non-poor often benefit from these laws. Former New York City mayor Ed Koch, for example, was known to have paid $441.49 per month for an apartment worth $1,200 in the early 1980s. One high-profile politician is another recent example of a member of the high-income club who has benefited from rent control.[19] In fact he enjoyed four units in Harlem even using one of them as an office in violation of rent control rules. A study of Cambridge, Massachusetts, revealed rent-controlled units were concentrated among educated professionals with few poor, elderly, and student recipients.[20] Professionals often track down and ferret out these great deals better than the poor. Apparently, landlords are predisposed to renting to tenants they expect have few problems paying rent and those that can afford the largest bribes.

BAILOUTS OF INDUSTRIES AND HOME OWNERS

Protecting Failing Businesses and Jobs

One of the greatest strengths of markets is how they reward innovative technologies and businesses that provide good values to consumers. The market system picks winners and losers on this basis. This great strength is also the source of much discontent for those whose jobs and businesses are creatively destroyed. Predictably, those whose lives are overturned often believe markets are unfair to them and thus call upon government to protect them.

There has been a recent dramatic rise in government bailouts of failing businesses. Federal bailouts (2008 dollars) of businesses since 2008 include[21]:

- Bear Stearns ($30 billion),
- Fannie Mae and Freddie Mac ($400 billion),
- AIG (American International Group) ($180 billion),
- GM, Ford, and Chrysler ($25 billion),
- TARP (Troubled Assets Relief Program, $700 billion),
- Citigroup ($280 billion), and
- Bank of America ($142 billion).

The list of bailouts is long and could easily be the subject of an entire book.

Proponents rationalize bailouts for various reasons. One is that businesses are "too big to fail," which means their failure endangers other businesses and thus could spur an economy-wide meltdown. Industries important to national security such as aeronautical firms, banking, and telecommunications are often placed in this category. Protection from foreign competition is another argument for rescue based on it being unfair when it erodes domestic profits and jobs. Calls for protection often accompany claims that foreign government subsidization of businesses offers unfair advantages. Another rationale is that bailouts are only temporary and will be removed quickly once unforeseen events or recessions conclude. A more recent rationale is that government can partially take over management of businesses such as automakers and redirect them into more profitable enterprises.

There are many criticisms of bailouts. One is that businesses mostly fail due to creative destruction and therefore bailouts strangle this vital weeding out of poorly run businesses. Successful businesses are built to withstand good times as well as bad and so bailouts reward bad management. Bailouts also signal to badly run businesses that they can be less concerned about creative destruction. Government promotes "moral hazard" whereby rescuing inefficient businesses promotes weaker businesses in the future. Lenders and owners are encouraged to be less interested in monitoring business risk. Inefficient businesses attract more capital simply because they are given political preference, but capital becomes scarcer for efficient businesses thus raising overall risk in the economy. Rescues today thus create bailouts tomorrow as long as markets are stopped from weeding out inefficient businesses today.

Politicians are predisposed to cater to immediate benefits from bailouts and ignore longer-term harm. Saving jobs today is immediately gratifying for bailed-out businesses as well as politicians. Owners, creditors, and their employees understandably prefer bailouts rather than losses associated with restructuring. One estimate is that UAW union workers earn $70 per hour—substantially above $25.35 earned by the average private sector worker.[22] Obviously, union workers fear salary reduction and fewer jobs that might follow restructuring by new management. Their rent-seeking efforts have been rewarded with bailouts.

Despite its recent bailout, GM remains unlikely to pay its pension costs in upcoming years. GM's rescue by government left intact $100 billion of unfunded long-term liabilities in what is the world's largest "private" sector pension plan.[23] GM's 531,500 pensioners are supported by 87,500 current employees thus meaning that each worker must support six pensioners. Rescue purposively ignored this imbalance thus shoving its resolution to the future. Investors and creditors that continue backing GM are probably banking on future bailouts. Bailouts restructure the profit-loss nature of markets into one where favored businesses are entitled to profits, but also are entitled to bailouts when they fail.

Skeptics often claim businesses should be rescued because otherwise their plants and factories will simply go out of existence. This argument assumes that businesses would entirely fold without bailouts. This is true only when they have so little value that no one would bid for them. If true, it should even be clearer they should be shuttered since only productive assets draw bidders. Recall that markets can only be efficient when government does not stall the creative destruction process.

Bailouts do not clearly promote fairness because politicians determine which businesses receive rescue. Two traits guide bailouts. One is that inefficient businesses receive bailouts since otherwise they would not require rescue. Bailouts require politicians to pick winners and losers on the basis of something other than efficiency. This is another example of the principle that government does not mimic how markets reward the efficient. The other trait is that businesses are politically powerful since otherwise they would not attract political support. Of course, all businesses become more interested in all matters of politics as played out by political donations and other activities thought to place them within the list of favorites.

Taxpayers ultimately pick up rescue funding as tax bills rise today and tomorrow. Debt is deferred taxation that places burdens on the backs of future taxpayers. Bailouts also "glue" resources to inefficient businesses thus stalling their flow to more efficient businesses. Many customers, workers, and owners of more efficient businesses are harmed despite this fact being difficult to recognize as proponents of bailouts focus on immediate benefits to those bailed out.

That proponents rarely discuss harm associated with bailouts is most telling. It is understandable that proponents ignore harm to taxpayers and efficient businesses since it introduces greater ambiguity into claims that bailouts promote fairness in our society. Bailouts promote fairness only when debate clearly delineates winners from losers for all citizens to clearly understand. Public support or disapproval would then be based on full disclosure of benefits and costs rather than claims that benefits come with little or no harm.

Protecting Home Owners

The recent housing market bubble has created new programs aimed at keeping home owners in their houses. The $8,000 first-time home buyer tax credit of 2009 was designed to pull future demand to the present thus pushing housing prices up today. The tax credit was not primarily aimed at the poor since it was made available for single taxpayers with incomes up to $125,000 and up to $225,000 for married couples. The Home Affordable Modification Program (HAMP) provides financial relief for home owners facing foreclosure, but this program has so far failed to produce many success stories.[24]

These are attempts at promoting fairness based on the argument that falling prices and home owner equity are not the fault of home owners. We have seen record highs in both defaults and delinquencies. Combinations of the following reasons are involved in protecting home owners.

- Lenders deceived buyers into signing loan agreements without sufficient income to make future payments.
- Falling home prices stem from market outcomes unfair to home owners.
- Markets are failing to maintain home prices at levels consistent with their true value.
- Financial markets created hybrid mortgage instruments that caused an economy-wide meltdown.
- Greedy financial institutions caused the housing market meltdown and home owners got caught in the melee.
- Allowing so many foreclosures endangers the overall economy.
- Housing prices will eventually return to past levels.

Government has thus introduced policies that lower both loan size and interest rates, provide tax subsidies for home purchases, and increase regulation of lenders.

It takes a great leap of faith to believe government can judge whether housing prices are correct or not. Rather, falling prices are a symptom rather than a cause of a surplus in the housing market that will only be eliminated when prices fall to equilibrium. Falling prices are symptoms rather than causes of more houses on the market than buyers. Prices want to fall simply because supply and demand are out of whack, but of course home owners dislike falling values of their housing investments.

Government has given itself the unenviable task of attempting to prop up housing prices through raising demand for housing. This is predictable for two reasons. One is that there are so many unhappy home owners awaiting rescue. The other is that government pushed up prices for many years. Housing has experienced a vast amount of government intervention consistent with the American dream of home ownership. A few of the more visible programs are:

- tax deductions for mortgage interest payments,
- tax deductions for property tax payments,
- creation of Fannie Mae and Freddie Mac to purchase mortgages from lenders,
- FHA insurance and VA guarantees,
- subsidized interest rates and payments for first-time buyers,
- low interest rate policies of the Federal Reserve, and
- encouraging lenders to lower minimum down payments.[25]

These policies have numerous supporters that include home owners, lenders, realtors and construction and home supply industries. These parties cheered wildly as government raised housing prices only to complain loudly when they began free-falling from the ensuing price bubble.

Misperceptions persist about how past government actions contribute to today's problems.[26] Conventional thinking is that expanded regulation is the cure-all for greed believed behind housing market problems with little thought that bad business practices were enabled by government. However, the ratio of financial legislation that increased regulation to legislation that decreased it is 4:1.[27] A recent study tracks financial regulatory spending on the theory that financial deregulation would show falling regulatory budgets.[28] Spending in inflation-adjusted (year 2000) dollars on finance and banking grew over the past 50 years: from $190 million in 1960 to $2.3 billion in fiscal 2010. Despite claims that President George W. Bush's administration (2001–2009) led the charge for deregulation, real spending for finance and banking regulation grew 26 percent during his administration.

Fannie Mae and Freddie Mac are government-sponsored enterprises (GSEs) chartered and regulated by government with implicit guarantees that the U.S. Treasury backs their debt. In effect, they acted like private businesses, but under protection of Congress. GSEs are partly responsible for the financial market mess because Congress encouraged them to buy subprime mortgages from banks. Normally, banks would refuse such loans or require larger down payments or higher interest rates. But, banks quickly passed high-risk loans to Fannie Mae and Freddie Mac thus at least partially enabling a housing price bubble fuelled by rising demand for homes. These GSEs were taken over in September 2008 in a move acknowledging they were really undercover government programs all along with little motivation or ability to be efficient businesses. Taxpayers are stuck with a bill of at least $160 billion, though some place it closer to $1 trillion.[29] Future costs are undoubtedly higher as long as Congress is unwilling to shutter Fannie Mae and Freddie Mac.

Recent findings of the Republican members of the Financial Crisis Inquiry Commission placed blame on Fannie Mae and Freddie Mac for part of our housing mess. They concluded:

> The GSEs were not the only means by which the government supported the financing of high-risk mortgages. Through the GSEs, FHA loans, VA loans, the Federal Home Loan Banks, and the Community Reinvestment Act, among other programs, the government subsidized and, in some cases, mandated the extension of credit to high-risk borrowers, propagating risks for financial firms, the mortgage market, taxpayers, and ultimately the financial system.[30]

Fairness issues again arise over citizens who pay for rescues of home owners today and tomorrow. This is further complicated when rescues reward home owners who took on the most risk and experienced the highest default rates. More prudent home owners took on smaller loans and saved more of their income for contingencies such as lost jobs or falling housing prices. Prudent home owners are thus required to pay for excesses of the less prudent since they don't receive bailout money or the newer tax breaks offered to those in danger of foreclosure. It is difficult to argue that the more prudent should rescue the less prudent.

Many home owners couldn't resist drawing down home equity accompanying rapidly rising housing prices. For example, a home purchased for $150,000 becomes an ATM machine of sorts when its value rises to $250,000. Home owners were flooded with offers for refinancing homes with many taking on larger mortgages as they cashed out some or all of their equity. It is easy for home owners to believe that refinancing into a $250,000 mortgage is a safe bet when they believe housing prices only rise and never fall. Some purchased cars, boats, vacations, and other fun items, despite not earning higher incomes. Of course, housing prices eventually fell with imprudent owners—those who cashed out the most equity and took the most risk—being devastated the most. Many ended up "underwater" holding mortgages larger than home values. More prudent owners lost wealth as well, but were better cushioned because they didn't take on larger mortgages, held more savings in reserve, or only drew down smaller chunks of home equity.

A recent article overturns conventional wisdom that the poor are the biggest defaulters.[31] The rate at which the rich have stopped paying mortgages greatly exceeds that of the rest of home owners. Roughly 14 percent of home owners with loans above one million dollars were delinquent in their payments on primary residences, second homes, and investment properties. About 8 percent of borrowers with loans below one million dollars were delinquent. Some delinquencies were "strategic defaults" meaning borrowers chose to walk away even though they had sufficient funds to make payments. Programs helping high income borrowers are consistent with previous discussion that income transfers naturally flow toward the politically powerful and that many are not poor.

Other unintended examples of harm arise. Some renters would have loved to have purchased houses from those in foreclosure, but of course this would mean current home owners would have received prices deemed below what they perceived fair. Future home owners paying higher prices are losers and current home owners are winners in this example. Rescuing imprudent home owners today is of course consistent with government that focuses on creating short-term winners while ignoring those it harms today and tomorrow.

Bailing out home owners poses a significant moral hazard when they come to expect future bailouts. In effect, home owners are rescued from past bad decisions by government thus making past investments more profitable than they otherwise would have been. Government merely subsidizes past decisions that turned sour. Home owners thus become to expect that they should earn all gains when housing prices rise, but are rescued when prices fall. We would all like such protection for all decisions. But, bailouts encourage even more risk-taking and bad investment decisions in the future.

It is ironic that rescues are inconsistent with original intentions of policies that pushed housing affordability. Policies included lower down payments, lower mortgage rates, and encouraging private lenders to make loans to those who previously would never have been able to borrow. These actions quickly raised demand for housing that eventually contributed to a full-blown housing price bubble. Longer-term consequences—housing price bubble—thus eventually became out of sync with initial intentions of making housing more affordable. Government efforts then abruptly changed course attempting to stop housing price reduction with a new goal of propping up housing prices rather than supporting the initial goal of affordability by allowing prices to fall. Government again picks winners—current home owners being rescued by attempting to push up prices—and losers—renters who miss out on lower housing prices, taxpayers who fund rescues, and prudent home owners.

SIX

Misconceptions of Tax Fairness

KEY POINTS IN THIS CHAPTER

- Ninety-two percent of all taxes—individual income, social insurance, and corporate income—are based on income.
- Our tax system mostly ignores benefits and costs when billing taxpayers.
- Disconnecting tax bills from value citizens receive from government leads to misconceptions over fairness.
- Taxing on the basis of income rather than value from government is a major reason why government cannot be efficient.
- Forty percent of income tax revenue comes from the top 1 percent of earners. The bottom 50 percent pay 3 percent. There are 46.6 million citizens who earn income but pay no income taxes.
- Tax collection data stop short of revealing who bears their burdens.

In 2011, $2.3 trillion of federal taxation, or roughly $7,467 per person, was collected.[1] Figure 6.1 displays the four principal types of taxes.

- Individual income refers to taxation of personal income of individuals. The largest category of taxation, this tax accounted for 47 percent of tax revenues.

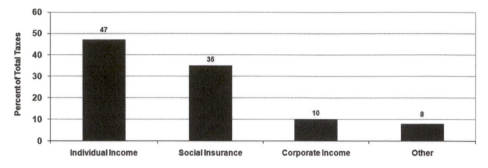

Figure 6.1 Federal Tax Revenue Sources: Fiscal Year 2011. (*Source:* Congressional Budget Office.)

- Social insurance refers to payroll taxes collected for Social Security, Medicare, and unemployment compensation. This source accounted for 35 percent of tax revenues.
- Corporate income refers to taxation of income of corporations. It provided 10 percent of tax collections.
- Other includes estate and gift taxes, custom duties, and taxes on sources such as alcohol, tobacco, telephone usage, and highway, waterway, and airport usage. These taxes accounted for 8 percent of tax collections.

Our discussion focuses on the top three tax sources—individual income, social insurance, and corporate income—that account for 92 percent of all taxes. Discussion of social insurance taxes—one-third of all taxes—takes place in chapter 9.

MARKETS USE THE BENEFIT PRINCIPLE

Markets price according to the *benefit principle.* Only those who benefit from production are required to pay. If Ken decides not to purchase season tickets to the local ballet company, he does not contribute to the ballet company. Mary, however, contributes to the local football team when she purchases tickets to watch games from the bleachers. Payments also rise with greater consumption—Mary pays more than Ken if she buys more hamburgers than Ken.

The benefit principle guides markets toward efficient outcomes. Consumers scrutinize purchases when they recognize they are personally responsible for paying for products they consume. They recognize that greater consumption requires more of their income in payment. Bad values are rejected following comparisons of price with perceived benefits. Mistakes are corrected quickly because consumers don't enjoy wasting income.

Markets cannot require non-users to subsidize users. A pizzeria that remains in business selling large pizzas for $25 cannot charge $10 because its owner will not find charitable citizens who enjoy subsidizing his customers. Market prices must mirror benefits since otherwise consumers walk away. Consumers understand they must pay and thus carefully pick and choose from sellers that understand the importance of providing good values to customers.

Few question fairness of this pricing system. Everyone is responsible for paying for their own consumption and for their own mistakes. The benefit principle is thus synonymous with equity when fairness is defined as charging consumers costs of products they consume. Fairness also means non-users do not subsidize consumption of others.

GOVERNMENT REJECTS THE BENEFIT PRINCIPLE

Government does not mimic markets and thus it does not connect tax bills with benefits. What is meant by benefits requires clarification. It is common to think of benefits only as dollars from Social Security payments or unemployment checks. But, benefits are all values received by citizens from government programs. Benefits take the form of a $650 Social Security payment or values received when enjoying public museums, driving on public roads, or knowing medicine has passed scrutiny of the Federal Drug Administration.

Further, government uses the *ability-to-pay* principle to assign most tax bills.[2] This principle views equity in two different directions. "Horizontal equity" requires that individuals with identical abilities to pay be assigned identical tax bills. "Vertical equity" requires that tax bills rise with ability to pay in one of the following three ways.

- Progressive where tax bills rise faster than increases in income; for example, an individual with an income of $20,000 pays $2,000 in taxes (10%), but an individual earning $30,000 pays $4,000 in taxes (13.3%).

- Regressive where tax bills rise slower than increases in income; for example, an individual with an income of $20,000 pays $2,000 in taxes (10%), but an individual earning $30,000 pays $2,500 in taxes (8.3%).

- Proportional where tax bills are a fixed percentage of income; for example, an individual with an income of $20,000 pays $2,000 in taxes (10%), and an individual earning $30,000 pays $3,000 in taxes (10%).

Table 6.1   Income tax brackets in 2010

Tax Rate	Single	Married
10%	$0–$8,375	$0–$16,750
15%	$8,375–$34,000	$16,750–$68,000
25%	$34,000–$82,400	$68,000–$137,300
28%	$82,400–$171,850	$137,300–$209,250
33%	$171,850–$373,650	$209,250–$373,650
35%	over $373,650	over $373,650

Income tax brackets for 2010 are displayed in Table 6.1. Tax rates rise with higher income brackets under our progressive system. Each rate applies only for income within a given bracket. The first $8,375 of income for a single earner is taxed at 10 percent, additional income between $8,375 and $34,000 is taxed at a 15 percent rate, additional income between $34,000 and $82,400 is taxed at 25 percent, additional income between $82,400 and $171,850 is taxed at 28 percent, additional income between $171,850 and $373,650 is taxed at 33 percent, and additional income above $373,650 is taxed at 35 percent.

Let us compute tax bills for five single income earners using our tax code.[3]

- William earns $10,000 and is assigned a tax bill of $1,081.25, or 10.8 percent of income.

- Janice earns $30,000 and is assigned a tax bill of $4,081.25, or 13.6 percent of income.

- Bernice earns $60,000 and is assigned a tax bill of $11,181.25, or 18.6 percent of income.

- Sam earns $100,000 and is assigned a tax bill of $21,709.25, or 21.7 percent of income.

- Oscar earns $400,000 and is assigned a tax bill of $117,643.75, or 29.4 percent of income.

Average tax rates, which are measured by dividing income into tax bills, rise with income because this is a progressive tax system.

Table 6.2 displays income and tax distribution data of our five-person society. Tax bills rise from $1,081.25 for William up to $117,643.75 for Oscar. A total of $155,696.75 in taxes is collected. The share of all taxes paid by upper-income earners can be quite large. Oscar shoulders

Table 6.2 Income and tax distribution of five-person society

	Income ($)	Tax Bill ($)	% Share of All Taxes	% Share of Income
William	10,000	1,081.25	0.69	1.67
Janice	30,000	4,081.25	2.62	5.00
Bernice	60,000	11,181.25	7.18	10.00
Sam	100,000	21,709.25	13.94	16.67
Oscar	400,000	117,643.75	75.56	66.67
Total	600,000	155,696.75	100.00	100.00

76 percent of all payments. The other 24 percent is divided between Sam paying 14 percent, Bernice paying 7 percent, Janice paying 3 percent, and William paying 1 percent. The final column displays percent shares of total income of $600,000. Oscar's 67 percent share is the largest, followed by Sam with 17 percent, Bernice with 10 percent, Janice with 5 percent, and William with 2 percent.

The top 1 percent of tax returns paid 40 percent of all federal individual income taxes in 2007—thus 1 out of 100 taxpayers funded $40 of every $100 in taxes.[4] The top 5 and 10 percent of taxpayers paid 61 percent and 71 percent, respectively. The top 50 percent paid 97 percent thus leaving the bottom 50 percent paying 3 percent of all income taxes. These data are useful when discussing the perennial issue of "do citizens pay their fair share?"

Our tax system is more progressive than these data indicate. Roughly 46.6 million tax returns faced a zero or negative tax liability in 2007.[5] Roughly one-third of all tax returns were nonpayers and these citizens are not counted in the above statistics on who pays taxes. These are people whose exemptions, deductions, and credits wiped out tax bills and were refunded any dollars paid in from paychecks.[6] About half of nonpayers received payments in what amounts to a "negative tax." These payments are sent to low-income earners on the theory that payments encourage them to continue working rather than quitting work and seeking public assistance.

Finally, it should be understood that regressive and proportional income tax systems are also consistent with the ability-to-pay principle. The commonly held belief that average tax rates—tax bills divided by taxable income—must rise with income in order to be consistent with the ability-to-pay principle is untrue. Tax payments rise with income under progressive, regressive, and proportional tax systems.

Consider again our five-person society. Tax bills under a 10 percent proportional tax are:

- William pays $1,000,
- Janice pays $3,000,
- Bernice pays $6,000,
- Sam pays $10,000, and
- Oscar pays $40,000.

Oscar's tax bill is thus 40 times larger than William's ($40,000 vs. $1,000), rather than 109 times ($117,642.75 vs. $1,081.25) under our current system. The rate of rise is slower than under a progressive tax code, but nonetheless tax bills rise with income. Chapter 10 discusses the merits of a proportional income tax, or what is commonly known as a "flat tax."

WHY REJECT THE BENEFIT PRINCIPLE?

Three reasons are commonly given for rejecting the benefit principle. One is that benefit taxation places an undue burden on the poor. This is the most common justification. Consider funding a public road. Rather than focus on road users that directly benefit from roads, tax bills are based on incomes of users and non-users alike. Citizens are taxed little, much, or not at all with bills revealing nothing about benefits. In contrast, market prices such as private tolls are clearly connected to benefits and never charge non-users. Public education provides another example. Even though parents with children are primary beneficiaries, tax policy makes it irrelevant that some families have many school-age children and other families have few or no children. Whether children attend private schools is also irrelevant.

High implementation costs are a second reason. Even if tax agents knew benefits of thousands or millions of beneficiaries of programs, differential tax schemes would be costly to implement. Mary, for instance, might find much value in public roads, museums, public housing, and space exploration, but not public schools, publicly funded radio and television, and government research on obesity prevention. Each program would require separate tax bills as well. A multitude of different tax bills that vary across citizens would be costly to implement even if necessary benefit calculations are possible.

Lack of knowledge is a third problem. Advocates of the ability-to-pay principle argue the impossibility of accurately assessing benefits from using roads, visiting museums, attending schools, or any other program. Even if individuals knew their benefits, citizens would likely lie when asked to declare benefits since they understand tax bills rise in tandem with stated benefits.

Problems associated with application of the benefit principle carry a ring of truth. Taxes based on benefits might deplete incomes of the poor, especially when our government funds so many programs. Most of us would also be hard-pressed to reveal dollar values of benefits from programs. There are also considerable incentives to understate benefits hoping to lower tax bills. It is also questionable that government would even be capable of orchestrating such an array of different taxes, especially given that it lacks ability or motivation to be efficient.

But, let's think a bit further about conventional wisdom. Consider the impossibility of measuring benefits. Arguing that "we can't measure benefits" is an admission that we can't compare benefits with costs of its programs—a rather unsettling admission to be sure. Of course, advocates of government programs rarely concede that they are not really sure if benefits outweigh costs of their programs. But, in effect, the argument that we can't accurately measure benefits implies just this. Moreover, it also becomes rather problematic for government efforts aimed at promoting fairness if we can't accurately measure benefits from its programs.

It is not always so difficult to determine benefits, however. Markets do it all the time. Consider whether a private business builds a new road. The builder can only collect payments from those willing to pay tolls and will carefully study whether it can provide the road at reasonable profit. Risk is that too few users show up and is obvious when funds come from his own pockets. Investors will also look carefully over shoulders of the builder. The market thus carefully compares benefits with costs as it determines whether to undertake the project.

Private schools provide another example. Private schools exist because parents would not pay tuition unless they believed benefits outweighed costs. It is no secret that the best schools charge the most. This is just restatement of the benefit principle that prices and benefits are aligned when markets allocate resources. Health care is another where customers compare benefits with costs. Again, the best doctors tend to charge the most, or at least have the longest waiting lists, in another restatement of the benefit principle. Even spending on protection arises in the private sector as demonstrated by private purchases of security officers, firearms, locks, alarms, and watchdogs. Prices rise with benefits in markets where customers have great interest in determining whether benefits outweigh costs.

Many functions of government are thus mirrored in markets whereby customers carefully scrutinize benefits along with costs. What is different in markets, however, is that consumers undertake decisions with the understanding that they are personally responsible for paying for benefits. Arguments against the benefit principle ironically lead us back to the title of chapter 4: "Government: The Last Place to Look for Efficiency." Citizens are encouraged to overconsume when their tax bills are not directly connected to values from their consumption. The example of a fixed-price food buffet explains how citizens view government when they perceive more benefits come with little personal responsibility for payment.

In sum, rejection of the benefit principle is argued on the grounds of fairness, but its rejection is also rejection of efficient government. Citizens have very limited interest in cost-benefit analysis that would be naturally pursued in markets where additional consumption comes with clear price tags tied directly to associated costs. Thus, many government programs would never be pursued in markets. Those programs that would be pursued would be of different size. The question remains if the ability-to-pay principle lives up to its promise that it is fairer than the benefit principle.

REDISTRIBUTING INCOME THROUGH TAXES

The ability-to-pay principle opens a very wide door for income redistribution. All programs become transfer programs. Again it is important to define terms. Government defines transfers as simply dollar payments to individuals through programs such as Social Security, Medicaid, and Medicare. This is far too narrow. An individual who enjoys public museums but contributes nothing or little to its provision is the recipient of an income transfer. This largesse is possible because someone who doesn't enjoy museums does contribute.

Consider again a road funded by taxes. Income transfers are possible because road users are subsidized by taxing non-users. Consider transfers that arise on Robert, who receives $100 in benefits from the road.

- A tax bill of $20 assigns Robert an $80 transfer.
- A tax bill of $150 assigns Robert a −$50 transfer.
- A tax bill of $100 assigns Robert a $0 transfer.

Any of the three scenarios can arise since Robert's tax bill is unrelated to his benefits. The −$50 transfer means his $150 tax bill enables a $50 transfer to another person. The +$80 transfer means someone transfers income to Robert.

It is problematic to assess fairness of this tax system to Robert or anyone else. While Robert may receive a −$50 transfer from the public road, he may receive a +$75 transfer from a public swimming pool when he is an avid swimmer. The final value of net transfers requires the impossible task of adding up transfers from many programs. Citizens can't possibly know their own tallies. This conclusion can be rather unsettling for those who have never questioned the fairness of using the ability-to-pay principle to fund government. But, this conclusion nonetheless is valid and should not be ignored if we are truly interested in assessing fairness of our tax system.

Let us pursue this matter further. Citizens are not provided itemized tax bills displaying costs of each program. When Robert pays income tax of $5,000, he does not receive an itemized tax bill showing $500 goes toward national defense, $300 to education, $250 on interest on the national debt, and so forth. The essential question of whether Robert's tax bill of $5,000 is fair or not requires information on how benefits from each program compare to his costs. For example, Robert's tax bill of $500 for national defense may or may not compare favorably with his benefits. This comparison is essential before we can determine whether he receives a positive, negative, or zero income transfer from this program. But, citizens have little ability or even interest in uncovering this information because they have no legal ability to refuse payment for any specific program.

Again, markets provide a stark contrast. Payments for utility bills, private schools, toll roads, hamburgers, cars, vacations, and clothes each involve itemized bills. A $950 rent payment, for instance, clearly links benefits with payment for housing. Members of gyms quit when fees outweigh benefits. An income tax bill, however, does not connect to any benefit except all government programs and citizens have little ability or interest in separating the tax bill—benefit puzzle into its many pieces.

The bottom line is that our tax system creates myriad transfers that invisibly take place without clear recognition by any citizen. Our ability to assess tax equity is very muddy indeed. Individual citizens can not assess fairness of a system that they don't even recognize takes place. Politicians have no better information. No one has a clue. Unfortunately, the muddiness by which we necessarily must assess equity under this tax system is rarely acknowledged. Again, this can be a rather unsettling conclusion for those who have never carefully questioned fairness of our income tax system.

Consider again our five-person society using the 2010 tax code. Simple inspection reveals tax bills (average tax rates) rise quickly with income under our progressive income tax:

- William pays $1,081.25 (10.8%),
- Janice pays $4,081.25 (13.6%),
- Bernice pays $11,181.25 (18.6%),
- Sam pays $21,709.25 (21.7%), and
- Oscar pays $117,643.75 (29.4%).

A total of $155,696.75 in taxes is collected with Oscar shouldering 76 percent of that total—one person out of five pays roughly three-fourths of all taxes.

It is unclear whether this tax system is fair or not without comparing benefits received from programs funded by $155,696.75.[7] The fact that Oscar's average tax rate of 29.4 percent is higher than William's tax rate of 10.8 percent reveals little about fairness. William may receive benefits above, below, or equal to his $1,081.25 payment and the same goes for how tax bills of Janice, Bernice, Sam, and Oscar compare with benefits they receive. This exercise reveals little about fairness because it ignores values citizens place on government they fund with their tax payments.

Ratios of federal spending per dollar of taxes in Table 6.3 offer a very rough description of income transfers between citizens and states in 2005.[8] New Mexico citizens received the highest average transfer of 2.03, which means they received $2.03 in federal spending for every $1 in taxes paid. The difference of $1.03 came from citizens of other states. Rhode Island's value of 1.00 means they paid $1 in tax for every $1 of spending and thus did not receive transfers from citizens of other states. New Jersey citizens were awarded the lowest transfer of 0.61, which means they contributed 39 cents of every tax dollar to citizens of other states. New Jersey citizens thus received negative transfers. Citizens of the District of Columbia received the largest transfers: they received $5.55 in spending for every $1 in taxes paid—quite a positive transfer!

The data in Table 6.3 demonstrate the unequal nature of transfers across states. Thirty-two states and the District of Columbia were net gainers, one state experienced no transfers, and seventeen states were net losers. States with many federal workers and retirees are states with above-average federal spending directed at them. Many people in each state may be well above or below the average for their state. Finally, numbers do

Table 6.3   Federal spending in each state per dollar of federal taxes in 2005

State	Ratio	Rank	State	Ratio	Rank
New Mexico	2.03	1	Vermont	1.08	26
Mississippi	2.02	2	North Carolina	1.08	27
Alaska	1.84	3	Pennsylvania	1.07	28
Louisiana	1.78	4	Utah	1.07	29
West Virginia	1.76	5	Indiana	1.05	30
North Dakota	1.68	6	Ohio	1.05	31
Alabama	1.66	7	Georgia	1.01	32
South Dakota	1.53	8	Rhode Island	1.00	33
Kentucky	1.51	9	Florida	0.97	34
Virginia	1.51	10	Texas	0.94	35
Montana	1.47	11	Oregon	0.93	36
Hawaii	1.44	12	Michigan	0.92	37
Maine	1.41	13	Washington	0.88	38
Arkansas	1.41	14	Wisconsin	0.86	39
Oklahoma	1.36	15	Massachusetts	0.82	40
South Carolina	1.35	16	Colorado	0.81	41
Missouri	1.32	17	New York	0.79	42
Maryland	1.30	18	California	0.78	43
Tennessee	1.27	19	Delaware	0.77	44
Idaho	1.21	20	Illinois	0.75	45
Arizona	1.19	21	Minnesota	0.72	46
Kansas	1.12	22	New Hampshire	0.71	47
Wyoming	1.11	23	Connecticut	0.69	48
Iowa	1.10	24	Nevada	0.65	49
Nebraska	1.10	25	New Jersey	0.61	50
			District of Columbia	5.55	

Source: Tax Foundation, Census Bureau.

not reflect deficit spending and thus future transfers are unaccounted here because some citizens will bear more of their costs in the future than other citizens.

Again, this exercise reveals how little information we have to answer fundamental questions regarding fairness of our income tax system. Is it fair that citizens of New Mexico receive the highest transfers of any state while New Jersey citizens receive the largest negative transfers? Do the poor receive the largest positive transfers while the rich receive the largest negative transfers? Assessment tools require vast improvement before serious assessment of fairness can proceed. Meanwhile, we have the income tax to thank for blocking serious study of tax fairness.

A recent study sheds further light, albeit very dim light, on the issue. It concludes that city dwellers in expensive cities in the Pacific, Great Lakes, and Northeast bear a disproportionate federal tax burden.[9] Their federal tax bills are 27 percent more than workers with similar skills in less expensive and more rural areas. A major reason is that our progressive system taxes more of their income at higher rates even though their higher incomes often don't reflect higher standards of living. It is well understood that high cost of living areas have higher salaries. But, their tax burdens are even more burdensome when it is discovered that many of their tax dollars are transferred to more rural areas. The study concluded that high-cost areas transferred $269 billion in higher taxes to low-cost areas in 2008 alone. This is additional evidence of "invisible" income transfers. Notice this study is unable to clearly demonstrate whether the poor receive the largest positive transfers.

RENT-SEEKING IN TAX POLICY

Skeptics at this point will quickly argue that the ability-to-pay principle is fair because lower tax burdens for the poor take place in a world where the poor receive the largest share of benefits from government—that is, taxes are low but benefits are high for the poor. Perhaps, but there is little reason to suspect programs are primarily aimed at the poor. Recall that rent-seeking theory predicts programs are aimed at the well connected rather than the fact that someone is poor.

Political support goes to powerful special interest groups. Federal flood insurance was shown in chapter 4 to direct many benefits to high-income property owners. Discussion in chapter 5 showed that monopoly rights for distribution of all eggs in British Columbia secured higher prices for sellers. Pork barrel spending examples have also been discussed many times whereby narrow special interest groups receive benefits at the cost of many citizens. Rescues of failing automakers are another example of benefits not being directed at the poor.

It does not require much imagination to apply the theory of rent-seeking to tax policy. Rents may be secured in the same way they are awarded through beneficial legislation or public spending. Citizens prefer lower tax burdens than higher tax burdens. Chapter 8 describes how "tax preferences" decrease taxes through deductions, credits, and exemptions to individual groups at the expense of the many. Specific industries, such as automobile, steel, or financial institutions, lobby for reduced tax bills. Greater tax deductions for owners of old buildings or old cars indicate a few of many possibilities.

Whatever form rent-seeking takes, the result is always to transfer income. Reconsider Robert, who receives $100 in benefits from a new public road. He clearly gains with tax reduction, but assessing fairness of the tax change becomes a muddy exercise. We now have two determinants of tax bills rather than one: income and whether or not some citizens receive tax reduction that other citizens do not enjoy. Another complication is that tax bills of others might rise to make up for tax losses from Robert. And still another complication arises when tax reduction reduces government programs that Robert or others enjoy. Again, simple comparison of tax bills between citizens reveals little about tax fairness as rent-seeking loosens connections between tax bills and income.

These facts are not well appreciated. Just because it is easy to collect income data and inspect how they vary across incomes does not mean it is particularly useful in assessing whether government is fair or not. This exercise does not clearly reveal who receives the best or worst deals from government and therefore sheds little light on how well government promotes fairness. There is little reason to believe that ignoring value from government yields fair tax policy because debate focuses on incomplete disclosure of who gains and who loses from government.

Again, this conclusion will be rather unsettling to those who have been happy to implicitly assume that comparing tax bills in isolation of value from government offers a useful guide to tax fairness. This mentality leads to a false sense of security about our ability to assess tax fairness. Chapter 10 discusses tax reform measures that would improve the ability and motivation of government to be efficient and fair. Unfortunately, widespread misconceptions regarding tax fairness contribute to why so little fundamental tax reform has taken place over the years.

TAX SHIFTING

An enduring myth is that tax burdens always fall directly on those paying taxes. Paul O'Neill, former secretary of the U.S. Treasury, provided the following commentary on the confusing and complex nature of how government collects taxes:

> For a long time we've maintained what I think is clearly a fiction—the idea that somehow corporations and businesses pay taxes. The clear

economic truth is that businesses and corporations don't pay taxes, they just collect them for the government.[10]

Analysis of tax incidence examines who really bears burdens of taxation by questioning whether taxes are passed onto other parties. For example, taxes imposed on businesses may be passed onto consumers. Consider taxes on cigarette sales. Smokers bear much of the tax in higher prices. Businesses appear to pay the tax, but businesses merely collect taxes before sending them to the government treasury.

Tax data are easy to collect, but unfortunately stop short of revealing who bears burdens. Burdens can easily be passed onto consumers with few options such as consumers of cigarettes and gasoline. Consumers with many options flee higher prices. Rising prices of hamburgers lead diners to purchase more chicken, salad, tacos, and pizza thus giving business owners greater pause before hiking prices.

Taxes on movie theaters lead more customers to rent movies or watch more TV thus leaving more burden on owners. Owners, of course, attempt to pass burdens onto customers by hiking prices on popcorn and soda. Even this strategy has its limits when moviegoers have alternatives such as bringing their own food and soda, eating before movies, or simply forgoing their usual popcorn and soda.

Often, taxes on business owners are shifted. Consider a tax on each worker employed by business owners. Politicians might claim this tax is fair because it is placed on owners, but this simply mandates who must collect the tax. The reality is that workers are compensated in salary and benefits such as health care, vacation, sick leave, and pension benefits. Betty, for instance, might receive $75,000 in total compensation, split between 50,000 in annual income and $25,000 in benefits. The new tax forces owners to rearrange compensation components so that Betty still receives total compensation of $75,000.

Income tax shifting is rarely uniform across taxpayers. Burdens are especially heavy on low-income workers since they have fewer alternatives for earning income and thus have little leverage when it comes to asking employers to "eat" the tax for them. Highly paid consultants can more easily shift taxes onto clients in the form of higher fees as they push burdens onto clients.

Taxes on corporations are also shifted to varying degrees. The corporation tax yielded $230 billion in 2010, but it is incorrect to believe this burden was entirely imposed on owners. Owners shift as much of the tax onto workers through reduced compensation, customers through higher prices, and vendors through reduced payments. Owners bear whatever they cannot shift. Workers bear much of the tax because capital is highly mobile across countries as it searches for lower tax rates. The United States has the second-highest corporate income tax rate—combined state and federal is 39 percent—of any advanced economy.[11] It is roughly 50 percent higher than most European countries. Workers lose when the tax system creates incentives for relocation or outsourcing simply because tax rates are lower in other countries.

A recent *New York Times* article echoed similar insights about how businesses pass on regulator costs onto customers. After spending millions of dollars fighting new regulations banks quickly turned efforts toward using regulations to their advantage. Managers were not shy about passing higher costs onto customers. Jamie Dimon of JPMorgan Chase stated:

> If you're a restaurant and you can't charge for the soda, you're going to charge more for the burger. . . . Over time, it will all be re-priced into the business.[12]

An example is free checking, which may go the way of the dodo bird as banks scamper for ways to recover higher costs imposed by new regulations. Despite conventional wisdom that business owners carry all burdens of regulation, owners are busy attempting to shift burdens onto others that include customers, workers, and other businesses. The poor and non-poor are affected along the way. Owners carry burdens that they cannot shift onto others.

In sum, tax shifting is mostly ignored in assessing tax fairness. Despite promises that businesses or the wealthy fund government programs, consumers and workers often bear much of the burden. Higher-income individuals can also shift taxes more easily than lower-income individuals. Enduring misperceptions regarding who bears tax burdens are unlikely to yield fair tax policy, especially when we ignore what benefits different individuals receive from government.

TAX CUTS "FAVOR" THE RICH?

Ten friends dine together each week at a nice restaurant and agree to pay for the meal using the income tax system to guide how they split its payment.[13] For example, if the total bill is $100, the following payment structure roughly mimics our progressive income tax system: the first four diners pay nothing, the fifth pays $1, the sixth pays $3, and the next three pay $7, $12, and $18, respectively; the tenth pays $59. This is a close approximation to how our progressive tax system sets tax bills.

This arrangement worked well until the restaurant owner awarded their longtime loyalty with a $20 reduction in their bill. The normally tranquil group then erupted into bitter conflict. The four who always paid nothing were outraged when some suggested they not share in the $20 windfall. The other six replied it was fair because they entirely subsidized meals of the four. They also pointed out that free meals for the four diners would continue. The four diners then became more outraged, replying it was only fair they receive the $20 since they deserved it most.

A fight ensued in which the four diners who paid nothing eventually won. They happily divided the $20 among themselves. The other six diners were so disappointed they decided to never dine with the other four again. It turns out the four never dined together again as they came to understand their meals never tasted as good when they had to pay for them.

Readers need only revisit past debates over who deserves tax cuts to understand relevance of this story. The majority of a tax cut must go to high-income earners if we believe it is fair to return tax payments in proportion to what was paid in. Poor citizens receive little or no monies under this notion of tax fairness. Of course, some people believe the poor need these dollars more than the rich.

It is unlikely this debate yields a fair outcome as long as so much misunderstanding exists about tax fairness. The appropriate, but mostly unasked, question is: How much more should the rich pay than the non-rich? It is also appropriate to acknowledge current shares paid by various income groups in this debate. Furthermore, debates regarding fairness focus on taxes rather than the connection between tax bills and benefits received thus further complicating any assessment of fairness. It is difficult to believe our tax system is fair when these critical issues are ignored.

ABILITY TO PAY (UN)FAIRLY TAXES EFFORT?

Tax systems penalize effort when tax bills are based on income. Let us consider two twins, Emily and Erin, each having identical IQs, graduating from the same medical school with identical grades, and receiving identical job offers. Emily pursues a highly technical position earning a very high salary but has few hours left for anything other than work. Erin chooses a job where she earns substantially fewer dollars but works only 30 hours per week. Erin spends considerable time learning to surf and reading all the books she never had time for during her many years in higher education.

We all know Emily is assigned a tax bill many times Erin's. Emily outearns Erin and receives a higher bill. But, income differences do not necessarily reflect differences in ability to pay. Emily and Erin received identical job offers. Personal choices rather than different abilities can create different incomes. Income thus can offer little more than a "rubber yardstick" when it comes to measuring differences in ability to pay.

There is nothing inherently fair about tax bill differences in this example. Advocates of highly progressive tax systems will find it difficult to argue that transferring income from those who work harder to those who work less is somehow fair under this example. Our tax system thus encourages perverse economic behavior when it encourages some able-bodied individuals to work less simply because they are rewarded with tax reduction when they do. In addition to lower tax bills, Erin's ample free time probably allows her to enjoy more public programs such as museums, parks, and hiking trails. Such income transfers are rarely acknowledged.

Citizens whose hard work enables high incomes also become less interested in working or at least become more interested in hiding income from taxation. High-income individuals who work less include doctors and those in other professions that offer their services to those with little income. Longer waits for medical appointments are one symptom of higher marginal tax rates when doctors choose more free time and there is little reason to believe that they will only cut back their working hours for their rich patients. Thus, the tax system itself encourages highly productive citizens to expend effort and time on tax avoidance rather than working hard and their efforts affect citizens other than themselves. Those subject to high tax rates may also harbor ill feelings toward those being taxed less. Of course, those with lower tax bills may also become more interested in seeking larger income transfers through larger government.

SEVEN

Vocal Advocates Encourage Inefficient Government

KEY POINTS IN THIS CHAPTER

- Our tax system creates vocal advocates who believe benefits from government programs come at little or no cost to them. What is rational for individual citizens, however, is not efficient for society.

- Vocal advocates focus on benefits and not costs of government programs and thus encourage government to be inefficient.

- Growing progressivity of our tax system creates a growing number of "vocal advocates" interested in expanding government.

- Heightened awareness of costs of government and a larger role for state and local governments encourage government to be more efficient and fairer.

Market pricing promotes efficient outcomes because only those benefiting from products are required to pay for them. Product prices directly connect supplier costs and values of demanders. But government does not mimic markets thus presenting a very high hurdle for making government efficient. Our tax system encourages citizens to be "poor shoppers" that focus on benefits and not costs of government programs.[1] Citizens that recognize benefits from programs are partially or completely paid by someone else are encouraged to demand quantities they would never choose if they were fully responsible for their costs.

Readers are reminded that benefits from government take many forms. While it is common to think of benefits only as dollars received from programs such as Social Security, benefits flow from all programs. For example, public museums, roads, and the Federal Drug Administration all convey benefits of various forms and to varying degrees to citizens.

Markets work well because exchanges between demanders and suppliers are voluntary and mutually advantageous. Product prices allow consumers to pick and choose good values over bad values. Consumers can easily walk away from products they don't want or are offered at prices out of whack with perceived value. The voluntary nature of the exchange process between voters and government is necessarily weaker. Refusal to pay taxes is illegal. Citizens have very limited ability to refuse paying for government they have little use for or even object to.[2]

The tax system thus opens a very wide door for transferring income. In markets, income transfers are voluntary and referred to as charity. Many charities exist. But citizens cannot so freely refuse income transfers through government. While not entirely "sitting ducks" to those seeking transfers, citizens must lobby, vote, or move in their attempts to stop transfers they oppose. Majority rule means a minimum 51 percent majority yields a maximum minority occupied by 49 percent of citizens. Voting minorities may thus be comprised of many citizens displeased with government. Fifty-one percent of voters might transfer income to themselves from the other 49 percent. Unlike market consumers who can simply refuse, dissenters have little choice but pay for programs they would never voluntarily choose.

Presidential elections reveal how large minorities can be. In 2004, George W. Bush received 62,028,285 votes (51%) to John F. Kerry's 59,028,109 votes (49%). In 2008, Barack Obama received 66,862,039 votes (53%) to John McCain's 58,319,442 votes (47%). Thus, voting minorities include many citizens.

VOCAL ADVOCATES

Our tax system encourages some rather perverse behavior because taxes do not signal value or costs to citizens. Consider, for example, parents wanting elementary education, Social Security recipients wanting monthly checks, and campers demanding national parks. Citizens naturally become obsessed with quantities of programs they enjoy, such as levels of school funding, size of Social Security checks, or sizes of support payments with little thought about how the benefits they value are connected to the costs of those programs.

Shopping without concern over costs, and with inability to refuse taxes, results in inefficient outcomes for society. Citizens become *vocal advocates* of expanding their favorite programs because they understand their advocacy does not obligate them to pay all additional expenses. Vocal advocates understand great values when they receive them. Benefits from sending kids to schools are huge when parents don't directly pay for associated costs.

Consider, for instance, visitors of federal museums in Washington, D.C., who receive tremendous bargains. The Smithsonian Institution is the world's largest museum complex and research organization composed of 19 museums, 9 research centers, and the National Zoo. Admission is free. Museum lovers recognize tremendous deals when they see them as demonstrated by its many vocal advocates. Of course, not all citizens are museum lovers and many vocal advocates are citizens in the Washington, D.C., area due to advantages of local proximity.

Citizens who are not vocal advocates can't opt out of paying for programs. Many have little incentive to complain when they understand how unlikely their complaints will result in trimming or shutting down programs they don't value. They may also be reticent to complain when many vocal advocates can't fathom complaints about their favorite programs. Vocal advocates believe favorite programs are underfunded and that critics simply lack common sense.

Also, citizens are encouraged to become uninterested in monitoring quality or program costs. Vocal advocates themselves have little incentive to scrutinize costs under a tax system that disconnects benefits from costs. Program expansion becomes most important. Those who are not vocal advocates can't opt out and may not particularly enjoy fighting vocal advocates with strong incentives to fight critics of their favored programs. Costs are spread over the population at large thus providing little financial incentive for individual critics to complain. Benefits, however, are more narrowly focused onto the group of vocal advocates thus providing strong incentives to fight critics.

Vocal advocates are easy to spot. They write letters to newspapers and politicians; display bumper stickers touting public education, parks, and museums; and picket public spending reductions while demanding expansion of favorite programs. Schools, parks, dog parks, Social Security, and public health care are programs commonly advocated. Vocal advocates rarely mention excessive cost or reform that enable cost-reduction and more efficient operation. Few complain that public monies are wasted on their programs or that administration by public employees is inefficient. Why would vocal advocates act otherwise when their benefits are not directly connected to their tax payments?

Consider parents with children in public schools. Tax bills do not directly rise with numbers of children. Parents are vocal advocates with little incentive to question spending other than to advocate its expansion. In stark contrast, parents with children at private schools are keenly aware of tuition costs thus encouraging them to compare costs with perceived value. Parents understand tuition rises with spending expansion. They are also "smart shoppers" because they can easily exit private schools whenever they conclude benefits are less than costs.

Vocal advocates are often public employees because their immediate benefits—salaries—are huge in relation to costs they personally bear. Newspapers run many stories written by government employees describing chronic underfunding of programs they administer. They extol the many benefits of their programs but rarely discuss cutting costs under the implicit assumption that all functions are necessary. A business owner claiming consumers spend too little on their products would engender quick laughs. But somehow it is easier to believe government is underfunded when uttered by vocal advocates.

UNLIMITED BUFFET

Consider two alternative payment methods at a food buffet. The first assigns each food item its own price tag connected to its costs to be paid by diners. Food trays will be filled with smart choices by diners personally responsible for paying for each item. Some diners prefer expensive items such as steaks more than meatloaf and hamburgers, but they must pay more. Second and third trips back to the buffet come with additional charges. Owners understand customers can easily exit to other restaurants and that diners don't want to subsidize food chosen by other diners. Diners return when they receive good value for their money.

The other payment method is "all you can eat" where payments are based on income above a minimum level. Food trays quickly become too small when there are no additional costs for choosing more food. Low-income diners receive "great values" with some receiving "free lunches" when they earn income below the minimum level. Many vocal advocates emerge who busily return to the buffet for seconds, thirds, and fourths. They demand more choice, especially expensive items such as steaks, omelet stations, and fancy baked goods.

This discussion demonstrates that what is optimal for individuals is not necessarily optimal for society. Overconsumption is inevitable under a tax system that disconnects costs from value since it encourages individuals to consider only benefits rather than what it costs to provide them. "Trough-feeding" is encouraged whereby diners demand more simply because they are not personally responsible for additional costs. No buffet is too large under a payment system that creates many vocal advocates.

But, many diners will shun restaurants funded on the basis of income. In fact, no restaurants employ this business model. Trim diners with small appetites surely find the experience of subsidizing diners with larger appetites too costly. Some diners will also avoid these restaurants simply because they understand they lack self-control when it comes to eating. High-income diners—especially those without gargantuan appetites— also find these very bad deals. All-you-can-eat food buffets exist, but they charge fixed prices thus representing good values to customers interested in large quantities and varieties of food. But, most restaurants are not run on this business model because customers don't want to subsidize other diners.

Why would it be any different for government? Our tax system encourages voters to demand programs they would never want if they were required to cover their costs. In other words, voters spend their own money wisely, but are more than willing to spend other people's money on items they would never pay for themselves. But, few voters apparently blame our tax system for encouraging inefficient government since otherwise there would be stronger support for its reform.

Several reasons explain why so few citizens blame our tax system for inefficient government. One is that voters mistakenly believe it unambiguously promotes fairness. Chapter 6 discussed how a tax code based on income provides a false sense of security over its fairness. This false sense of security leads to contentment that inevitably encourages citizens to not scrutinize its role in causing government to be both inefficient and unfair. Unfortunately, it becomes difficult for citizens to understand the role that the tax code itself plays in causing their growing disappointment with government.

Another is that voters have problems understanding how prices in markets promote efficient outcomes by connecting values to costs. Misunderstanding of how markets promote efficient outcomes through its price system goes a long way toward explaining myths that government can somehow promote efficient outcomes. Apparently, knowledge that diners overconsume at fixed-price buffets does not lend itself to understanding how our tax system leads to overexpanded government. What is common sense to diners is somehow lost when citizens don't apply the same principle to government.

VOCAL ADVOCATES ARE GROWING

Figure 7.1 displays a very significant trend in recent IRS data.[3] Since 1987, the share of all federal income taxes paid by the top 1 percent of taxpayers rose from 24.8 percent to 40.4 percent in 2007. This is the highest percentage on record and remarkably, its share now exceeds the share paid by the bottom 95 percent of all taxpayers. In 2007, the bottom 95 percent paid 39.4 percent of federal income taxes, down from 58 percent in 1987. Just 1.4 million taxpayers (top 1%) pay a larger share of the income tax burden than the bottom 134 million taxpayers (bottom 95%) combined. Thus, our income tax is increasingly progressive.

Earlier discussion also showed that our income tax system is much more progressive than these data indicate. A record 52 million filers—36 percent of the 143 million who filed a tax return—had no tax liability.[4] Federal tax policy has become so generous that a family of four earning up to about $52,000 can expect to have their income tax liability erased entirely. These numbers also exclude millions of Americans whose low incomes did not require tax filing. Nine of ten states with the largest percentage of nonpayers are in the South and Southwest. These include Mississippi (45%), Georgia, and Arkansas (41% each), and Alabama, South Carolina, and New Mexico (40% each). States with the lowest percentage include

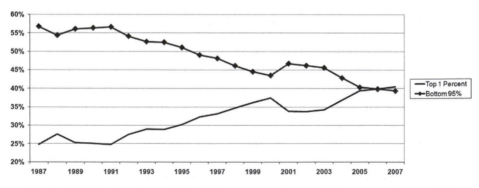

Figure 7.1 Tax Burdens of Top 1 Percent vs. Bottom 95 Percent. (*Source:* IRS Data.)

Alaska (lowest at 21%), Massachusetts (27%), Connecticut (27%), New Hampshire (28%), and Wyoming (28%).

Ironically, rapid reduction in citizens from tax rolls is out of sync with many Americans' notions of tax fairness. A poll in 2009 found that 66 percent of Americans agree with the statement: "Everyone should be required to pay some minimum amount of tax to help fund government."[5] Thus, it appears a majority understand that giving "free lunches" to many citizens is undesirable despite that fact that many more "free lunches" are being served. Rapidly growing progressivity creates a growing number of vocal advocates that push for government expansion that few would accept if they were directly responsible for its payment.

TAX ILLUSION

Tax complexity encourages the illusion that government costs less than it actually does. Prior to 1942, the IRS collected tax after the year was over. Writing one $7,000 check painted a clear picture of what government cost. Taxes are now withheld from paychecks: a $7,000 annual bill becomes 52 weekly payments of $134.62. An unintended consequence is that it encourages citizens to want more government when tax bills appear smaller.[6]

Taxes are also collected at grocery stores, gas stations, bars, sporting events, and department stores, and are attached to utility bills, cell phone bills, and interest income. Tax sources are plentiful and few of us could reasonably be expected to come close to tallying up overall tax bills. Cable and phone bills are notorious for a confusing maze of charges, fees, and contributions that few consumers understand.

Our tax code is at least partially designed with the goal of quietly collecting as many tax dollars as possible in order to dull senses of taxpayers. French Minister of Finance Jean-Baptiste Colbert (1619–1683) famously quipped:

> The art of taxation consists in so plucking the goose as to obtain the largest amount of feathers with the least possible amount of hissing.

Few politicians, government workers, or vocal advocates would prefer a system that allows greater clarity about what programs cost. Citizens also fund all programs together in what can be thought of as a huge "blob" of spending. Tax bills don't easily connect to any one program. Remember consumers in markets rarely prefer to spend their own money this way because they understand that picking and choosing between good and bad values allows for efficient choices.

One solution is to separate tax payments into several partitions: payments for defense, education, highways, transfers, etc. For instance, each citizen might send five separate checks to five separate government agencies on April 15. Taxes could be allocated to individual bureaus, with largest tax sources being broken up. The Department of Defense, for example, might receive 25 percent of personal income taxes, or possibly all of income taxes collected from the top one-fifth of earners. Citizens would then be better able to view defense or other programs as "bargains" or "extortions."

Another proposal establishes a taxpayer savings account (TSA) that holds future tax dollars for every taxpayer, overseen by government.[7] The TSA substitutes for tax withholding and would open eyes of taxpayers wider about how many of their dollars fund government. Dollars taken out of each paycheck would be deposited in TSA accounts rather than the U.S. Treasury. Taxpayers would receive a low interest rate thus allowing it to grow while awaiting tax payments on April 15. Taxpayers would then shift monies from their TSAs to the U.S. Treasury on April 15 with remaining funds earning interest in their personal accounts. TSAs instill a form of individual ownership of tax dollars that is generally lacking under our current system.

These reforms, however, suffer from a status quo problem. Vocal advocates are unlikely to favor changes. Parents with school-age children are unlikely to prefer placing their program under greater public scrutiny. Under the first reform, taxpayers with no children might be unhappy knowing $3,500 funded public schools. Or, taxpayers who dislike parks might be displeased that $450 went to public parks. These reforms challenge the status quo by encouraging greater scrutiny—especially when taxpayers learn that government costs more than they previously thought.

Yet, reforms that encourage more scrutiny are valuable for society as they encourage government to be more efficient and fairer. Efficiency rises when citizens have better information on both costs and benefits of programs. Efficient choices require full disclosure of benefits and costs. But decisions are also fairer to the extent full disclosure allows citizens to clearly understand how government programs provide benefits with costs. Greater clarity on who gains and who loses provides more informed decisions regarding fairness. Our current tax system is a major roadblock for understanding how well government promotes fairness.

DEBT ILLUSION

Government debt reflects deferred taxation. Those with credit card debt understand dollars charged today are promises to pay tomorrow. If voters mistakenly believe debt today does not require taxes tomorrow, they believe government costs less when financed through public debt than through taxation. This misunderstanding results in higher demands for government programs when citizens underestimate future tax burdens associated with debt.[8]

One significant difference between private and public debt also encourages government expansion. Private debt, as in credit cards, is the liability of the credit user. Even when users die before paying off debt, creditors can secure payment from that individual's estate. This is not true for public debt because no legal mechanism exists that forces citizens to repay public loans incurred during their lifetime. Meanwhile, public debt represents unpaid costs of past programs and thus reflects unpaid costs from "long ago" programs.

Expanding public debt should give pause to future taxpayers. It is largely the result of economic stimulus packages that contributed to the record 16 percent rise in federal spending to $3.2 trillion, in 2009.[9] The U.S. Treasury provides a daily tally of "The Debt to the Penny and Who Holds It."[10] Figure 7.2 displays federal debt per person in 2008 dollars. Real debt per person grew from $4,007 in 1980 to $39,067 in 1999—an 875 percent increase. As of August, 27, 2010, total federal debt was

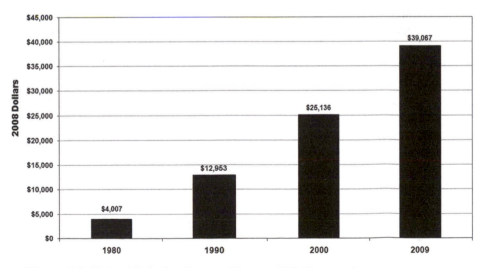

Figure 7.2 Federal Debt Per Person. (*Source:* U.S. Treasury.)

$13,375,222,710,985.08, or roughly $42,000 per U.S. resident. In other words, future citizens owe this amount.

BUDGETARY "TRICKS"

Illusions regarding taxation, spending, and public debt are enabled by various "tricks" of budgeting. The Federal Impoundment Act of 1974 created a "current services budget" that allowed spending increases to be called spending "cuts." Current services budgets are estimated spending increases consistent with current levels of service. Budget analysts estimate continuation of current services by making assumptions regarding the economy (e.g., inflation and unemployment) and public programs (e.g., numbers of beneficiaries). A budget "cut" arises whenever spending falls below continued current services. For example, if a $2 billion increase next year would maintain current service levels, a budget "cut" of $900 million arises when only $1.1 billion of additional spending takes place.

This budgetary definition encourages spending expansion. Vocal advocates can proclaim spending increases are "cuts" when, in fact, increases fall below current service estimates. President Ronald Reagan was accused of cutting federal "spending to the bone" in the early 1980s, when, in fact, he proposed that spending rise by less than current services estimates. While President Reagan was a budget "cutter" under parlance of congressional definitions, spending rose during his tenure. Budget jargon is a useful tool for those seeking government expansion.

The current services budget also enables spending expansion by placing spending in out-years. Spending $450 billion can be budgeted in many different ways that include $450 billion disbursed immediately or over the next 10 years. Today's budget only shows that portion disbursed during today's budget year. For example, if the first year's commitment is for $50 billion to be spent, only that sum is placed on that year's budget. The remaining $400 billion commitment arrives in budgets of following years thus placing them outside the current year's budget deliberations. Moreover, estimates of current services in later years immediately rise in tandem with higher future spending thus "baking into the cake" future spending increases that are not counted as spending increases. A recent manipulation of the "budget window" occurred when "costs" of health care bills were structured on 10 out-years of revenues, but only 6 years of spending.[11] This "trick" created an illusion that the health care proposal was much less burdensome than its reality.

The Gramm-Rudman-Hollings Act of 1985, called GRHI, is a case study in failure to control public debt. GRHI required a balanced budget by 1991 to be enforced by automatic cuts in spending. But, before the ink was barely dry, it was clear GRHI was not going to be enforced. The revised 1987 Gramm-Rudman-Hollings Plan, called GRHII, pushed a balanced budget out to 1993. By the time GRHII was approved, it became obvious it would fail as well, and, consequently in 1990, the Budget Enforcement Act of 1990, called BEA, replaced GRHII with a new plan that pushed the deadline to 1994. As a way of making reparations for previous failures, Congress promised that the BEA would produce budgetary surpluses in 1994 and 1995. The BEA failed to reach promised goals too.

An understanding of budget definitions explains why these laws failed. Each new balanced budget plan redefined some portion of the budgetary process. One change permitted spending and tax receipts to be shifted between different fiscal years. For example, a Pentagon payday was moved to September 29, 1989, which is in fiscal year 1989, from October 1, 1989, the first day of fiscal year 1990. This shift lessened spending by that amount for fiscal year 1990 and increased, by the same amount, spending in the previous year. GRHI and GRHII made policy makers only responsible for current and future deficit numbers and therefore increases in past levels of budget deficits above targeted levels would not trigger spending reduction. Similarly, farm price support payments during fiscal year 1990 were shifted back in time to fiscal year 1989 and this move made it $4 billion easier to reach the fiscal year 1990 deficit target.

Deficit targets could also be met by taking budgetary savings out of future budgetary years, or what are called "out-years." For example, if the current policies of a certain spending program called for spending increases of $50 million a year for the next five years, reductions of $10 million during each of the out-years could be used to decrease current spending levels by the sum of those savings, or $50 million. Promised savings are only promises and, because there is no requirement that promised savings actually occur during out-years, savings rarely materialize.

Creating two sets of books—on-budget and off-budget—is another "trick" that fosters illusions of smaller government. On-budget spending of $3.2 trillion, but off-budget spending of $557 billion, took place in fiscal 2011.[12] Large off-budget spending items include Social Security, Medicare, and the U.S. Postal Service. Similar treatment for Fannie Mae and Freddie Mac allows them to appear to be private corporations despite being taxpayer-supported entities. Taxpayers are stuck with an estimated bill for these "private corporations" of at least $160 billion, though some place it closer to $1 trillion.[13] Separating off-budget programs from the on-budget books promotes the illusion that taxpayers fund less government than they actually do.

The point is that spending, tax, and debt illusions are encouraged by budgetary gimmicks thus allowing vocal advocates to more easily expand government. Again, government expands beyond efficient levels whenever citizens believe benefits come with costs lower than actual. But, government's promotion of fairness also suffers since it becomes even more difficult to recognize the connection between benefits and costs of programs. Thoughtful assessment of fairness requires full disclosure of benefits and costs of government.

MANY GOVERNMENTS HELP

Problems posed by our tax system can be substantially mitigated by a federal system with many small governments. The primary difference between a system of one large centralized government and a federal system is that only in the latter can citizens readily move from one jurisdiction to another when they are dissatisfied with their local government. Ability to exit provides the ultimate threat that dissatisfied citizens may wield against governments they dislike.

Exiting is clearly a "last resort" and, for this reason, exiting jurisdictions has been described as "voting-with-your-feet."[14] Research indicates that like-minded citizens assemble together under such freedom of movement based on evidence that residents of small governments tend to be fairly uniform in their preferences for government. Families congregate in communities with many swimming pools, good schools, and playgrounds. Senior citizens congregate where there are many adult education classes, recreation centers, and stringent noise ordinances.

Two beneficial consequences of many smaller governments are obvious. First, citizens locate in communities served by governments that offer their preferred assortment of programs. This outcome requires no extensive planning on the part of politicians but rather citizens voluntarily sort themselves among communities. Second, politicians are more responsive when unhappy citizens have ready ability to relocate. In effect, the ability to "flee" governments empowers citizens with more leverage in the political process because they have power to erode tax bases by their exiting. This is no different from what businesses face each day in competitive markets and explains why consumers are happiest when they face many competitors rather than a monopoly.

Recent evidence indicates citizens are more sensitive to high taxes than ever before. One study found that from 1998 to 2007, more than 1,100 people every day moved from the nine highest-income-tax states such as California, New Jersey, New York, and Ohio and relocated mostly to the nine states with no income tax, including Florida, Nevada, New Hampshire, and Texas.[15] The same study found that no-income-tax states created 89 percent more jobs and had 32 percent faster personal income growth than their high-tax counterparts. The authors concluded that many movers are high-income and were reacting to both current tax rates and expectations of higher future tax bills with expanding budget deficits.

Another example is when Cleveland Cavaliers' basketball star LeBron James was recently offered a five-year deal of $95.5 million by the Miami Heat versus a six-year deal of $124.5 million offered by Cleveland. The difference becomes fairly small—$4 million—after factoring in income tax differences between Florida and Ohio, as well as tax rates associated with earning income on the road in different states.[16] James faced a state income tax of 5.925 percent and a Cleveland city tax of 2 percent, but no income tax in Florida. James eventually chose Miami with widespread speculation that differences in tax rates played an important role.

Tax differences also influence spending on high-tax items such as liquor and cigarettes. Consider, for instance, New Hampshire, which does not separately tax alcohol sales. About one-half of New Hampshire's hard liquor is sold to out-of-state customers indicating that nearby residents prefer its tax policy on alcohol over their own.[17] Price differences are clearly tempting: buyers can purchase one-liter bottles of Ketel One Vodka for $20.99 rather than $27.39 for the same vodka but in a three-quarter-liter bottle in Boston, Massachusetts. The state of California estimated that cross-border smuggling of lower-tax cigarettes saved smugglers $180,000 in sales tax for a load of cigarettes in a 14-foot truck.[18] Losses were believed to approach the mid- to high hundreds of thousands of dollars in a 24-foot truck.

A federal system of many governments provides a check on tax policies. A federal system is a world of intergovernmental competition. Politicians have strong incentives to keep taxpayers happy since when one government attracts a new taxpayer, another government loses a taxpayer. Governments also engage in substantial "courting" of businesses since their relocation generates tax revenues and jobs for their jurisdictions. This discussion does not mean all citizens are content with every policy of their local government. A family, for instance, may be happy with local public schools, but unhappy with road maintenance. But, on balance, citizens will be content to the extent that they are unable to gain higher satisfaction by relocating to another jurisdiction. Other factors, such as climate, geographical preferences, and proximity to family, also influence locational decisions.

Centralization of government encourages larger government. The potential gain from moving from one state government to another falls as the size of the federal government expands. This point becomes obvious after contrasting two examples where governments spend $3 trillion.

- Case A: Federal government spends $2 trillion and $1 trillion is spent by state and local governments.
- Case B: The federal government spends $1 trillion and state and local governments spend $2 trillion.

State and local governments are clearly much more important in Case B. When citizens are dissatisfied with their state and local government, it is more likely that migration provides relief in Case B. "Voting-with-your-feet" simply cannot change two-thirds of government policies under Case A, but, under Case B, only one-third of policies are unaffected by migration. Research strongly supports the view that government centralization encourages larger government.[19]

A federal system also discourages rent-seeking whereby politicians are lobbied for income transfers. The following example demonstrates that income transfers are easier to secure when government is more centralized because costs are more thinly spread across more taxpayers. Suppose that 500 swimmers lobby for a swimming pool to be built, at a cost of $25 million, in their local community of 50,000 citizens. Also suppose that there are 10 million citizens in their state. When the tax base is comprised of 50,000 citizens, average cost per citizen is $500. Average costs per citizen fall to $2.50 when costs are spread over all citizens in their state. Vocal advocates encounter less resistance with average tax increases of $2.50 than $500. Extension to all citizens in the nation would result in even less resistance to government expansion plans of vocal advocates.

Understanding of markets again goes a long way toward explaining why intergovernmental competition promotes efficient and fair outcomes. Lack of competition enables "fat and happy" sellers that care more about themselves than their customers. There is no reason to believe this works differently when applied to government. Few of us prefer dealing with monopolists, but somehow this basic knowledge does not so easily transfer over to our understanding of government. Our federal government is, in effect, a monopoly government from which citizens have very limited ability to flee policies they strongly dislike.

A federal system of many competing governments also lowers the ability of special interests to secure income transfers. A federal system allows citizens greater ability to shield themselves from programs they dislike by simply "voting-with-their-feet" to another government. Income transfer policies that survive under a federal system are also more voluntary in nature and thus considered "fair" by more citizens.

EIGHT

Tax Preferences: Government Playing Favorites

KEY POINTS IN THIS CHAPTER

- Tax preferences are tax reductions that favor various activities and thus also discourage non-favored activities.

- They are a substantial, growing, and mostly hidden government presence that encourages the false impression that government is smaller than it really is.

- Tax preferences lower economic efficiency because they are the visible hand of government overturning the invisible hand of markets.

- Tax preferences provide "cover" for transferring income to favored citizens.

- Assessment of fairness requires full disclosure of both benefits and costs of tax preferences.

Anyone who has filled out income tax forms knows that deductions, credits, deferrals, and exclusions are provided that decrease taxable income. They are referred to as tax preferences and represent a substantial, growing, and mostly hidden government presence that should be examined alongside its more visible spending programs. They include all tax policies that result in revenue losses for the public treasury. The General Accounting Office (GAO) found they more than doubled in number as their value tripled (2004 dollars) to $730 billion over 1974–2004.[1] The Congressional Budget Act of 1974 required their inclusion in the U.S. government budget.

Tax preferences are important for three reasons.[2] One is their existence gives the public the false impression that government is smaller than it really is. Government size is an important issue that requires complete accounting of its activities. GAO concludes that despite past calls for reforming tax preferences, little progress had been made. GAO stated:

> Although tax preferences are substantial in size, little progress has been made in the Executive Branch to increase the transparency of and accountability for tax preferences.... Over the past decade, however, the Executive Branch has made little progress in integrating tax preferences into the budget presentation, in developing a structure for evaluating the performance of tax preferences, or in incorporating tax preferences under review processes that apply to spending programs, as we recommended in 1994.[3]

Another reason is they distort costs of different economic activities thus lowering economic efficiency. Finally, they rarely promote equity because they are promoted without full disclosure of benefits and costs. Government's inability to promote efficiency or equity extends to its tax preferences.

A total of $1,079,359,000,000 in tax preferences—roughly $3,480 per capita—were granted in fiscal year 2011.[4] Some apply only to individual taxpayers and some only to corporate taxpayers, but revenue losses are substantially larger for individual income taxpayers. Corporations took advantage of $102 billion in tax preferences in fiscal year 2011. State and local governments are the largest beneficiaries of corporate tax preferences.[5]

The 14 largest tax preferences account for 75 percent of total revenue loss.[6] The 4 largest tax preferences in 2011 were:

- A total of $177 billion from excluding employer contributions for medical insurance premiums and medical care from taxable income. Total compensation includes benefits and salary thus exclusion of medical benefits are tax preferences. The self-employed also may deduct part of their health insurance premiums. Estimated costs over 2011–2015 are $1,054 billion.

- A total of $105 billion from deductibility of mortgage interest on owner-occupied homes from taxable income. Owner-occupants may deduct mortgage interest on primary and secondary residences as itemized nonbusiness deductions. The deduction is limited to interest on debt of no more than $1 million. Interest on up to $100,000 of other debt secured by a lien on a principal or second residence is also deductible. Estimated costs over 2011–2015 are $638 billion.

- A total of $67 billion from 401(k) plans.[7] In 2009, employees can exclude up to $16,500 of wages from taxable income. Employees age 50 or over can exclude up to $22,000 in contributions. Taxes on investment income are deferred until withdrawn. Estimated costs over 2011–2015 are $361 billion.

- A total of $47 billion from deductibility of nonbusiness state and local taxes. Taxpayers who itemize can deduct taxes from taxable income for state and local income taxes and property taxes. Estimated costs over 2011–2015 are $300 billion.

HOW DO THEY WORK?

The important distinction between tax rates and taxable income helps us understand the role of tax preferences in government policy. Tax rates measure how many dollars in taxes are collected from a given level of income. If an individual with an income of $50,000 pays $5,000 in taxes, the corresponding (average) tax rate is 10 percent (= $5,000/$50,000) of income. Taxable income is defined as what portion of income is subject to taxation. Tax collection of $5,000, for instance, is determined by multiplying the tax rate, 10 percent, by taxable income of $50,000. Many different combinations of tax rates and taxable income may thus generate the same tax collection. Tax collection of $500 results when a tax rate of 5 percent is applied against taxable income of $10,000 or when a 10 percent tax is applied against taxable income of $5,000.

Tax preferences lower tax bills by either lowering tax rates or decreasing taxable income. Excluding employer contributions for medical insurance premiums and medical care decreases taxable income. Excluding mortgage interest from taxable income decreases taxable income. The capital gains tax is an example of taxing short-term income gains at different rates than long-term income gains (assets held over one year). In 2010, capital gains for individuals at the highest income tax bracket were taxed at 20 percent (long-term gains) versus 39.6 percent (short-term gains). At the lowest income tax bracket, capital gains were taxed at 10 percent (long-term gains) versus 15 percent (short-term gains).

The following example shows why tax deductions offer less tax relief than equal amounts of tax credits. Suppose there are only two sources of income in our hypothetical economy: apple production provides $400 in income and production of guitars enables $200 of income. Taxable income is $600 and, at a tax rate of 35 percent, tax collection equals $210 (= 35 percent × $600).

Tax preferences lower tax rates or taxable income. Remembering that tax collection was $210, let us now compare a tax deduction for guitar income versus a tax credit for guitar income.

- A tax deduction for all guitar income lowers taxable income by $200. Taxable income is $400 and, at a tax rate of 35 percent, the new tax bill equals $140 rather than $210.
- A tax credit equal to guitar income equals $200. Taxable income remains $600, but $200 is directly subtracted from tax collection of $210. Thus, the new tax bill is only $10.

The tax deduction of $200 lowered tax collection by $70, but the tax credit of $200 lowered tax collection by $200. Tax credits thus offer more tax relief than equal amounts of tax deductions.

Values of tax deductions also vary under progressive income tax codes. There are six different marginal tax rates in 2010 with rates rising with income brackets: 10 percent, 15 percent, 25 percent, 28 percent, 33 percent, and 35 percent. Tax deductions of $1,000 provide tax reduction that varies from $100 (= 10 percent of $1,000) to $350 (= 35 percent of $1,000). This is the inevitable result of a progressive income tax code. As discussed before, higher-income taxpayers pay most of the income tax and thus receive the substantial bulk of tax preferences.

Tax relief, however, is not confined to tax preferences. Across-the-board tax reduction is an alternative that does not differentiate between income sources. Reconsider our economy with income of $600 from apples ($400) and guitars ($200). At a 35 percent tax rate, tax collection was $210. Lowering the tax rate to 25 percent generates $150 in tax collection, or tax relief of $60. Across-the-board tax reduction does not single out any income source for tax reduction. Tax preferences, in contrast, are preferential in nature—hence, they are called "tax preferences." Across-the-board tax reduction takes a "shotgun approach" without any particular preference for tax reduction, but tax preferences are "rifle shots" aimed at reducing taxes of particular activities.

OPPOSITE OF TAXATION

Taxation discourages activity. A tax on coffee production discourages consumption because sellers shift as much of the tax as possible onto consumers through higher prices. Consumers buy less coffee as prices rise. They will drink more soda, tea, and other beverages. This same logic is used to discourage smoking—price hikes cause many smokers to smoke less. Some might even quit smoking.

Tax preferences encourage activity because they provide tax relief for preferred activities. They act like discount cards of supermarkets that highlight price reductions on sales items such as hamburger, watermelon, and laundry detergent. Shoppers are guided to purchase more sales items thus demonstrating business owners exert some control over consumer choices. Grocers could offer shoppers discounts on specific items or they could offer 5 percent reductions on all items. The former approach steers customers to specific sale items much like tax preferences. The latter does not designate preferences and is an across-the-board price reduction.

The mortgage interest deduction is a straightforward example of how politicians push resources into housing.[8] If, for instance, $12,000 in interest payments are deducted from taxable income, tax bills fall $3,000 for citizens facing tax rates of 25 percent. This tax preference lowers costs of purchasing homes and so pushes citizens into home ownership and to take on larger mortgages than otherwise. Home owners are not the only beneficiaries. Other "winners" include lenders and businesses selling furniture, paint, plumbing services, bookkeeping, yard supplies, and insurance. Many jobs have been enabled by this tax preference that pushes resources into housing markets.

Downsides of tax preferences are explained by the law of unintended consequences. When tax preferences direct resources into preferred activities, resources are redirected out of nonpreferred activities. This is the proverbial "no free lunch" truth. More resources in housing mean fewer resources in—to name only a few—education, vacations, automobiles, health care, and defense. Pushing resources into housing are resources that can't be used for education. Fewer education loans mean higher interest rates, even though few citizens connect higher interest rates and less lending in education markets with tax preferences for home owners. Nonetheless, tax preferences create winners and losers.

Tax preferences are never argued for on the basis that they create harm for "losers." Losers include many citizens too, but are harder to isolate and rarely receive explicit acknowledgment. Losers are those dealing with the fact that resources are pushed out of markets from which they benefit. Adverse effects are surely subtle and arise with little knowledge of those adversely affected thus enabling advocates to assert tax preferences come with little to no cost to anyone else. Again, government creates winners and losers when it offers tax reduction to some and not others.

The following example explains how income distribution is affected. Consider an economy with five citizens, each of whom is assigned an annual tax bill of $100. Assume Karen now receives a $25 tax credit that drops her tax bill to $75. This provides her a positive income transfer as long as there is no corresponding change in her benefits from government programs. Recall that benefits include everything of value that citizens receive from government programs—for example, government checks (e.g., Social Security) and enjoyment from using roads and public museums. Karen naturally becomes a vocal advocate of this tax preference because she enjoys the same benefits as before but with a lower tax bill.

But, Karen's positive transfer must be balanced out by one or more negative transfers. Prior to Karen's tax preference, tax collection of $500 came from each citizen paying $100. Each citizen was responsible for 20 percent (or $100/$500) of the tax bill. After the tax preference, Karen's share falls to 15 percent (or $75/$500), but burdens rise to 21.25 percent (or $106.25/$500) for the other four when they are equally responsible for making up revenue losses from taxing Karen less.

This tax preference creates one winner and four losers. Negative transfers are borne by the other four citizens since they must now pay $5 more in taxes but receive no additional benefits in return. Other situations may arise such as reductions in public spending or increases in public debt that further complicate how tax preferences affect the welfare of citizens today and tomorrow.

EXPENDITURE PROGRAMS IN DISGUISE

Tax preferences provide benefits in much the same way as public spending programs. Consider how cash payment of $25—an expenditure program—is similar to reducing Karen's tax bill by $25. Assume five citizens share equally in funding a new $25 expenditure benefiting Karen and that, prior to this expenditure, all citizens received $100 in benefits from government. Karen now receives $125 in benefits at a cost of $105. The other four citizens still receive $100 in benefits, but are now taxed $105 each. Again, one winner and four losers from this spending program thus demonstrating positive transfers to one or more citizens require other citizens to bear negative transfers.

The point here is that government can promote preferred activities in several ways. For example, coffee consumption could be promoted through the following three methods.

- Regulation: businesses must provide workers and customers "free" coffee.
- Public Spending: government provides "free" coffee to all businesses.
- Tax Preference: businesses receive tax preferences for coffee expenses.

All three methods encourage coffee consumption. All three methods lower consumption of substitutes such as tea, soda, and water. Winners are those who like coffee and whose jobs are connected to coffee consumption or production. Losers include those not so fond of coffee; consumers, workers, and business owners in markets that experience an outflow of resources; and taxpayers required to pay for public spending or pick up revenues lost through tax preferences.

Options are endless with tax preferences. Preferences could be offered for only decaffeinated coffee, instant coffee, vanilla-flavored coffee, coffee sold in one-pound containers, whole bean coffee, or coffee harvested in South America. Each creates its own unique set of winners and losers that, in effect, divide our economy into two sectors: preferred and non-preferred. Tax preferences are very busy underneath the surface of our economy invisibly pushing resources toward preferred areas and sucking them out of non-preferred areas. Again, government creates winners and losers.

Across-the-board tax reduction could also promote coffee. But, coffee advocates are less interested in this option because it does not directly encourage coffee consumption. Some citizens will simply not drink much more coffee because they prefer to spend their tax cut on other items they prefer more. Tax preferences are sometimes called "directed tax cuts" that quite visibly create a line between preferred and non-preferred activities. They represent the very visible hand of government directing citizens toward activities receiving preferences.

Sometimes government does not direct citizens with much precision. For example, state governments have been ramping up proposals to tax candy as a way of lowering budget deficits. But, the distinction between candy and food can be hard to define. Some states tax Butterfinger candy bars, but not Kit-Kat wafers due to some states exempting foods with flour in them.[9] In Colorado, Kit-Kats are untaxed, but Twix bars are taxed. Other problems include taxing of flour tortillas, but not corn or whole wheat. These examples again demonstrate tax preferences create preferred and non-preferred areas, but predicting exactly how they influence behavior can be problematic.

Consider the 10 percent federal tax on tanning services introduced in recent health care legislation. While the tax was argued on the basis of helping pay for health care, its administration apparently was given little thought. Ultraviolet tans are taxed, but spray tans aren't. It also turns out taxing tanning is not so simple especially given recent trends by owners that have added tanning services to their video rental, dry cleaning, gym, salon, and other businesses.[10] Tanning services have been added to smooth out revenues from recent turbulent ups-and-downs in customer traffic. The fact that tanning services at health clubs are exempt has also led some owners to add gym equipment as a means of becoming "health clubs." Restructuring businesses into "health clubs" demonstrates that tax preferences push resources into preferred activities and away from non-preferred. Meanwhile, tax preferences create many opportunities for lawyers and accountants to sell their services to clients wishing to take advantage of tax reduction.

Special interest groups exhibit great interest in winning tax preferences. They are groups of voters that unite with the ultimate goal of securing policies beneficial to the group at large. For example, a group may be formed around the goal of securing lower tax burdens on single parents. Successful lobbying may, for instance, result in greater tax deductions for day care expenses, car pools, lunches, or extension to tuition at private schools. Gardeners may push tax credits for tree planting. Tanning businesses might lobby for a law that defines a "health club" as a business with two treadmills or three stationary bicycles. Large industries, such as automobile, steel, or financial, lobby for tax preferences too. A tax bill of $900,000, for instance, may be deferred for later payment or simply "forgiven" by a special provision of the tax code.

Winners are vocal advocates because they correctly understand tax preferences to be income transfers. Losers might not realize they are transferring income to winners or, even if they do, they rarely have much incentive to complain when losses are thinly spread over many citizens. Tax reduction of $25 million secured by a steel producer can be spread over many millions of taxpayers. Tax preferences may receive little opposition when marketed as policies promoting the society at large. Among energy firms, renewable energy businesses receive more than four times as much tax reduction as the oil and gas industry.[11] All policies create winners and losers even though it might be hard to understand that dollars pushed into favored areas means fewer dollars spent in unfavored areas or that other citizens must cough up lost tax revenues or experience reduction in government programs they enjoy.

Tax preferences provide "cover" for transferring income. Businesses that manufacture bicycles, for instance, may be rewarded in the following three ways.

- Public Spending: all U.S. bicycle manufactures receive checks of $1 million.
- Regulation: all foreign bicycle manufacturers must use U.S.-made tires, shocks, and brakes if they import bicycles into the United States.
- Tax Preference: all U.S. bicycle manufacturers receive tax credits for all purchases of tires.

Public spending suffers from being very obvious and it shows up directly on the budget as a spending increase. Spending clearly favors a particular special interest group—U.S. bicycle manufacturers. Regulation and tax preferences are more subtle. Neither show up directly on the budget and many citizens might even believe they are "free" if they even know they exist. Of course, regulation benefits bicycle manufacturers, but pushes up prices thus demonstrating its harm on consumers. Tax preferences push resources into bicycle markets and away from other markets thus creating winners and losers as well.

Recent federal stimulus legislation is a case study in how to transfer income to special interests. Tucked into one bill were $32 billion in tax preferences for NASCAR track developers, restaurant owners, movie producers, and other special interests.[12] The one for NASCAR allowed track owners to depreciate property development costs over 7 years rather than the 15 years allowed for most other businesses. Of course, Congress could have simply cut a check to NASCAR track owners, but tax preferences made it appear less like pork barrel spending.

Bailed-out companies such as General Motors receive tax preferences as well. A recent *Wall Street Journal* article put it this way:

> General Motors Co. will drive away from its U.S.-government-financed restructuring with a final gift in its trunk: a tax break that could be worth as much as $45 billion.[13]

General Motors received its highly visible bailout, but also was awarded less visible tax preferences in what amounts to "double-dipping" from government.

OVERTURNING THE INVISIBLE HAND

Tax preferences are the visible hand of government overturning the invisible hand of markets. Tax preferences promote inefficient outcomes either because government lacks motivation and ability to promote efficient outcomes or because tax preferences simply reflect income transfers to special interest groups. *The Economist* magazine put it most succinctly when it argued:

> A pathological optimist, or somebody nostalgic for Soviet central planning, might argue that the whole point of the myriad breaks, deductions, allowances, and assorted other tax preferences that clog rich countries' tax systems...is to improve economic efficiency. The whole idea, you see, is to allocate resources more intelligently.[14]

Skeptics might believe tax preferences promote equity despite rewarding inefficiency. However, this remains unlikely as long as their costs are misunderstood. Public debate based on valid cost-benefit comparisons is critical for both clear assessment of efficiency and equity.

Consider the home mortgage interest deduction. Despite conventional wisdom, home ownership is not so dependent on large tax preferences. Canada, Australia, and England each have roughly the same home ownership rates as the United States, but do not allow mortgage interest to be deducted from taxable income. Cross-country research has not found a significant link between mortgage interest deductions and home ownership rates.[15] The implication of this research is that most current home owners would still own homes without the deduction, but, as argued below, they would tend to live in less expensive homes rather than become renters.

About one-fourth of tax returns claimed the mortgage interest deduction in 2008.[16] The average deduction was $12,221. Home ownership rates are much higher than this, but not all home owners find tax-savings large enough when they have small mortgages or insufficient income to claim the deduction on itemized tax forms. Still others have already paid off mortgages and thus don't qualify.

This tax preference has pushed U.S. citizens into buying larger and more expensive houses than they might otherwise have bought. It helps explain why the average square feet of new homes rose from about 1,500 to 2,200 over 1973–2006.[17] The percentage of new homes with garage parking for at least three cars also doubled from 10 percent to 20 percent over 1992–2005. The $1 million deduction ceiling encourages extravagant housing. Other factors surely contributed to our growing tastes for housing, but tax preferences are a most significant factor.

One downside to promoting home ownership is its effect on unemployment. Unemployment has been linked to home ownership since it ties citizens to specific locations and thus leads them to search less broadly for jobs than otherwise.[18] One study finds no relationship for both young households and old households, but it exists for middle-aged households. This result makes sense since younger people are less attached to geographical areas than middle-aged households and thus have fewer obstacles to moving farther away when seeking jobs. Older people would not be as interested in moving since fewer are in the labor force and they have stronger community roots. Again, good intentions in government policy rarely come without harm.

The tax preference also pushes citizens to save less because it pushes more of their income toward servicing mortgage payments. Borrowers are encouraged to take on more debt to maximize tax savings. Borrowers thus have less equity in their homes and they become more vulnerable to falling housing prices. There would be fewer "underwater" mortgages—when owners owe more than houses are worth—without this tax deduction simply because fewer home owners would have chosen such small equity-stakes in their homes. The proportion of "underwater" home owners was as high as 23 percent in 2009, or nearly 11 million households.[19] These borrowers are also more likely to default simply because they have no remaining equity stakes in their homes.

Some citizens would be better off saving more of their income, taking on smaller mortgages, owning fewer houses, renting rather than buying, investing in stock and bond markets, or simply paying down other debt such as on credit cards. Credit card debt, for instance, has been relegated to the non-preferred area of the economy since 1986 when tax law removed its tax preference. That is, interest paid on mortgages can be deducted from taxable income, but interest on credit card debt cannot. It remains unclear clear why it is fair to allow the deduction for mortgage debt but not credit card debt, especially given that poor individuals are less likely to be home owners.

It has been estimated that owner-occupied housing now receives an effective tax rate of zero percent.[20] It is little wonder so many dollars have flowed into a market subject to no tax. Estimates of tax rates on alternative investments demonstrate how effective government has been at driving resources into housing and out of nonhousing markets:

- housing (0%),
- noncorporate business (17%),

- corporate business (26%),
- business sector in general (22%), and
- economy-wide total (14%).

In order to encourage housing, nonhousing had to be discouraged.

Tax preferences on housing have been very busy rearranging our economy, but most citizens are unaware of the harm done to nonhousing sectors. Pushing tax rates on housing to zero percent provides this market with a huge advantage over its alternatives. This is similar to pushing prices downward on beef while, at the same, policies push prices on chicken, vegetables, and fish upward. Consumers eat much more beef and much less chicken, vegetables, and fish. Even though advocates might believe they are only encouraging beef, policy discourages chicken, vegetables, and fish. This is exactly how tax policies pushed housing but "starved" nonhousing investment.

Encouraging so many resources into housing encourages housing price bubbles. Growth of subprime mortgages was one highly visible symptom—not a cause—of how successful government was in pushing resources into housing. Subprime loans are high-risk loans made to borrowers with characteristics linked to high rates of default. These borrowers might have poor credit histories, unstable employment, or significant health and marital difficulties. Lenders deal with risk by lending at higher rates and requiring borrowers to make large down payments. However, the enormous flood of resources into housing could only be lent out by lowering standards and digging deeper into loan application pools. They began lending—more loans and larger loans—to applicants they previously would have either rejected or required large down payments from. Rising home ownership rates were applauded as housing prices rose and few questioned whether government's encouragement of 27 million subprime and other nontraditional loans was a recipe for future disaster.[21] Fannie Mae and Freddie Mac—government-sponsored enterprises—also facilitated this expansion by purchasing or guaranteeing many of these loans. Of course, the subprime loan market story ended badly with high default rates and many "underwater" mortgages when the housing bubble burst.

The capital gains tax preference is another major encouragement for housing. Up to $500,000 of capital gains is excluded from taxable income for homes used as a principal residence for two out of the past five years. This provision lowered tax bills by $31 billion in fiscal 2011. Home owners also benefit from deductibility of residential property taxes on owner-occupied homes. Again, tax preferences reward home ownership and encourage even more resources to flow out of investments not receiving the same preference. These preferences contributed to the housing price bubble since many dollars entering the housing market were fleeing from the stock market bubble of the late 1990s. Housing's preferential tax treatment thus encouraged dollars to flow out of stock markets even faster thus pushing share prices down faster and farther. Despite common beliefs that housing was a "fail-safe" investment compared to stocks, beliefs were obviously unfounded. But, citizens were encouraged by tax preferences to think this way about housing.

Resources are wasted when tax preferences push resources toward less efficient uses. Previously unprofitable areas of the economy suddenly become "profitable." Consider, for example, a landscaping business that could never make a profit prior to receiving a tax credit. The tax credit now decreases expenses enough to push it to profitability. The process of creative destruction would have led to bankruptcy thus allowing employees and resources to flow to other more efficient businesses in landscaping or some other industry. Tax preferences can offer "life support" for businesses that cannot stand on their feet. Meanwhile, overall efficiency of the economy suffers whenever politicians "glue" resources to less efficient businesses. This discussion is subtle and easily overlooked, but nonetheless tax preferences are just another example of how government promotes inefficiency.

President Ronald Reagan once said:

If it moves, tax it. If it keeps moving, regulate it. If it stops moving, subsidize it.

The following tax credits are recent attempts that began in 2009 to revive housing prices.

- The $8,000 First-time Home Buyer Tax Credit available for buyers who had not owned a principal residence during the three-year period prior to the purchase. The tax credit was equal to 10 percent of the home's purchase price up to a maximum of $8,000 and applied to homes priced at $800,000 or less.

- The $6,500 Move-Up/Repeat Home Buyer Tax Credit available for buyers who had owned and lived in their previous home for five consecutive years out of the past eight years. The tax credit was equal to 10 percent of the home's purchase price up to a maximum of $6,500 and applied to homes priced at $800,000 or less.

These tax credits attempted to overturn the invisible hand of markets. Housing prices were attempting to fall due to the fact that buyers were outnumbered by sellers at current prices. Again, rather than support movement toward efficiency, government pushes back by attempting to overturn the direction of markets. Meanwhile, tax credits affected timing of purchases since more sales today mean fewer tomorrow. These tax credits also had their share of abuse. For example, 1,295 prison inmates received tax credits worth close to $9 million and 14,100 other ineligible tax filers wrongly received at least another $27 million in tax credits.[22] One home was used by 67 applicants.

Reform efforts to overturn the recent explosion of tax preferences—in housing and elsewhere—have mostly failed. Recall that the General Accounting Office (GAO) concluded that little progress had been made by government.[23] The president's Federal Advisory Panel on Federal Tax Reform in 2005 concluded that:

> Tax provisions favoring one activity over another or providing targeted tax benefits to a limited number of taxpayers create complexity and instability, impose large compliance costs, and can lead to an inefficient use of resources.

and

> A rational system would favor a broad tax base, providing special treatment only where it can be persuasively demonstrated that the effect of a deduction, exclusion, or credit justifies higher taxes paid by all taxpayers.[24]

This report was quickly shelved upon completion along with most previous attempts to reform tax preferences.

RARELY FAIR

Tax preferences introduce much greater complexity into assessing tax equity. Consider, for example, two families: the Smiths and the Jones each earning $100,000. Taxable income is thus equal in a world without tax preferences and they would each pay the same tax bill. Both would pay $17,362.50 in taxes under the 2010 income tax brackets for married couples. Their average tax rates are 17.4 percent (= $17,362.50/$100,000).

But, if the Smiths are home owners paying $25,000 in mortgage interest payments and the Jones rent, they quickly become quite unequal. Taxable income for the Smiths becomes $75,000, but remains $100,000 for the Jones. Tax bills are thus much higher for the Jones at $17,362.50, despite the fact they earned the same income as the Smiths. The Smiths pay $11,112.50 in taxes and so receive tax reduction of $6,250 due to housing tax preferences. The average tax rate for the Smiths now falls to 14.8 percent versus 17.4 percent for the Jones. We may compare tax rates of these two families, but they are not directly comparable because each has different percentages of income subject to taxation. Moreover, the Smiths might enjoy more or fewer government programs than the Jones thus making assessment of tax equity an even muddier exercise due to preferential treatment of housing decisions by the Smiths.

It is natural for those receiving tax preferences to believe it only fair they receive them. They are "vocal advocates" of their tax preferences. But, there really is no magic formula that can unambiguously separate winners from losers so that everyone agrees that fairness is achieved. This is especially true given that losers are rarely acknowledged. Moreover, tax preferences are necessarily directed toward higher-income taxpayers since they pay the bulk of the income tax. Many poor individuals do not own houses and therefore cannot take advantage of this tax preference. About 30 percent of tax filers enjoyed lower tax bills from home mortgage interest deductions and more than 55 percent of total tax reduction went to the 12 percent of taxpayers who had cash income of $100,000 or more.[25] Moreover, only 54 percent of taxpayers who pay interest on their mortgages receive tax reduction and most of these are higher-income taxpayers who fill out the longer tax forms that itemize the various tax preferences.

Returning to preferential treatment of housing provides another example where it is difficult to argue that government is clearly fair. Consider how the mortgage-interest deduction varies by tax bracket assuming a 30-year fixed rate loan at 5.5 percent.[26] A $250,000 mortgage allows home owners income tax reduction (tax rates): $3,416 (25%), $3,826 (28%), $4,510 (33%), and $4,783 (35%). A $500,000 mortgage allows home owners income tax reduction (tax rates): $6,833 (25%), $7,653 (28%), $9,020 (33%), and $9,566 (35%). Housing tax preferences thus provide income transfers that rise with income and size of mortgage. Again, despite common beliefs that government is busy transferring income to the poor, this case demonstrates something quite different.

Home owners who pay interest on home equity loans and lines of credit are allowed to deduct interest payments from taxable income. A home worth $300,000 financed by a $200,000 loan allows up to $100,000 in home equity that may be tapped through loans secured by the property. This provision encourages taxpayers to use their homes like ATM machines because they may deduct from taxable income all interest expenses. U.S. home owners cashed out $80 billion at the peak of the housing bubble in 2006.[27] It makes no difference if such loans finance vacations, medical expenses, cars, clothing, or trips to Las Vegas casinos—interest on home equity loans is deducted from taxable income. Other borrowers, however, have no such ability since interest payments on their loans are not deductable.

Tax preferences that exclude interest on home equity loans encourage home owners to draw down more equity in their homes than otherwise. Government thus encourages home owners to take greater risks simply because the tax code makes it cheaper to do so. Clear symptoms of this encouragement are identical to our previous discussion of allowing interest to be deducted from home mortgages: less housing equity, rising rates of home foreclosures, and more "underwater" loans. Consider, for example, the cushion afforded to home owners who did not cash out home equity in the above example of the $200,000 loan on a property worth $300,000. Prices would have to fall below $200,000 before the home owner was pushed "underwater."

Some home owners were more prudent. They may have put more money down on their home purchases or simply cashed out little or no home equity during the housing price boom. They may have been more risk-averse or simply less eager to use their homes like ATM machines and go on shopping sprees. They are not the focus of recent attempts by government to overturn the harm from past intervention into housing markets. Again, it is difficult to argue it is fair to focus additional tax preferences (e.g., the $6,500 Move-Up/Repeat Home Buyer Tax Credit in 2009) to those who were less prudent, especially when this forces the more prudent to fund income transfers to the less prudent.

Many point to private lenders as causing so much harm. But, as discussed above, growth of the subprime market owes much to government, despite many blaming lenders. Subprime loans are one symptom of government intervention that pushed so many resources into housing markets and encouraged lenders to lower lending standards. It is easy to sympathize with citizens who lost so much equity and those who lost their homes. But, it remains unclear how much blame should be assigned lenders who made subprime loans or to borrowers who accepted such loans. Both were encouraged by government to pursue these behaviors and, of course, intentions were noble. The role that government played in enabling a housing price bubble with its many policies aimed at encouraging housing is one misunderstood backstory of our housing market crisis. Much unintended harm came from well-intentioned government intervention that was promoted on promises of benefits with little to no harm.

BOTTOM LINE

Tax reform rarely touches tax preferences. Their beneficiaries are "vocal advocates" who understand that reform might raise their tax bills. *The Economist* magazine again offers a most relevant take on this subject:

Once tax codes have degenerated to the extent they have in most rich countries, laden with so many breaks and exceptions that they retain nothing of their original shape, even the pretence of any interior logic can be dispensed with.

and

No tax break is too narrow, too squalid, too funny, to be excluded on those grounds: everybody is at it, so why not join in?[28]

Remember our tax code fosters an "eating-at-that-trough" mentality for "vocal advocates" who believe their benefits come at little cost to themselves or anyone else. They rightfully fear that if they are the first to volunteer to give up subsidies others might not follow suit.

Again, most citizens have little grasp of true costs of government under our tax system where individual payments do not clearly reflect program costs or values from government programs. It is also predictable that citizens and businesses seek tax preferences. But, society as a whole suffers a loss of efficiency when government pushes resources into preferred areas and out of non-preferred areas. It is also difficult to argue that tax preferences promote fairness because they make assessment of tax equity even more difficult by spreading tax reduction unevenly across recipients. Moreover, while advocates might believe benefits come with little to no cost, many are harmed along the way. Tax preferences thus rarely promote efficiency or fairness as long as there is incomplete disclosure of their benefits and costs.

NINE

Unfunded Liabilities of Future Citizens

KEY POINTS IN THIS CHAPTER

- Government debt represents unpaid bills from past government programs that totaled $13.1 trillion in 2010. Debt is predicted to grow to 185 percent of GDP by 2035.
- Government debt reflects unfunded long-term liabilities of taxpayers since no plan is in place for its repayment.
- The term *insurance* to characterize Social Security and Medicare is misleading since these programs transfer income between citizens.
- Unfunded long-term liabilities of Social Security and Medicare are predicted to rise 2,438 percent—from $0.13 trillion in 1980 to $3.3 trillion in 2015 (2007 dollars).
- Past tax increases, balanced budget laws, and promises of fiscal responsibility have not resolved the coming fiscal train wreck.
- Resolution requires a consensus over what is the appropriate size of government.

Future citizens are stuck with a growing bill for the costs of today's programs. Total debt in 2010 was $13.1 trillion, of which $4.2 trillion was intergovernmental debt held by federal agencies and $8.9 trillion was held by the public.[1] Intergovernmental debt—debt government owes to itself—mostly resides in Social Security and Medicare trust funds. Government debt reflects unfunded long-term liabilities of taxpayers since no plan is in place for its repayment. Previous chapters have argued that full disclosure of benefits and costs of government programs is necessary for any thorough examination of efficiency or fairness. Unfunded long-term liabilities should not be ignored in our examination.

This chapter tackles two critical issues. First, Social Security and Medicare are examined—programs about which the public expresses deep concerns. A recent Gallup poll found that 60 percent of workers believed they would not receive Social Security benefits upon retirement, the highest percentage since this question was first asked in 1990.[2] It is unlikely these programs will cease to exist, but they surely require reform in the near future. Second, rapid growth in government debt is examined with special focus on its implications for the size of government. We will discuss why the solution to the debt problem requires an open and clear debate regarding whether it reflects overspending or undertaxation. This question must be answered before we can resolve the coming fiscal train wreck from long-term unfunded liabilities of citizens.

SOCIAL INSURANCE

The Social Security Act of 1935 was the first large-scale social program in the United States. Prior to the Great Depression, government's role in the economy was principally one of providing for national defense and protection of private property. Economic collapse, however, has often been a catalyst for growing support for a government that more actively intervenes into markets. Social Security provides retirement insurance for senior citizens as well as payments to disabled workers, their dependents, and widows or widowers. Medicare, which was created in 1965, provides health insurance to senior citizens.

One argument for social insurance programs is that private insurers set premiums too high for various individuals and therefore it is only fair that government should transfer income to them. Remember markets allocate resources on the basis of efficiency and not fairness and therefore private insurers will not provide this transfer function. However, the term "insurance" to characterize Social Security and Medicare is misleading. Social insurance programs perform two functions.

- The "insurance function" arises when individual benefits are financed by payments of beneficiaries and is identical to the function performed by private insurers.

- The "transfer function" arises when individual benefits are paid by someone else—a function not performed by private insurers—and explains
why social insurance programs should never be confused with private
insurance programs.

Conventional wisdom is that social insurance programs are insurance programs, but this chapter makes clear they act more like transfer programs
than insurance programs.

Paternalism provides another rationale. Some argue that too many citizens will not voluntarily purchase health insurance or save for their own
retirement even when they have sufficient resources to do so. Paternalists believe mandatory enrollment into social insurance programs is appropriate because it is in the best interests of society that citizens carry
insurance.

Mechanics of Social Insurance

It is useful to understand how private insurance works before tackling
the mechanics of social insurance. Consider retirement insurance, or what
is commonly referred to as pensions. Their mechanics may be thought of
in terms of inflows and outflows. Similar to a savings account, workers
contribute dollars for future pension benefits. Pension companies invest
pension contributions and, upon retirement, return to workers accumulated
pension contributions plus interest earned. Liabilities of pension funds are
thus projected promised future payments to contributors and depend on
actuarial assessment of life expectancy, retirement age, and promised retirement benefits. Value of assets, however, depends on size and frequency
of contributions and expected rates of return when invested by pension
fund managers. Fully funded plans are solvent when future pension payments are guaranteed by invested contributions.

Social Security and Medicare are financed through payroll taxes. Employers and employees pay equal shares of 6.2 percent for Social Security
and 1.45 percent for Medicare. The combined tax rate of 15.3 percent
thus consists of payments by both employee and employer of 7.65 percent
each. Self-employed workers send in the full 15.3 percent since they are
both worker and boss. Social security taxes are only levied up to an income threshold—$106,800 in 2010—that rises with inflation each year.
All earnings are subject to the Medicare tax.

Employers shift their share onto workers. Recall that Chapter 6 explained
that tax codes merely mandate who must collect tax payments, not which
party must bear burdens. Employers shift taxes onto workers by decreasing

salary or benefits so that overall compensation remains the same. For example, an employer that contributes $2,000 in social insurance taxes for a worker will lower salary and/or benefits by the same amount. Burdens rest on workers despite conventional wisdom that burdens are equally shared between employers and workers.

Consider, for example, Ingrid, who earns $80,000 this year. Ingrid's paycheck will show deductions of $4,960 (Social Security portion) and $1,160 (Medicare portion) for a total of $6,120. Ingrid's employer will send in $6,120 too since he is legally responsible for sending in half of the total tax. Ingrid's employer is forced to deliver $6,120 of her overall compensation in the form of the social insurance tax. Thus, Ingrid bears a tax of $12,240 (15.3 percent of $80,000) even though tax records show that Ingrid paid $6,120 and her employer paid $6,120. Ingrid sends in $12,240 when self-employed.

A much-misunderstood element of social insurance is its "pay-as-you-go" funding requirement introduced in 1939. In contrast to fully funded pension funds, social insurance programs are only required to have funds sufficient to meet obligations in the current year. They are not required to be solvent in any long-term sense. Whenever tax receipts exceed payments to beneficiaries, "surpluses" occur and, whenever benefit payments exceed tax receipts, "deficits" occur. For example, $500 billion of tax receipts and $300 billion in benefit payments would result in a $200 billion surplus for that year. A deficit of $200 billion would occur in a year in which there were $400 billion in tax receipts and $600 billion in benefit payments.

Surpluses are not required to be saved to meet future liabilities of programs. The $200 billion surplus in the above example is not saved. In fact, even if surpluses were saved and invested in trust funds, their value would still be insufficient to meet future expected claims of beneficiaries.

Trust funds are the main source of confusion surrounding social insurance. Social Security and Medicare are funded through their own trust funds. It is common to believe that payroll taxes are sent to trust funds, but this does not occur. "Trust fund" is a misleading term because payroll taxes are sent to the general fund of the U.S. Treasury where they are indistinguishable from income taxes, corporate taxes, excise duties, and all other revenues. Trust funds receive credits in the form of intergovernmental debt that represent IOUs from the U.S. Treasury in years in which tax receipts exceed payments to beneficiaries. The $200 billion surplus in the previous example would result in an IOU of the same amount and would be deposited in the trust fund.

Social Security and Medicare trust funds are simply pieces of paper promising to make good on future claims without equivalent dollars being saved by the U.S. government. This is the definition of an unfunded long-term liability. So where do surplus dollars go if not to the trust funds? Though surpluses could lead to reductions in overall federal taxation, empirical evidence indicates social insurance surpluses have financed overall expansion of federal spending.[3] Social insurance surpluses are borrowed by the government to finance current spending in other areas of the budget. Future citizens have been handed the bill to make future repayment.

The Congressional Budget Office (CBO) projects that, in 2010, Social Security's outlays will begin exceeding its tax receipts.[4] Tax revenues are projected to again exceed outlays, but only for a few years. CBO anticipates that starting in 2016, annual spending will regularly exceed tax receipts and that its trust fund will be exhausted in 2039. Current projections have Medicare outlays regularly exceeding tax receipts starting as soon as 2012, while its trust fund is projected to run out by 2029.[5]

The state of social insurance trust funds is displayed in Figure 9.1. Trust funds are shown (2007 dollars) from 1980 to 2015.[6] The Social Security trust fund has risen from $0.08 trillion to $3.14 trillion over this period. The Medicare trust fund has risen from $0.05 trillion to $0.18 trillion, though it begins falling in 2012 reflecting projected and regular deficits beginning that year. Together, trust funds have risen from $0.13 trillion in 1980 to $3.3 trillion in 2015—an increase of 2,438 percent! Rapidly growing trust funds represent a fiscal crisis because they measure long-term unfunded liabilities of future citizens. Despite misconceptions that growing public trust funds represent growing financial health, they represent future claims on citizens under a "pay-as-you-go" system whereby not one dollar has been saved to make good on future claims.

Demographics are an important contributing factor for the rapidly approaching "day of reckoning" whereby Social Security and Medicare officials must begin redeeming trust fund IOUs. The elderly are an increasing percentage of the population that is also living longer. Between now and 2035, the number of people age 65 or older will increase by about 90 percent, compared with an increase of about 10 percent in the number of people between ages 20 and 64.[7] Fewer workers mean falling social insurance tax receipts and more beneficiaries mean rising payments. This explains the impending crisis that arrives when social insurance programs go from surplus to deficit—2012 in the case of Medicare and 2016 for Social Security. This is when tough questions must be answered about how government will make good on promises.

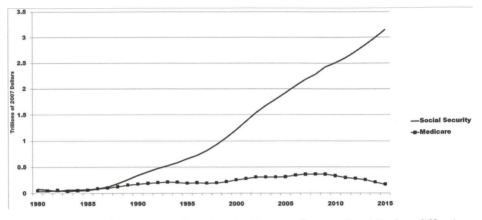

Figure 9.1 Social Insurance Trust Funds. (*Source:* Congressional Budget Office.)

It remains unclear how unfunded liabilities of future citizens will be met, but at least five options are available. One is to raise payroll tax revenues by either raising tax rates or the income threshold with which taxes are due. This option has been employed repeatedly over the years. Social Security was "saved" from bankruptcy in 1983 by increased payroll taxes, but obviously it was not saved in any long-term sense. Recent years have seen growing enthusiasm for removing the income threshold for Social Security taxes and this would clearly push the day of reckoning farther to the future. Of course, this would also raise non–social insurance spending and thus expand government as it expands unfunded liabilities of future citizens.

A second possibility is to raise other taxes. Recall current benefits are paid out of the U.S. Treasury's general fund and therefore, in practice, any tax finances current social insurance benefits. Recent interest in introducing value-added taxation (VAT) is clearly motivated by those interested in pursuing this strategy. Raising marginal income tax rates or placing higher taxes on gasoline or tobacco are other strategies that aim to fund unfunded liabilities of social insurance by raising other taxes on future citizens.

A third option is to directly reduce benefits. This option is unlikely because senior citizens are a powerful special interest group who believe benefits are "entitlements." Indirect reduction in benefits is more politically viable. Options include raising ages at which social insurance benefits are first available or altering cost-of-living formulae that expand benefits each year. Currently, age 62 is the earliest that one can begin collecting Social Security, with age 66 the age at which one collects full benefits. The full retirement age is set to gradually increase to age 67 by the early 2020s, but this can be changed by Congress. The fact that people are living longer is often used to justify extending the age at which benefits become available.

A fourth option is to lower spending on non–social insurance programs. Spending less on defense or education releases dollars for social insurance and of course creates "losers"—those who dislike having programs cut—and "winners"—social insurance recipients. A fifth option is to simply sell more government debt and continue placing burdens on future citizens. This approach creates winners—social insurance recipients—and losers—future citizens stuck with paying newly created long-term unfunded liabilities created to bail out past long-term unfunded liabilities now due.

It is ironic that social insurance programs do not save for retirement or future health costs of citizens. Recall that social insurance programs were argued on the basis that many workers would or could not save for retirement or future health costs. Government does not either it turns out. This outcome is consistent with the general themes that good intentions associated with government programs often fail to result in promised outcomes.

Social Insurance Programs Transfer Income

Social insurance programs transfer income in two fundamental ways. Intragenerational transfers occur because, within a given generation, some beneficiaries received better deals than others. When citizens, within a given generation, receive different benefit-to-tax ratios, transfers occur. Those with low benefit-to-tax ratios transfer income to those with high benefit-to-tax ratios. Most transfers are from high-income to low-income individuals because current benefit formulae are most generous for low-income workers.

This is in contrast to the common perception that social insurance programs are regressive. Such perceptions are based on the observation that high-income individuals pay a smaller percentage of income in payroll taxes than low-income individuals because taxes are only applied up to a threshold. This is true, but benefits need to be considered to recognize who receives the best deals. One study found that households in the lowest-income quintile received 20 percent of Social Security benefits and paid less than 2 percent of Social Security taxes.[8] Households in the top quintile, in contrast, paid 47 percent of all payroll taxes and received only 11 percent of total benefits. This program thus transfers income from higher-income to lower-income citizens.

The other source of transfer occurs *across* generations. Intergenerational transfers occur because current benefits are paid by taxes of today's workers. Workers of today transfer income to today's beneficiaries. Despite common perceptions that beneficiaries receive benefits funded by their own past tax payments, social insurance surpluses were never saved in trust funds. Transfers have been substantial. One study estimates that 80 percent of benefits of current retirees are transfers from today's workers.[9]

Intergenerational transfers also occur because earlier generations had lower tax rates. Consider, for example, an individual who retired in 1961 after paying social insurance taxes since 1937. Over this working life of 24 years, tax rates ranging from 2 percent to 6 percent were applied to income thresholds ranging from $3,000 to $4,800. A worker, however, who retired in 1991 after working the same number of years (since 1967) paid tax rates ranging from 8.8 percent to 15.3 percent on income thresholds ranging from $6,600 to $53,400. All workers who began earning income since 1983 have paid at rates of 15.3 percent; though it is quite possible rates will rise again on future citizens to meet unfunded liabilities of Social Security and Medicare.

Social Security and Medicare are thus social insurance programs that differ substantially from health, automobile, and property insurance provided by private insurers. Social insurance programs redistribute income between citizens and thus winners and losers emerge just as in any other government program. Some get great deals and others bad deals. Great deals have so far been awarded to lower-income citizens and workers of earlier generations.

Senior citizens are a powerful and growing special interest group and it is not surprising they receive such large income transfers. Rapid expansion of social insurance programs—as demonstrated by growing trust funds—demonstrates this power. Their power contributes to their rapid growth in income. While, in 1970, for example, 25 percent of all persons 65 years old and over had incomes at or below the poverty level, this percentage has fallen to 9.7 percent in 2008.[10] Clearly, beneficiaries of social insurance programs are not all poor and this observation raises important questions regarding whether it is fair to transfer so much income to them. Again, thoughtful answers to this question require full disclosure of benefits and costs of these programs both today and tomorrow.

Social Insurance Reform

Former congressman Dick Armey recently acknowledged the white elephant in the social insurance debate when he stated:

Americans should ask, if Social Security is such a great program, why is it mandatory? Workers should have the choice about whether they want to remain in the current system or invest in a personal saving retirement account, which would allow them to have complete control over their retirement funds and pass the remaining balance to family members. Let's have Social Security compete against other investment options.[11]

Privatization places provision of retirement and health care insurance in the hands of private insurers. There is, however, an important issue that must be addressed before this proposal can be seriously considered. Recall that social insurance programs provide two functions: insurance and income transfer. Privatization would be a fundamental redirection of these programs as private insurers would drop the income transfer function.

Consider the insurance function first. Remember that one rationale for social insurance programs is that some individuals will not voluntarily save for retirement and future health care costs. This concern could be met by a system where all workers invested some portion of their salaries in private pension and health funds much like IRA accounts.[12] Minimum standards regarding insurance coverage could be set by government, though readers by now understand this does not guarantee they will be pleased with results. Of course, concerns that politicians may exert undue pressure regarding where private firms invest funds are valid as well. Allowing politics to steer investments is unlikely to maximize returns for citizens or even guarantee solvent insurance programs as government has demonstrated with social insurance.

The design of a private system that transfers income is more problematic. One solution would be to simply disengage the insurance function from Social Security and Medicare and transform them into a government program that clearly admits that it transfers income. This would leave private insurers with responsibility for only insurance functions—something they can handle better than government. The transfer function remains with government where it belongs. This change also provides for a clearer debate over transfers because it no longer comingles insurance and transfer functions. This change encourages meaningful debate over the appropriate role for government in transferring income that is anything but clear under the current system. In effect, this change leads to fuller disclosure of what this government program actually does.

Privatization offers three advantages. One, private insurers are fully funded thus putting an end to expansion of unfunded liabilities owed by tomorrow's citizens.[13] Two, privatization expands program quality when it introduces competition into the market for retirement and health insurance. Social insurance programs are a federal monopoly that commands mandatory participation of virtually every worker. Privatization allows workers to choose among competing private programs. This would be similar to car insurance where customers are free to choose insurers they feel are best suited to their needs. Privatization thus promotes efficiency by handing over the insurance function to markets.

Three, privatization brings the distinction between insurance and transfer functions to the forefront of public discussion. Current debate is often based on many misconceptions regarding trust funds and tax fairness. This is particularly troubling given these programs account for the largest share of all government spending. Social Security and Medicare spending amounted to $678 billion and $499 billion, respectively, in a total budget of $2,094 billion in 2009.[14] These programs currently account for 56 percent of all spending and are only going to grow faster in the future.

Questions remain regarding the political viability of privatization because it creates a new budgetary environment. As discussed, surpluses in social insurance programs fund other government programs that many citizens enjoy. These programs are funded by issuing unfunded liabilities in trust funds to be paid by future citizens. Vocal advocates of these spending programs receive great deals and will be unhappy when favored programs no longer receive funding from social insurance surpluses.

Privatization proposals are also proof that past political promises have not been kept regarding long-term solvency. Most politicians have long assured constituents that rising trust fund balances are a good thing. They have fostered the impression that they do not reflect unfunded liabilities of future citizens. Constituents are sure to be displeased, especially when they believed their tax payments were saved and invested in accounts with their names on them. The truth can be devastating and it is predictable that politicians are reluctant to fully acknowledge how they run these programs.

NATIONAL DEBT

The budget deficit and national debt are often confused. Budget deficits reflect borrowing whenever government spending exceeds tax revenue in a given year. The budget deficit was an estimated $1.3 trillion in 2010, slightly below the previous year record in 2009. The estimated value of the federal budget deficit in 2009 was $1.4 trillion, which arose from the spending of $3.5 trillion and tax revenues of $2.1 trillion.[15] This indicates payment of $1.4 trillion of that year's spending was postponed to future citizens thus raising public debt by the same amount.

The national debt measures the sum of all unpaid public debt. While a budget deficit reflects the extent to which one year's spending exceeds tax revenues, the national debt reflects the extent to which payment for all past deficit-financed spending remains postponed to the future. Whenever government operates under a budget deficit, the national debt rises as well.[16] The national debt was $7.5 trillion in 2009.[17] History of our national debt is displayed in Figure 9.2. Rising to almost 109 percent of GDP in 1946, the national debt fell after World War II to a low of 24 percent in 1974. Since then, the national debt climbed to 53 percent of GDP in 2009. It is estimated to grow to 73 percent of GDP by 2015. The Congressional Budget Office predicts it will rise to 185 percent of GDP by 2035.[18]

Gross federal debt, which consists of all debt issued by the federal government, includes two broad categories: (1) debt held by federal government agencies and (2) debt held by the public. Gross federal debt in 2010, for example, was $13.1 trillion, of which $4.2 trillion was held by federal agencies and $8.9 trillion was held by the public.[19] This amounts to roughly $42,000 per capita in 2010 alone. Much of the debt held by federal government agencies resides in federal trust funds for Social Security and Medicare. Recall that when social insurance programs run surpluses, excess funds are sent to the U.S. Treasury where, in return, IOUs are sent to social insurance programs. These IOUs are federal debt securities since the Treasury borrows and promises eventual repayment by future citizens.

Largest holders of our public debt are: foreigners (51%), mutual funds (11%), state and local governments (8%), private pension funds (5%), state and local pension funds (3%), insurance companies (3%), and banks (2%).[20] Years of running budget deficits means the U.S. Treasury must

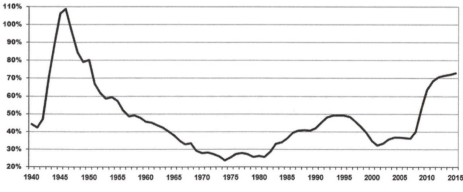

Figure 9.2 National Debt: Percentage of GDP. (*Source:* Congressional Budget Office.)

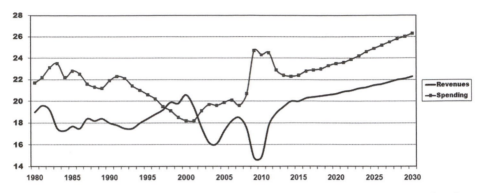

Figure 9.3 Revenues and Spending: Percentage of GDP. (*Source:* Congressional Budget Office.)

continually re-fund the national debt. Treasury securities are sold with maturities ranging from three months to thirty years and so debt is constantly maturing. Interest payments are predicted to grow from 1.4 percent of GDP in 2010 to 3.9 percent by 2035—an increase of 179 percent.[21]

Figure 9.3 presents recent and projected fiscal imbalances between government spending and taxation. Gaps between spending and taxation represent accompanying budget deficits. In 1980, spending and tax revenues as percentages of GDP were at respective levels of 22 percent and 19 percent, thus creating a budget deficit of 3 percent of GDP.[22] Spending then began to fall to a low of 18 percent of GDP in 2000 before rising to 25 percent in 2009. Spending is projected to rise to 28 percent of GDP by 2035. Revenues fell to a low of 15 percent in 2009, but are projected to rise to 23 percent of GDP by 2035. Government has thus operated mostly under budget deficits in our recent history and is projected to continue spending more than it receives in tax revenues for many years.

Undertaxation or Overspending?

Budget deficits are defined, and estimated, by budget accountants. But what does this accounting measure really indicate about the fiscal affairs of government? A budget deficit is first, and foremost, a residual: the difference between public spending and tax revenues. A budget deficit estimate, by itself, is relatively meaningless unless we know what levels of spending and tax revenues lie behind it.

This point is made clear when we consider how a budget deficit of, say, $1 trillion is consistent with the following three situations:

- spending of $3 trillion and tax revenues of $2 trillion,
- spending of $1 trillion and tax revenues of $0, and
- spending of $2 trillion and tax revenues of $1 trillion.

Viewing a budget deficit as a residual clearly indicates that budget deficits merely measure mismatches between government spending and tax revenues. Comparison of a budget deficit with spending suggests whether a budget deficit is small or large. A deficit of $1 trillion, for instance, may be considered huge when spending is $1 trillion or small when spending is $20 trillion.[23]

In theory, three options reduce or eliminate a budget deficit:

- increase taxes,
- decrease spending, or
- a mix of higher taxes and lower spending.

A budget deficit of $1 trillion may be eliminated by enacting a tax increase of $1 trillion, reducing public spending by $1 trillion, or combining a tax increase of $0.5 trillion with spending reduction of $0.5 trillion.

Any of these options may be recommended, but each option suggests a very different view regarding what is the underlying cause of a budget deficit. Budget deficits as residuals reflect symptoms rather than causes of fiscal imbalance. Thus, deficits represent either:

- undertaxation,
- overspending, or
- a mix of undertaxation and overspending.

A tax increase is logical when a budget deficit represents undertaxation. Spending reduction is logical when overspending is believed to be its cause. A mix of spending reduction and tax increase is the logical solution when a deficit reflects undertaxation and overspending.

This discussion easily fits within our recent fiscal history shown in Figure 9.3. Spending is projected to average 25 percent of GDP over 2010–2035. Taxation is projected to average 21 percent of GDP over the same period. Whether this divergence reflects undertaxation or overspending is subject to debate. If 25 percent of GDP is believed to be an appropriate spending level, raising taxes to 25 percent of GDP is logical. Those who believe budget deficits represent overspending argue spending should be reduced. Tax increases and spending reductions are advocated by those who believe budget deficits reflect both overspending and undertaxation. An appropriate solution requires the notion of an appropriate level of government spending.

Intergenerational Burdens from Public Debt

James M. Buchanan (1986 Nobel Laureate in Economics) argues that public debt is unfair to future generations.[24] Future citizens ultimately bear burdens associated with future payment of principal and interest and, unlike today's citizens, they do not enter into current agreements over issuance of today's public debt. This view argues that the ability to sell public debt provides today's citizens the ability to force future citizens to bear burdens of that debt. Issuance of public debt, in effect, allows current generations to award themselves income transfers by approving spending whose costs are paid by future citizens.

Future citizens not only inherit debt, they experience lower living standards as well. For every additional dollar of public debt, there is one less dollar of savings available for private investors. This effect is commonly referred to as "crowding out" and results in higher interest rates and less lending in consumer markets for mortgages, refrigerators, automobiles, clothing, etc., as well as for businesses seeking loans. An important implication is that the reduction in private investment results in slower capital formation. Smaller capital stocks lead to diminished future productivity and, in this way, public debt imposes burdens onto future citizens in the form of lower living standards.

Government debt also confuses citizens about the true nature of costs and benefits of government programs.[25] The fiscal illusion hypothesis was discussed in Chapter 7. It argues that citizens operate under the illusion that debt makes government appear cheaper than when it carries no debt. For example, citizens perceive that $100 billion of public spending costs less when funded by future citizens through public debt than through taxation of $100 billion on today's citizens. This view predicts citizens demand more government today when they can enlist future citizens to pay for it. Recall that no legal mechanism exists that forces citizens to repay public loans incurred during their lifetime. Under this view, public debt should be tightly controlled.

Do Tax Increases Reduce Deficits?

Conventional wisdom is that tax increases lead to lower budget deficits since deficits represent differences between public spending and tax revenues. Despite this common belief, tax increases rarely offer permanent reduction of budget deficits. The budget constraint view predicts spending rises whenever taxes are increased.[26] Simply put, increases in resources broaden spending opportunities. This view predicts government's ability to spend is constrained by its resources as defined by tax revenues and public debt.

Milton Friedman succinctly stated this view in the following way: "Government spends what governments receive plus whatever they can get away with."[27] This prediction follows from the view that there always exists a government program someone wishes to expand or create. Tax increases may cause budget deficits to rise, fall, or remain the same depending on how tax changes influence public spending.

Consider, for instance, a budget deficit of $1 trillion that occurs when government collects $2 trillion in tax revenue and spends $3 trillion. The following is a list of possible changes in the budget deficit that may occur following a $1 trillion tax hike.

- Budget deficit falls to $0 when spending does not change.
- Budget deficit falls to $0.5 trillion when spending rises by $0.5 trillion.
- Budget deficit remains at $1 trillion when spending rises by $1 trillion.
- Budget deficit rises to $1.5 trillion when spending rises by $1.5 trillion.

Further study of how taxes may influence spending is clearly warranted before assuming that tax hikes always lower budget deficits.

Causality between taxes and spending is the primary issue. Note that causality is different from association or correlation. Association is merely a statement about whether or not a relationship exists between two or more variables. For instance, money growth and inflation tend to rise and fall together and are therefore commonly believed to be correlated with each other. The belief, however, that money growth causes inflation is a statement of causality. Causality is therefore a more informative statement about relationships between variables and consequently is a more difficult relationship to verify.

Four causal directions are possible:

- taxes cause spending,
- spending causes taxes,
- taxes and spending cause each other, and
- taxes and spending are unrelated to each other.

When taxes cause spending, tax increases lead to spending increases and therefore budget deficits may or may not fall. If a tax increase leads to a smaller spending increase, the budget deficit falls by a smaller amount than the tax increase. If spending rises by more than the tax increase, the budget deficit rises. Finally, if spending rises by an amount equal to the tax increase, no change in the budget deficit occurs.

Politicians are not legally constrained to act in one way or another and therefore any of the four possible causal directions may approximate reality. But, many studies support the view that taxes cause spending.[28] Reasonable assessment of the empirical evidence is that, without further information, a tax increase exerts an ambiguous effect on a budget deficit since some question exists over whether or not spending changes. Removing this ambiguity requires tax hike legislation to include rules regarding how tax changes may be used by policy makers. For instance, a tax increase of $100 billion may be legislated with the stipulation that it not be used to finance additional spending. This stipulation is likely to only work when Congress agrees a budget deficit reflects overspending and not undertaxation. Of course, we previously saw that past budget balance laws failed miserably because Congress did not agree that it overspent.

BOTTOM LINE

The appropriate size of government is the critical but mostly unspoken issue. This issue guides the appropriate response to national debt since it answers the question of whether continual deficits reflect overspending, under taxation, or some combination of the two. Political discussion continually focuses on symptoms—budget deficits—and not causes—overspending or undertaxation. There is little reason to believe any long-term resolution of our public debt explosion is possible until this debate begins with a focus on the appropriate size of government.

Politicians who believe budget deficits reflect undertaxation rarely admit their preference. Few citizens enjoy being told they are undertaxed. Shifting focus toward symptoms—budget deficits—allows politicians "cover" when they believe overspending is not the problem. Empirical evidence also concludes that past tax increases have mostly enabled more spending.

Government's long-term unfunded liabilities pose major problems for future citizens. At first, programs appear cheap or even free, such as the case of social insurance programs that run surpluses that lead to rising trust fund balances. But, surpluses in social insurance do not imply longer-term solvency since no dollars were saved to fund their IOUs. The illusion that a rising trust fund balance is a good thing has been pedaled by politicians and other interested parties intent on spending today and pushing tax bills onto future citizens. Meanwhile, government continues to grow and citizens become increasingly dissatisfied with its performance.

The illusion that social insurance benefits are paid by past taxes of beneficiaries perpetuates the myth that social insurance reflects insurance. Taxes were never saved for this purpose, despite promises that this is exactly what these programs do. These are mostly income transfer programs rather than insurance programs. The cold reality is that many "vocal advocates" of government programs have been created along the way.[29] It has been estimated that 30 percent of U.S. households had at least one citizen receiving Social Security, subsidized housing, jobless benefits, or other government-provided benefits in the early 1980s.[30] By 2008, this grew to 44 percent and will grow as our aging population collects even more social insurance payments. Thirteen percent of households pay neither social insurance taxes nor income taxes.

It is not surprising that past tax increases, balanced budget laws, and promises of fiscal responsibility have not succeeded in resolving the rapidly approaching fiscal train wreck. Growing ranks of "vocal advocates" of government naturally resist efforts to trim their benefits or raise their taxes. There is little reason for optimism until a consensus arises over what is the appropriate size of government and how much income redistribution it should provide. These decisions, however, require acknowledgment that rapidly growing public debt levels reflect undertaxation, overspending, or some combination of the two. Acknowledgment that social insurance programs mostly transfer income is also necessary. Meanwhile, future citizens are stuck with a growing bill and further disappointment with their government.

TEN

More Efficient and Fairer Taxation

KEY POINTS IN THIS CHAPTER

- Tax reform opens the door for making government more efficient and fairer.

- The tax compliance industry is one of the largest U.S. industries. It hires the equivalent of 3.8 million full-time workers—roughly six times larger than the automobile industry.

- A flat tax is one reform with many advantages. It is simpler, encourages efficiency, improves tax equity assessment, and consumes fewer tax compliance resources.

- A pure flat income tax applies a single tax rate on all income. A modified flat tax applies a single tax rate only after reaching a minimum income threshold.

- A flat tax conforms to the vertical equity requirement that tax bills rise with income.

- A flat tax is imperfect, but is one reform that encourages government to be more efficient and fairer.

Our tax code is based on beliefs that it is fair to tax income and that tax rates should rise with income. Thus, it is not surprising that most taxation—92 percent—is based on income. In 2011, $2.3 trillion in taxes was collected—roughly, $7,467 per person—with personal income taxation (47%), social insurance taxation (35%), and corporate income (10%) all based on income.[1]

Previous chapters have argued that our tax code contributes to our disappointment with government. The Tax Reform Act of 1986 was the last significant tax reform. It reduced tax brackets from fifteen (11% to 50% tax rates) to four (15% to 28%) and removed many tax preferences. However, tax brackets have crept back to six (10% to 35%) alongside expanding tax preferences in the intervening years. Rapid expansion of long-term unfunded liabilities of government has spawned interest in tax reform.

Two reforms—flat income taxation and value-added taxation (VAT)—have garnered the most attention. VAT is a national sales tax added at each stage of production thus passing its burden onto customers in the form of higher prices. A flat tax fundamentally reforms the connection between tax bills and income. This chapter focuses on a flat tax because the public appears very committed to taxing on the basis of income and it is highly unlikely income taxation will be eliminated. Despite growing interest in VAT, its adoption would be unlikely to replace income taxation. Rather, VAT would raise additional tax revenue rather than substitute for taxes imposed on income.

JUDGING TAX SYSTEMS

Efficiency

Efficiency surrounds the question of whether the tax system itself pushes resources into less-productive areas of the economy. Previous discussion has argued that it is inefficient to tax income at different rates. For example, recall the 2010 tax code taxed income at the following rates for single earners.[2]

- The first $8,375 of income is taxed at 10 percent.
- Income between $8,375 and $34,000 is taxed at 15 percent.
- Income between $34,000 and $82,400 is taxed at 25 percent.
- Income between $82,400 and $171,850 is taxed at 28 percent.
- Income between $171,850 and $373,650 is taxed at 33 percent.
- Income above $373,650 is taxed at 35 percent.

Taxing income distorts incentives for earning income when it encourages workers to work less or hide income. Distortion rises with tax rates.

Paying 10 percent on the first $8,375 of income probably leads few workers to choose not to work—$1,000 of additional income provides take-home pay of $900.[3] But, an extra $1,000 in the 35 percent bracket provides take-home pay of $650 rather than $900. A difference of $250 is worth worrying about.

The simple rule of thumb is that taxes distort efficiency whenever workers take into account tax implications. Consider, for instance, a carpenter offered $1,000 for installing a custom door. Prior to taxation, decisions are solely based on demand and supply for his services. He compares $1,000 against his costs and accepts or rejects the job. Costs include materials, commuting, and having to forgo other jobs. He accepts when benefits—$1,000—compare favorably to his costs.

Taxation lowers take-home income. At 10 percent, after-tax income of $900 is compared to costs that have not changed. At 35 percent, $650 compares much less favorably to costs. Despite $1,000 being offered, after-tax income falls as tax rates rise. Everyone understands that $650 buys less than $900, and both are worth less than taking home $1,000.

Tax codes thus encourage some workers to reduce their tax bills. One avenue is to work less, and this possibility is more attractive to higher-income individuals that already meet life's necessities. Higher-income individuals also have more of their work penalized by higher tax rates. So, after-tax income from an additional $1,000 is much higher for workers in the 10 percent tax bracket than those in the 35 percent tax bracket.

Another avenue is tax evasion. Evading taxes on $1,000 saves $100 at the 10 percent bracket, but $350 at the 35 percent bracket. The progressive income tax code thus encourages working "off the books." A carpenter offered $1,000 might prefer $1,000 in cash that never finds its way onto his tax form. This example demonstrates unintended consequences of progressive income taxation: it is intended to raise more tax revenue by taxing higher-income workers at higher rates, but it encourages tax evasion that lessens income tax collection.

Tax preferences also distort choices. Chapter 8 discussed how tax preferences are a significant, but mostly hidden, government presence. They lower tax bills by decreasing tax rates or taxable income on preferred activities but not others. For example, suppose our carpenter receives tax preferences whereby income from installing custom doors is untaxed, but all other work is taxed according to the 2010 tax code. One thousand dollars in income provides take-home pay of $1,000 as long as he installs custom doors, but from $900 to $650 for all other income of $1,000. Our carpenter will surely prefer installing custom doors over other jobs.

One tax preference is provided for rehabilitating homes built prior to 1936, but not for homes built in or after 1936. The rehabilitation tax credit— 10 percent for buildings and 20 percent for certified historic structures— thus increases demand for workers hired at pre–1936 job sites and decreases demand for others. Advocates argue these buildings deserve more restoration. But, income decisions are now distorted because wages are pushed up for those working at pre–1936 jobs sites but lowered for other homes. The tax code is thus busy influencing behavior that has nothing to do with the fundamental value of work. Workers simply find it more financially attractive to work at pre–1936 job sites because of the tax code.

Recall that chapter 6 showed that our income tax encourages citizens to want government to be inefficient. Individual citizens are not charged more for services they value more or that cost more to provide. Tax bills simply rise in sync with income. Previous discussion of grocery shopping showed that shoppers receive many great deals when they are not personally responsible for paying for every item placed in carts. Shoppers understand that prudence reaps little individual reward similar to the all-you-can-eat buffet whereby diners eat more and waste more food when they are not charged for each item. Citizens would choose very differently—smaller government—if they were faced with connecting their benefits with true costs associated with government programs.

Also recall that more citizens are receiving similar great deals from government. Since 1987, the share of all federal income taxes paid by the top 1 percent of taxpayers rose from 24.8 percent to 40.4 percent in 2007.[4] This is the highest percentage on record and now exceeds the share paid by the bottom 95 percent. Our income tax system is actually more progressive than these data indicate. Fifty-two million filers—36 percent of the 143 million who filed a tax return—had no tax liability due to tax preferences.[5]

Removing a growing proportion of citizens from taxation disconnects more citizens from considering costs as well as benefits from government. But, as mentioned many times before, what is efficient for an individual is not always efficient for society. More "vocal advocates" of government cannot be expected to push for more efficient government. Rather, they want even better deals for themselves and thus push for increasingly inefficient government from the point of view of society.

In sum, our tax code is busy directing resources into and out of markets through distorting decisions and encouraging citizens to want less efficient government. There is little reason to suspect final outcomes are more efficient than when directed by the invisible hand of markets. In effect, our tax code moves supply and demand around as it makes some activities more valuable than others simply because of taxation rather than from values determined by demanders and suppliers. Again, government does not mimic markets and therefore rarely can be expected to promote outcomes more efficient than markets.

Fairness

Tax codes owe their structure to perceptions of fairness. Our progressive income tax system is built on the belief that ability to pay is a more important principle than taxing on the basis of benefits. Recall that, while most people think of benefits only in terms of dollars such as social security payments or unemployment checks, all programs confer benefits to one or more citizens since otherwise there would be no demand for programs. Benefits include a $650 Social Security payment or enjoying public museums and roads.

Chapter 6 explained that our progressive income tax creates myriad of transfers that invisibly take place without clear understanding by citizens. Consider three alternative tax bills on Robert, who receives $100 in benefits from a public road.

- A tax bill of $0 assigns Robert a $100 transfer.
- A tax bill of $150 assigns Robert a −$50 transfer.
- A tax bill of $100 assigns Robert a $0 transfer.

Assessing fairness of this tax system is problematic when we ignore benefits. Moreover, while Robert may receive a −$50 transfer from the road, he may receive a +$75 transfer from a public swimming pool. Finally, tally of net transfers requires adding transfers from thousands of programs. There is no reason to suspect any citizens or government officials have the ability to perform the necessary calculations required to fully assess who gains and who loses.

The following are among the many reasons we have addressed as to why perceptions about fairness of our tax code are misplaced.

- Rent-seeking explains why income transfers are often aimed at the well-connected rather than the fact that someone is poor.
- Tax preferences lower taxable income for some but not for others.
- Taxes can be partially or entirely shifted onto others.

- Despite employers and workers "sharing" social insurance tax bills, burdens are entirely borne by workers in most cases.
- Progressive income taxation penalizes effort when personal choices create different incomes because those who work and earn more have more of their income taxed at higher rates.
- A growing portion of costs of today's government programs are imposed on future citizens.

Our ability to assess tax equity is very muddy and rarely acknowledged. Dictionaries include a variant of "freedom from bias or favoritism" to define fairness. This definition also describes what many parents hope to achieve when dealing with their children. Tax codes that achieve this definition of fairness would also be careful to avoid picking favorites, which by its very nature is a process that also picks non-favorites. Favorites are awarded income transfers that harm those less favored. Despite common illusions that our tax code is fair, our code in practice often picks favorites that would rarely fit the illusion of fairness that so many believe exists in theory.

Complexity

No one promotes making tax codes more complex, but growing complexity is the one constant we all observe over time. Anyone who has paid taxes knows records must be kept; tax forms obtained, read, understood, and filled out; and, in many cases, friends, accountants, and lawyers called in to help complete necessary paperwork.

The IRS's Office of Taxpayer Advocate Service (TAS) has declared:

> The most serious problem facing taxpayers is the complexity of the Internal Revenue Code.... The only meaningful way to reduce these burdens is to simplify the tax code enormously.[6]

TAS estimates that taxpayers spend 7.6 billion hours a year complying with IRS requirements—a figure that does not even include millions of hours taxpayers spend when responding to an IRS notice or audit. They conclude that the tax compliance industry is one of the largest U.S. industries. It hires the equivalent of 3.8 million full-time workers—roughly six times larger than the automobile industry![7] Costs of complying with the individual and corporate income tax requirements in 2006 amounted to $193 billion—or roughly 14 percent of income tax revenue.

TAS argues that America's taxpayers deserve a simple and less burdensome tax system. They report that nearly 61 percent of individual taxpayers and 74 percent of unincorporated business taxpayers pay someone to determine their taxes. Since 2001, there have been more than 3,250 changes to the tax code, an average of more than one a day. The tax code now contains 3.7 million words—a number that has more than tripled since 1975. The *CCH Standard Federal Tax Reporter,* a leading publication that summarizes administrative guidance and judicial decisions on taxation, is published in 25 volumes that take up nine feet of shelf space. There are also two businesses that publish daily newsletters that report on new tax code developments often running 50–100 pages per day.

Further, TAS offers many reasons for worry. One is that honest taxpayers too often make inadvertent errors, causing them to overpay their tax that sometimes leads to IRS enforcement action for mistaken tax underpayments. Even honest taxpayers apparently have much to fear under a complex system difficult to comprehend.

Another concern raised by TAS stems from the multitude of competing tax preferences. For example, at least 11 incentives encourage taxpayers to save for and spend on education, but eligibility requirements, definitions of common terms, income level thresholds, phase-out ranges, and inflation adjustments vary substantially. There are 16 tax incentives that encourage taxpayers to save for retirement, but again they are subject to different sets of rules governing eligibility, contribution limits, taxation of contributions and distributions, withdrawals, availability of loans, and portability. TAS argues that it is unreasonable to expect taxpayers to learn details of 27 education and retirement incentives to determine which ones provide the best fit.

TAS also takes aim at the Alternative Minimum Tax (AMT). The AMT was prompted by a widespread reporting in 1966 that 155 high-income taxpayers paid no income tax. The AMT requires taxpayers to compute taxes twice—once under the regular rules and again under the AMT regime. Taxpayers are required to pay the higher of the two amounts. Its original intent was to prevent wealthy taxpayers from escaping taxation through heavy use of tax preferences. But, the original tax loopholes that enabled such tax reduction were repealed years ago. TAS estimates that 77 percent of the additional income subject to tax under the AMT is attributable simply to family size or residing in a high-tax state—circumstances unrelated to the original intent of the AMT. TAS concludes Congress has been unwilling to repeal the AMT because they don't want to lose its additional tax revenue. In 2010, 27 million taxpayers paid $102 million in

AMT taxes.[8] Meanwhile, the AMT contributes to complexity of our tax system.

The Earned Income Tax Credit (EITC) is another example discussed by TAS. It is a very complicated tax preference claimed by about 22 million taxpayers each year. It provides low-income workers with government checks as a way of encouraging them to keep working. Maximum EITC benefits for the 2010 tax year are:

- $5,666 with three or more qualifying children,
- $5,036 with two qualifying children,
- $3,050 with one qualifying child, and
- $457 with no qualifying children.

Eligibility requirements and computations are complex thus leading to improper claims by taxpayers and to improper denials by the IRS. Recently, TAS found that even when the IRS initially denies EITC claims, taxpayers ultimately obtained EITC payments in 43 percent of cases. Complexity also explains why 72 percent of taxpayers who claim the EITC hire tax preparers.

TAS concludes that small business owners face a particularly bewildering array of laws, including a patchwork set of rules that governs the depreciation of equipment, numerous and overlapping filing requirements for employment taxes, and a vague set of factors that governs the classification of workers as either employees or independent contractors. These complications lead to long-standing battles between businesses and the IRS, with no obvious "correct" answers in many cases.

One more unintended consequence deserves mention. Tax complexity erodes confidence in our tax system as citizens come to believe "others"—such as the rich, corporations, or even their neighbors—somehow escape taxation. Suspicions that "others" escape taxation are enough to erode confidence and lead to even greater demands for tax preferences—and hence more tax complexity, less efficiency, and even muddier assessment of tax equity—on the argument that "everyone else does it too."

FLAT TAX

A pure flat income tax is so simple that its filing requirements can fit on a postcard.[9] The term "flat" refers to a single tax rate applied to all income. Our current income tax code has six tax rates—10 percent, 15 percent, 25 percent, 28 percent, 33 percent, and 35 percent—each applied to different income brackets. Unlike our current code that offers many tax preferences, all income is taxable under a pure flat tax.

Under a flat tax of 20 percent, Anne, who earns $100,000 in income, would owe $20,000—20 percent of income. Michael, who earns $10,000, owes $2,000, or 20 percent of $10,000. Average tax rates are identical for Anne and Michael—20 percent—and equal the flat tax rate.

A flat tax is consistent with the ability-to-pay principle since tax bills are solely based on income. It is also consistent with the "horizontal equity" notion whereby equals receive identical tax bills. If Bob and Janice each earn $50,000, each owes $10,000 in taxes under a 20 percent flat tax. "Vertical equity" is also maintained because tax bills rise with income. Anne's $100,000 of income yields a $20,000 tax bill, but Janice's $50,000 tax bill yields a $10,000 tax bill. It is a proportional tax whereby tax bills are a fixed percentage of income—20 percent in this case.

A modified flat tax is likely to be acceptable to more citizens than the pure one just described.[10] It remains simple and taxes income at a single rate only after reaching a minimum income threshold. For example, all income below $25,000 could be tax free at a 0 percent rate. All income above $25,000 is taxed at a single rate.

Consider a modified flat tax of 20 percent with a taxable income threshold of $25,000.

- Michael owes no tax on income of $10,000 since he fails to meet the $25,000 threshold.
- Bob and Janice earn $50,000 and so each owes $5,000 on taxable income of $25,000.
- Anne's income of $100,000 yields a tax bill of $15,000 on taxable income of $75,000.

Again, tax bills rise with income. Tax collection of $25,000 comes from taxing three out of four individuals—bills for Michael, Bob, Janice, and Anne are $0, $5,000, $5,000, and $15,000, respectively. Anne bears 60 percent of all taxes, Bob and Janice bear 20 percent each, and Michael owes no taxes.

Flat Tax Advantages

A modified flat tax has many advantages. One is that all income, above the threshold, is taxed at the same rate. Resources flow to their most productive uses rather than to areas enjoying tax preferences. It also greatly simplifies equity assessment. Equals are truly treated equally because no one is better able to take advantage of tax preferences. Home owners, for instance, do not receive preferential treatment over renters. Home owners with larger mortgage costs don't receive greater preferences over those with smaller mortgage costs. No one receives preferential treatment, but all receive the same tax break of no taxes on income below the income threshold.

A second attribute stems from its sheer simplicity. Public discussion of tax equity under a modified flat tax focuses on only two issues: the one tax rate and the income threshold. Both are extremely flexible—easily changed without mountains of tax legislation and forms. Both can be easily raised or lowered. Simplification enables a more productive debate on tax equity when compared to the muddy one under our current tax code. The flat tax leaves little room for confusion about how taxes vary with income. There is also less reason to suspect that "others" are somehow getting better deals by taking greater advantage of tax preferences. There are no tax preferences other than the one that all citizens receive: income below the threshold is untaxed.

A third attribute is that compliance consumes fewer resources. Tax forms can be placed on a postcard and few citizens will require services of tax specialists. Recall that TAS found that the tax compliance industry employs 3.8 million workers making it one of the largest U.S. industries. Compliance costs amounted to $193 billion in 2006 alone. Surely more productive work could be found for many of those employed in an industry that owes much of its size to the complexity of our tax code.

A fourth attribute is that elimination of tax preferences allows for tax rate reduction. Recall that tax collection equals tax rates multiplied by taxable income. Suppose that taxable income equals $100 million under a complex tax system with many tax preferences. Under an average tax rate of 30 percent, tax collection equals $30 million, or 30 percent of $100 million. Now suppose elimination of tax preferences raises taxable income to $140 million. Collection of $30 million—a "tax neutral" change—requires a tax rate of 21.4 percent, which amounts to a 29 percent reduction.

Previous discussion has argued the benefits of decreasing tax rates. Unlike tax preferences, across-the-board tax reduction does not play favorites and thus does not steer resources into less efficient areas of our economy. Lower rates raise economic incentives to work, save, and invest. Increases in after-tax income encourage more work. Savers also benefit when they are able to keep more of their income. Same goes for investors. Moving from our complex tax system with high tax rates to a modified flat tax with one lower tax rate (applied at the income threshold) is the rare government policy that promotes a more efficient economy.

A fifth attribute is that it meets the vertical equity requirement that tax bills rise with income. Consider six individuals with very different incomes under a flat tax rate of 20 percent and a $25,000 taxable income threshold.

- Joan earns $22,000 and pays $0.
- James earns $26,000 and pays $200.
- Kerry earns $50,000 and pays $5,000.
- Larry earns $100,000 and pays $15,000.
- Daphne earns $250,000 and pays $45,000.
- Gwen earns $1 million and pays $195,000.

Total tax collection is $260,200 with the following percentage shares: Joan (0%), James (0.1%), Kerry (1.9%), Larry (5.8%), Daphne (17.3%), and Gwen (74.9%). Gwen's tax bill at $195,000 is roughly 4 times that of Daphne's tax bill of $45,000, 13 times that of Larry's $15,000, 39 times that of Kerry's $5,000, and 970 times that of James's $200. Different examples may be made, but the point remains that tax payments meet the vertical equity requirement.

Tax compliance incentives are a sixth attribute. Incentives to evade taxes fall with tax rate reduction. Taxes on an additional $1,000 of income fall from $350 to $200 when tax rates fall from 35 percent to 20 percent. The U.S. underground economy is estimated at roughly 7 percent of GDP, or $1 trillion in 2009, and provides an estimate of how much of our economy evades taxation.[11] The IRS estimated the tax gap—difference between taxes owed and paid—was $345 billion in 2005 and demonstrates that less tax evasion could reap substantial revenues.[12]

Still at 7 percent of GDP, the U.S. underground economy is small when compared to Greece (25%), Italy (22%), Spain (20%), and Portugal (20%). A recent article describes how tax authorities in Greece resorted to studying satellite photos to uncover just how many residents of Athens, Greece, owned swimming pools.[13] Only 324 taxpayers checked the appropriate box on their tax return admitting to ownership. Tax authorities estimated 16,974 owned pools. Greece provides a case study of tax evasion that is deeply embedded in every crevice of its economy.

Finally, a flat tax yields more efficient government if it enables more citizens to recognize costs of providing government. Recall rising progressivity of our tax code: since 1987, the share of all federal income taxes paid by the top 1 percent of taxpayers rose from 24.8 percent to 40.4 percent in 2007.[14] Thirty-six percent of those filing tax returns also had no tax liability due to tax preferences.[15] Disconnecting citizens from taxation encourages citizens to focus on benefits from government rather than both costs and benefits of its programs. This is how vocal advocates of government are born.

Although vocal advocates enjoy receiving great deals from government, this is rarely efficient for society. Vocal advocates favor more government spending today and may have few regrets about expanding unfunded liabilities of future citizens as discussed in the previous chapter. A modified flat tax that shields fewer citizens from taxation creates fewer "vocal advocates" who are also less happy about deals they get from government programs. Thinking more about connections between benefits and costs leads to a more efficient and leaner government whose performance will be less disappointing.

Flat Tax Problems

Transition problems are inevitable when moving from today's complex tax system to a simple or modified flat tax. Many decisions have been encouraged by our code filled with so many tax preferences and tax rates. Previous chapters discussed how tax preferences have encouraged larger houses and larger mortgages. Tax complexity also encourages a huge tax compliance industry that would begin unraveling. Some citizens became accountants, tax attorneys, and finance experts simply because there was growing demand for people to navigate the complex tax code.

It is difficult to argue we should scrap plans for a flat tax simply because we want to protect so many jobs connected to tax complexity. Nonetheless, some citizens who were drawn into tax preferred activities would lose as the tax code becomes less important in determining careers of citizens. Prices of housing and other activities previously favored by tax preferences might also fall.

No one could ever list all the effects—intended and unintended—that stem from our current complex tax system. None of us have the imagination to fully predict what changes this world would experience under a flat tax code. We do know, however, resources would flow toward more efficient uses thus growing our economy as a result. Resources would flee from areas of our economy that had been favored by our complex tax code. The invisible hand of markets would guide more resources in ways that none of us could ever imagine. Demanders and suppliers would direct more of the economy rather than government.

Concerns have been voiced that housing markets would tumble. We have previously argued that countries with little to no tax preferences for housing do not suffer from low rates of home ownership. Nonetheless, the housing market would undoubtedly change and, along the way, some citizens will lose and others will gain. Losers probably include those who took on high debt levels, multiple houses, and expensive houses and those whose income was associated with housing. Gainers are those who would enjoy falling housing prices, such as those who previously could not afford a house, and those—consumers, investors, and business owners—whose lives were not closely tied to housing. Citizens today and tomorrow would gain as well when they are no longer burdened with costs of government programs aimed at cleaning up problems from previous programs that encouraged citizens to overinvest in housing.

Another problem lies with expectation that a flat tax will evolve into a "tax increase machine." History demonstrates that fundamental tax reform such as the 1986 Tax Reform Act rapidly unraveled into a more complex tax system. In November 2005, the report of the president's Federal Advisory Panel on Federal Tax Reform laid bare the facts:

> Since the 1986 tax reform bill passed, there have been nearly 15,000 changes to the tax code—equal to more than 2 changes a day. Each one of these changes had a sponsor, and each had a rationale to defend it. Each one was passed by Congress and signed into law.[16]

The 1986 tax change lowered numbers of tax rates from 15 to 6 and eliminated or reduced many tax preferences. Of course, no tax law is permanent and this fact explains why a flat tax might evolve back into the very structure it was intended to replace. Meanwhile, the fact that it eliminated tax preferences makes tax rate increases very tempting to those seeking additional tax revenues since more income becomes taxable.

Experience with VAT demonstrates tax rate increases often follow tax reform. VAT rates of nine of ten developed countries have risen substantially since their introduction.[17] These include:

- Denmark from 9 percent to 25 percent,
- France from 13.6 percent to 19.6 percent,
- Germany from 10 percent to 19 percent,

- Italy from 12 percent to 20 percent,
- Japan from 3 percent to 5 percent,
- Spain from 12 percent to 16 percent,
- Sweden from 17.7 percent to 25 percent,
- Switzerland from 6.5 percent to 7.6 percent, and
- United Kingdom from 8 percent to 17.5 percent.

Canada is the lone exception—its rate fell from 7 percent to 5 percent. VAT systems did not replace income tax systems but rather were used to generate additional tax revenue. These countries have highly progressive income tax systems with top income tax brackets ranging from 41.7 percent (Switzerland) to 59.7 percent (Denmark).

VAT systems are also loaded with tax preferences similar to our income tax system. Tax preferences are awarded the same ways—to help the poor (e.g., food expenses), promote social goals (e.g., solar and wind energy), and reward special interest groups. All are fraught with complexity and rampant tax evasion. VAT is also hidden in final prices to consumers thus further disconnecting taxpayers from costs of government and enabling inefficient government programs.

Similar concerns surround introduction of a flat income tax in the United States. What would begin with a low flat tax rate might evolve into a rising flat rate as pressures continue building to fund our expanding long-term unfunded liabilities of government. Proposals to raise the flat rate or to reintroduce a progressive tax rate system can be expected by those who believe the government undertaxes rather than overspends.

BOTTOM LINE

Many misconceptions surround flat taxation, which is not surprising given that this book focuses on myths of fair and efficient government. A flat income tax enables clearer assessment of tax fairness and promotes a more efficient economy. Still, a flat tax will never please all citizens, but remember perfection only exists in theory. Shortcomings exist but should be discussed alongside advantages to provide balanced discussion of whether it would fund a government that provides citizens greater satisfaction with its role in promoting fairness and efficiency.

Uncertainty over the new world that would emerge certainly frightens many. For example, many industries other than tax-preferred ones such as housing would grow as resources flow to more productive areas of the economy. Fewer jobs in tax compliance would be another symptom of change. It is common to focus on short-run transition issues that would emerge, but over time the economy would be more efficient with greater job opportunities. Of course, many citizens and groups will argue for tax relief for activities they enjoy or wish to encourage. Failing businesses will argue for bailouts. Calls for preferential treatment will be hard to resist. Groups will declare they deserve tax favors, but remember our past inability to control these urges explains why we are now saddled with a complex tax code that is neither fair nor efficient.

It is worth remembering that flat taxation removes much of the clutter associated with our current tax system that creates so many jobs for those who deal with tax complexity. These workers unwittingly waste resources and would contribute more to society by following jobs created when resources flow out of the tax compliance industry. It is predictable that those making their livings off tax code complexity resist simplification, but again their resistance to change is understandable given how much their industry is likely to be destroyed by the opening up of creative destruction opportunities that will allow resources to flow toward more productive uses.

Skeptics will object on the grounds that a modified flat tax is unfair. It is often believed that the rich pay the same taxes as the poor under this system, but facts demonstrate otherwise. Taxable income can be set at the threshold that defines poverty thus removing low-income citizens from tax rolls. Tax bills clearly rise with taxable income and it will be no secret that the rich pay more than those earning less.

Also, skeptics will argue a modified flat tax does not make the rich pay their fair share, but it is worth understanding that much confusion exists over how progressive and flat tax systems differ. One study suggests great confusion.[18] College students in accounting courses were asked, "Are progressive tax rates more or less fair than flat tax rates?" Students much preferred a progressive tax rate system by a margin of four to one when asked this question in the abstract. However, students believed by the same margin that flat tax systems were fair when offered examples of tax bills and incomes for different taxpayers. It remains questionable whether most of the public understands that the rich pay more tax under a flat tax than do the poor. Confusion is predictable given that many citizens have problems understanding our complex progressive income tax code.

A modified flat tax also allows for a more thoughtful discussion of how many dollars in taxes citizens should pay. Our current system does not promote clear discussion on this issue. Again, this is understandable under a tax system that has spawned a tax compliance industry larger than the automobile industry. A more open and clear debate should be welcomed by all those truly interested in promoting tax fairness and a more efficient economy.

ELEVEN

Improving Government

KEY POINTS IN THIS CHAPTER

- Dissatisfaction with government is predictable given it is rarely fair or efficient. Solutions that improve government include:
  - debate the appropriate size of government,
  - acknowledge harm from government programs,
  - advocate government programs on their practice rather than theory,
  - admit government is inefficient by its very nature,
  - quit enabling inefficiency of businesses,
  - acknowledge unfunded liabilities of future citizens today,
  - make costs of government more visible, and
  - eliminate tax preferences and flatten tax rates.

This book has tackled the problem that government continues to grow despite growing dissatisfaction with its performance. This book is loaded with examples of wasteful programs that harm as well as benefit citizens. Only the most optimistic citizens believe recent expansion of government will live up to its many political promises that benefits come at little to no cost.

The good news is that it is clear why promises to improve government mostly fail. Promises rarely involve anything more than changing personalities or political parties that merely repeat mistakes of the past. Rethinking government is the only avenue open with true promise. Readers may remember that, "Duh! What do you expect?" was the response readers were to eventually offer when asked, "Why are we so dissatisfied with government?" Recognition of the causes for why government is rarely fair or efficient forms the basis for solutions.

This chapter outlines solutions that promote more efficient and fairer government. Of course, nothing is perfect and solutions enable improved rather than absolute satisfaction. Perfection does not exist in the real world and trade-offs between efficacy and political viability must be weighed. Ordering of solutions generally follows ordering of material in the book. Proposals point us in the right direction and require an honest debate that acknowledges our current predicament stems from myths that government is fair and efficient.

LIMIT GOVERNMENT SIZE

It's human nature to be distracted by the many problems we encounter on a daily basis. Few of us are immune to believing each problem deserves a specific government remedy that brings quick and effective relief. This thinking reflects the "trees" part of the "forest from the trees" question. "Trees" are specific programs—public spending on the arts, health care, or education, to name just a few. Each program has its fervent supporters. The "forest" part, though, involves how large of a role government should play in our lives.

"What is the appropriate size of government?" requires an answer. Conventional wisdom behind recent expansion of government reflects a very curious asymmetry. There is no logical basis for the view that all problems stem from markets and never from government. This misplaced logic explains much of our growing disappointment with government because programs are rarely fair or efficient. This view leads to expanding government as it ignores that current problems are at least partially caused by past government programs themselves. Repeating mistakes of the past rarely solves problems.

Public debate on government size enables better government by promoting fuller disclosure of benefits and costs of its programs. Currently, program advocates have little incentive to fully disclose costs and benefits when they don't directly compete for public funding.[1] Advocates enjoy free rein to push for programs based on promises of benefits with little to no costs rather than on the basis of why they deserve funding more than other programs. Competition for funding will unleash greater scrutiny of their claims of benefits with little to no costs by advocates of spending on other programs. Government will become more efficient and fairer when funding flows toward those who truly can demonstrate the widest gaps between benefits and costs.

Some spending programs are clearly more important than others. As President Barack Obama declared, recent "stimulus" spending packages represented "the largest new investment in our nation's infrastructure since Eisenhower built an interstate highway system in the 1950s."[2] There is clearly much support for improving what many citizens correctly believe is an aging infrastructure. But only $64 billion, or 8 percent of the total, went to roads, public transport, rails, bridges, aviation, and wastewater systems. More scrutiny on where the rest of the spending went would appear to be a useful endeavor that would be encouraged by placing government on an allowance. Questions should also be asked about why past expansion of government has failed to "correct" our aging infrastructure.

Placing a cap on government size may also force government to better provide its critical role in helping the truly needy among us. Capping government's allowance may force greater scrutiny on whether government is truly meeting its commitments to the needy by forcing supporters of spending on the non-needy to explain why they deserve higher priority than the needy.

An upper limit on government size also elevates debate over whether debt reflects overspending or undertaxation to the importance it deserves. The answer to this critical question leads to the solution. If spending exceeds its upper limit then spending reduction is the logical solution. Raising taxes is the solution when spending lies below its upper limit. Past efforts to rein in debt—the Gramm-Rudman-Hollings Act of 1985 (GRHI), the Gramm-Rudman-Hollings Plan of 1987 (GRHII), and the Budget Enforcement Act of 1990, for example—failed because questions of whether debt reflects overspending or undertaxation were not adequately addressed. Politicians viewed debt as the cause rather than the symptom of problems. Expect more of the same as long as "what is appropriate size of government" remains an unaddressed question.

Critics will claim that "the appropriate size of government" is either too abstract or a question that defies an answer. These responses explain much of our disappointment with government. It defies belief that the government that emerges from a debate that does not clearly assess benefits and costs within a limited public budget leads to much satisfaction with its performance. It makes no sense to argue that government is fair or efficient unless benefits and costs of its programs are fully disclosed. This book is full of examples of programs that were promoted on incomplete disclosure of benefits and costs.

One way to frame the critical issue of how large government should be is to compare sizes of government across countries. Figure 11.1 displays total (federal, state, and local) government spending as shares of GDP across 15 developed countries in 2008.[3] The average is 44 percent of GDP and the range is wide, demonstrating substantial variation in how large governments are across these countries. France spends the most—53 percent of GDP—and Switzerland spends the least—32 percent of GDP. The United States at 39 percent of GDP is the fourth lowest of this group. A relevant question asks whether citizens believe countries with larger or smaller governments are preferable to their own.

"Hauser's Law" offers additional insights into the appropriate size of government in our country.[4] W. Kurt Hauser observed in 1993 that federal tax revenues since World War II had always been roughly 19 percent of GDP, despite many changes in the tax code. Top marginal tax rates, for instance, varied between 28 percent and 91 percent over this period. Tax codes change, but somehow the amount of revenue collected by the government remained strikingly constant. Hauser's observation about the constancy of tax revenues strongly suggests evidence of a "natural" upper limit to how many dollars government commands in our economy.

Figure 11.2 displays federal revenues as a percentage of GDP over 1950–2010. Its average over this period is roughly 18 percent, which is

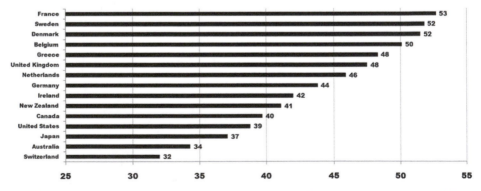

Figure 11.1 Government Size across Countries (2008): Percentages of GDP. (*Source:* OECD.)

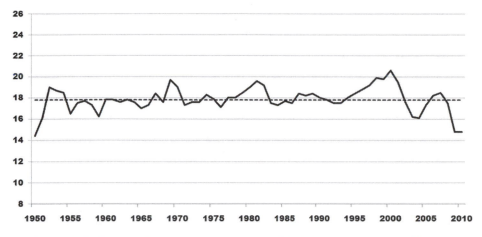

Figure 11.2 Federal Revenues: Percentage of GDP. (*Source:* Office of Management and Budget.)

slightly lower than the 19 percent observed by Hauser. Recent tax collections are on the low end, but not very different from the early 1950s. The evidence thus indicates that, despite numerous tax code changes over six decades, government tax collection appears to be constrained by a natural limit of around 18 percent of GDP.

This natural limit suggests that recent government expansion reflects overspending if citizens prefer budgetary balance over time—that is, public spending to be fully funded by tax revenues. Spending in 2009 and 2010 averaged 25 percent of GDP. Against the 18 percent of GDP average for tax collection, spending is roughly 7 percentage points above government's natural limit. This is a substantial $1 trillion in an economy with $14.2 trillion of GDP in 2009. The case for explicitly defining an appropriate size of government is really a harm-reduction strategy that constrains its ability to harm citizens by pushing inefficient or unfair outcomes to the tune of $1 trillion in 2009 alone.

Public debate on what constitutes an appropriate size of government may not result in capping spending at 18 percent of GDP. Of course, this book argues that costs are consistently underestimated thus leading to an overexpanded government. Nonetheless, it is critical to fully acknowledge the importance of the debate for improving efficiency and fairness of government. Any discussion that leads to fuller disclosure of benefits and costs of government leads to better government as it makes it easier to cast off ill-suited and unnecessary tasks.

Various think tanks have devoted much energy to proposing how best to cut wasteful government programs. These are excellent starting points for determining how best to trim government. Citizens Against Government Waste present many at http://www.cagw.org/. Cato Institute offers a department-by-department guide at http://www.downsizinggovernment. org/. Their website presents over $550 billion in cuts that include: Agriculture ($108 billion), Commerce ($1 billion), Defense ($150 billion), Energy ($11 billion), Education ($78 billion), Health and Human Services ($81 billion), Housing and Urban Development ($65 billion), and Transportation ($85 billion).

Consider Cato Institute's recommendation that farm subsidy programs be eliminated that effectively tax average families to fund a small group of well-off farm businesses. Cato discusses how the largest 10 percent of recipients receive 72 percent of all subsidy payments of $30 billion annually and that in 2007 the average income of farm households was $86,223, or 28 percent higher than the $67,609 average of all U.S. households. Cato argues that this program should be shelved since it is nothing more than an income transfer program for the well-to-do.

That government comes in many varieties—spending, taxation, tax preferences, regulation, and long-term unfunded liabilities—must be considered in any discussion of limiting government. Spending is government's most visible metric, but history demonstrates that containment of one area such as spending often leads to growth in other areas.[5] Other areas are more hidden than spending, but nonetheless exert costs as well as benefits too. For example, the annual cost of federal regulations increased to more than $1.75 trillion in 2008, a 3 percent real increase over five years, to about 14 percent of U.S. national income.[6] All areas of government need to be included in determining the limited role of government.

ACKNOWLEDGE HARM WHEN ASSESSING FAIRNESS

Benefits from government programs are quick and often easy to observe, but many of their costs often develop over time. It is easy to disassociate costs from benefits due to time delay and because they are often unintended. Disassociation leads to the vicious cycle whereby more government is believed to solve problems that are often connected to past government programs themselves. So government grows by attempting to overturn damage from its past policies. It repeats past mistakes with growing disappointment with government an ongoing symptom.

The following are among the many examples of the law of unintended harm that have been discussed.

- Minimum wage laws attempt to help low-income workers, but they also push some of those workers out of jobs.
- Rent control laws attempt to help low-income renters, but they also cause some of those citizens to pay higher rent.
- Tax laws that relieve citizens from paying taxes cause them to demand less efficient and larger government.
- Policies that pushed home ownership enabled a housing bubble that harmed citizens who purchased larger homes with more debt than they would otherwise have chosen.
- Policies that push home ownership harm renters and taxpayers stuck with paying for newer policies seeking to help those harmed from past policies that enabled foreclosures and price bubbles.
- Bailouts reward failure at the cost of the successful who do not receive funds and citizens footing the bills.

Unintended and adverse effects mostly stemmed from misunderstanding of how markets work. Misunderstanding allowed program proponents to believe benefits came at little to no cost and thus created "winners" and "losers" along the way. But, fairness cannot be thoroughly assessed without full disclosure of benefits to winners and costs to losers. Fairness is easy to claim when harm is not acknowledged and opens the door for using good intentions alone to justify programs.

Consider the case of government programs aimed at promoting home ownership. Private lenders are often accused of expanding subprime loans to home owners who were unlikely to have sufficient resources to withstand the aftermath of the price bubble. Previous chapters have argued that subprime loans are one symptom of government intervention into housing markets. It is easy to sympathize with citizens who lost so much equity and those who lost their homes. But, it remains unclear what blame should be assigned to lenders or to borrowers since their behaviors were enabled by government. It is also unclear whether it is fair to help less prudent home owners who took on more risk than the more prudent. The less prudent drew down more equity to finance spending, saved less, took out larger mortgages, and put smaller down payments than the more prudent. Similarly, it is unclear that government rescue of less prudent lenders is fair since it harms their more prudent counterparts. Recent government policies, nonetheless, help the less prudent, but at the cost of the more prudent.

The role that government played in enabling a housing price bubble remains the much misunderstood backstory. Far fewer loans to high-risk borrowers would have been made in the absence of intervention. It is also ironic that, while past policies encouraged housing by lowering costs, recent efforts to correct the long-term harm from those same policies attempt to push up housing prices to help current home owners. Higher prices harm citizens who wish to purchase homes today. Government efforts to promote equity often change course thus demonstrating that it not only creates winners and losers, but that the line drawn between winners and losers is subject to change.

"Cash for clunkers" is another example where proponents touted benefits with claims of little to no harm. Government provided rebates from $3,500 to $4,500 when purchasing new cars and nearly 700,000 cars were taken off our roads costing taxpayers $3 billion.[7] But, speeding up purchases today lowers car purchases tomorrow thus shifting lower sales farther down the road. Those prodded into buying cars with loans could have used monies to save more, buy used cars, lessen debt, or spend on other products. Most taxpayers could also think of better ways to use their dollars for themselves. This program also raised used car prices by decreasing supply thus harming low-income buyers who typically can only afford used cars. Skeptics will argue that destroying inefficient cars that pollute too much was the real reason behind the program. But, good intentions aside, it was an extremely inefficient program that would fail any test of fully disclosed benefits and costs.

Greater acknowledgment of harm would be unlikely to engender as much enthusiasm for government. Winners from today's programs understandably prefer that public debate not delve too deeply into who is harmed for fear that fuller disclosure might result in their favored programs being cut back or even shelved. But failure to clearly delineate winners from losers does not provide sufficient information with which to assess efficiency or fairness of government programs.

Focus on Practice Rather Than Theory

Although externalities (e.g., pollution), public goods (e.g., national defense), imperfect competition, and imperfect information pose hurdles for markets as they attempt to reach efficient outcomes, both markets and government fail to perfectly correct these problems. Government remedies exist in theory and include taxes, subsidies, regulation, and spending. But what is precise on a blackboard rarely finds its way to the practice of government. Government's ability to guide efficient outcomes is limited by motivation, as well as knowledge and expertise.

Markets mostly move toward efficiency naturally, unless government gets in the way. Government does not attempt to mimic markets and is thus called upon to overturn how markets work since otherwise there would be no need for government. Government cannot mimic how markets work because it never fears creative destruction and lacks necessary information and motivation. Ironically, lack of competition is viewed as an attribute in government and government is protected from competition in most areas in which it engages. It is unrealistic to believe it resists monopolistic urges to care little about keeping costs low or placing customers first.

Theorists also label government spending as "investment" rather than as simply taking resources out of markets to be spent by government. Recent spending "stimulus" programs are based on myths that politicians spend dollars more efficiently than markets and that public spending enriches the nation as a whole. These myths are very seductive, but evidence clearly indicates spending is often of the pork barrel variety that simply redistributes spending from one citizen to another. Many dollars are not redirected toward the poor. Government thus redistributes income and, along the way, directs dollars toward less efficient activities. Few recipients would have chosen to spend their own dollars on those same projects.

A swimming pool analogy clearly unveils the "investment" myth. Government spending entails taking dollars from the private sector. This is similar to attempting to raise the water level in a swimming pool by taking water from one end of the pool and dumping it in the other end. There is no reason to believe the water level will rise since water is simply being moved from one location to another. But, the fact that government is inefficient is reason enough for predicting the water level will fall. Government's bucket leaks water during its trip from one side of the pool to the other. Empirical evidence demonstrates that government spending shrinks rather than expands economic output.[8]

Projects that fit this description have been described within the $862 billion American Recovery and Reinvestment Act in 2009. Lawrence Lindsey places the spending "stimulus" in perspective of the 8 million people who became unemployed since the beginning of the recession and August 2010.[9] Each one of these people could have been handed government checks for $100,000 each, which would have "stimulated" their economic lives much better than the government stimulus package.

Recent auto bailouts provide another example. Despite widely conflicting claims of costs of providing new jobs ranging from $84,800 (1 million jobs) to $1,541,818 (55,000 jobs) per job, neither estimate indicates an efficient program.[10] Also, the $84.8 billion in government spending made citizens that much poorer and there were also fewer jobs in retail, construction, health care, and other industries. These forgotten citizens pay a heavy price as government props up inefficient businesses.

The evidence thus supports the theory that government rarely spends dollars more efficiently than consumers and producers in markets. Theory goes a long way toward creating many advocates of government who firmly believe that its expansion will somehow promote more efficient and fairer outcomes than markets. Taxes, subsidies, spending programs, regulations, and laws are contained in the theorist's bag of corrections. Promised benefits from these corrections are often disappointing when viewed against the weight of experience with the practice of government.

ADMIT GOVERNMENT IS INEFFICIENT BY ITS VERY NATURE

No politician runs for office without promising to restore efficiency in government. This is asking for trouble because it sets the stage for continuing disappointment with a government that cannot deliver efficiency. Overturning the myth of efficient government is thus an important ingredient to improving satisfaction with government.

Recall the five basic principles presented in Chapter 4 behind why government is inefficient. Principle 1 is that government is not called upon to mimic markets because it's illogical to call upon government to do what markets already do. Government is mostly called upon to overturn how markets promote efficient outcomes. Even when government is called upon to make outcomes fairer, this nonetheless requires government to promote inefficient outcomes.

The second principle is that it is a mistake to believe government is more efficient than markets. Markets are driven by an invisible hand, but the more visible hand of government can never know how to better match demand with supply. Markets are efficient because producers thirst for profits and thus keep costs low in order to remain competitive within a world where creative destruction is always lurking in the background. In contrast, government never fears creative destruction and is forbidden from earning profit. Misunderstanding markets apparently leads to misplaced beliefs that politicians are better at guiding efficient outcomes than markets.

The third principle is that monopoly government has little incentive to be efficient. Recall that lack of competition in markets is viewed as a problem, but an attribute in government. What is a problem in markets should also be a problem in government. There is little reason to believe government resists monopolistic urges to care little about keeping costs low and placing citizens first. Critics might argue that my book unfairly blames government workers and politicians. But, even the best and most dedicated individuals would be discouraged in their attempts to overturn this principle.

The fourth principle is that spending is often of the pork barrel variety whereby it transfers income from one citizen to another. "All politics is local" was coined by former U.S. Speaker of the House Tip O'Neill and demonstrates that politicians understand all too well that their success is directly tied to bringing "bacon" home to their constituents. Winners receive the "bacon" and losers fund it. Transferring income does not promote efficiency.

The fifth principle is that our tax system cannot direct citizens to efficient choices over the government they want. Unlike market prices determined by product value and costs, tax bills simply rise in sync with income thus creating great deals for some citizens and bad deals for other citizens. Individual citizens are not charged more for services they value more or that cost more to provide.

It is time to acknowledge the cold fact that government is inefficient by its very nature. Perennial promises by new and incumbent politicians that they will "clean up" government sound good but offer little true promise and unending disappointment with their results. It should also be understood that their inability to make good on these promises has little to do with their good intentions and much to do with the cold reality of the five principles behind why government by its very nature is inefficient. Even with the best intentions, politicians will mostly waste energy and time attempting to convert government into an efficient enterprise. Acknowledging government's inability to be efficient is consistent with previous discussion that limiting government size is a vital harm-reduction endeavor.

Privatization may promote more efficient operation of activities over which citizens believe government should retain some control. The post office, prisons, and airport security easily come to mind. Placing such functions in the hands of profit-seeking businesses will encourage more efficient operations. Competing businesses can bid for contracts under the direction of government. Of course, there is no guarantee that "crony capitalism" and inefficient bureaucratic oversight will not pose problems. But, it is better to be prepared for such complications rather than simply assume that government will properly handle privatization efforts.

QUIT ENABLING INEFFICIENCY OF BUSINESSES

Creative destruction plays a vital role in guiding markets toward efficient outcomes that "regulate" bad business practices. While some factors lie outside control of owners—state of economy, taxes, and regulations— businesses fail mostly because they could not efficiently cater to consumer preferences. Workers are often forced to relocate, retrain, and/or find employment in other industries. Sometimes lives improve and sometimes not. Meanwhile, markets are busy freeing up resources and opening new opportunities for owners, workers, and consumers of other businesses.

Although government in theory promotes competition, the more visible hand of government has been very busy enabling inefficient behavior. Recent years have seen a surge in "crony capitalism" whereby some businesses receive favors from government through tax breaks, liability caps, entry barriers, government contracts, and bailouts. Government thus influences who become winners and losers. Bailouts of failing businesses have become an all too common policy.

Proponents focus on winners—rescued businesses, and the many businesses that supply products to them and service their customers and local communities. But, fuller disclosure requires a listing of the many losers that include taxpayers as well as the businesses, including their customers and workers, not receiving subsidies. Bailouts harm many citizens along the way as they "glue" resources to less efficient businesses. This picture does not describe free markets thus leaving little reason to believe markets can be efficient when favored businesses are protected by government from creative destruction.

Despite recent promises that government has effectively "rescued" General Motors, there is every reason to predict its continued preferential treatment. Lowering $45 billion in GM's future tax bills is one clear demonstration of such treatment.[11] GM also remains unlikely to pay its pension costs in upcoming years since its "rescue" left intact $100 billion of unfunded long-term liabilities in its pension plan.[12] Investors and creditors that continue backing GM are probably banking on continued preferential treatment thus reinforcing government's role in defending inefficient businesses that is out of sync with the theory that government promotes competition.

The bottom line is that government needs to become a credible defender of efficient rather than inefficient businesses. Government can either choose to allow the market process to proceed and weed out inefficient businesses or intervene and "pick and choose" winners and losers. Government's record at promoting competition is so far very poor. But, the practice of government enabling inefficiency is consistent with the fact that government itself is either a monopolist or highly protected from competition.

The solution is to allow inefficient businesses to fail as dictated by the creative destruction process of markets. Nothing is perfect and markets make mistakes. Not all businesses are trustworthy and outright fraud arises at times as well. But, we also have a sophisticated legal system that can address all kinds of damages. Creative destruction keeps business owners in check over time rather than instantaneously. The invisible hand of markets guides us toward efficient outcomes, but it takes time and each step will rarely be perfect. Learning is an exercise sometimes best achieved through mistakes.

This recommendation is obviously a tall order for politicians. It is especially difficult when losers from bailouts and other preferences are not clearly acknowledged. This makes it appear that preferential treatment promotes both efficiency and fairness by helping politically powerful businesses and their associated workers and customers with little to no harm to anyone else. Fuller disclosure of benefits and costs will make it easier to resist subsidizing inefficiency when citizens more fully comprehend that preferential treatment often reflects inefficient and unfair government. Moreover, capping government size as described previously makes it easier to resist because it becomes clearer that losers are created when new programs favor some businesses and not others and also means that other programs must be cut when government has met its limit.

ACKNOWLEDGE UNFUNDED LIABILITIES OF SOCIAL INSURANCE

Social insurance—Social Security and Medicare—programs mislead citizens three ways. One, despite claims these programs are fair because employers pick up half of their costs, employers shift their shares onto workers. The combined tax rate of 15.3 percent on payroll consists of payments by both employee and employer of 7.65 percent each. Citizens are misled because they underestimate their costs for funding these programs.

Two, "trust funds" represent unfunded long-term liabilities of citizens rather than a growing pile of assets. Trust funds are simply pieces of paper promising to make good on future claims without equivalent dollars being saved and invested. Excess dollars fund non–social insurance programs. Combined trust funds in 2007 dollars are projected to rise from $0.13 trillion in 1980 to $3.3 trillion in 2015—an increase of 2,438 percent.[13] They represent claims on future citizens rather than real assets that can be drawn down in the future to make good on promises.

Three, they are not similar to private insurance programs. They are hidden income transfer programs because citizens are misled into thinking their benefits are entirely funded by their own past taxes. These programs create winners and losers because some citizens get great deals and other citizens receive bad deals. Great deals have so far been awarded to lower-income citizens and senior citizens. It remains unclear how future unfunded liabilities will be met, but at least four options are available: raising taxes, lowering benefits, lowering spending on other programs, and selling more debt.

Reform is stalled by these enduring misconceptions. Many politicians have long misled constituents by asserting that rising trust fund balances are a good thing. This is particularly troubling given these programs account for the largest share of all government spending. Social Security and Medicare spending amounted to $678 billion and $499 billion, respectively, in a total budget of $2,094 billion in 2009.[14] These programs currently account for 56 percent of all spending and are only going to grow faster in the future.

Privatization offers one solution. Private insurers are fully funded thus putting an end to expansion of long-term unfunded liabilities on tomorrow's citizens. Privatization allows citizens to choose among competing private programs similar to car insurance where customers are free to choose insurers they feel are best suited to their needs. Privatization thus promotes efficiency by handing over the insurance function to markets. Privatization also brings the distinction between insurance and transfer functions to the forefront of public discussion.

Of course, the private system would not transfer income. One solution would be to simply disengage the insurance function from Social Security and Medicare and transform them into a government program that directly transfers income. This would leave private insurers with responsibility for only insurance functions—something they can handle better than government. The transfer function remains with government where it belongs and this change encourages a meaningful debate over the appropriate role for government in transferring income that is anything but clear under the current system.

Long-term unfunded liabilities of citizens should be acknowledged today. Politicians stall reform because citizens are sure to be displeased when they are told past taxes have not been saved in accounts with their names on them. The truth can be devastating, but is essential for resolving this fiscal train wreck. Recent calls for changing retirement ages and size of checks or tax changes are merely means of furthering illusions that trust funds represent assets rather than long-term unfunded liabilities.

HEIGHTEN AWARENESS OF COSTS OF GOVERNMENT

Income taxation is an open invitation to inefficiency because citizens will demand programs in excess of those they would willingly choose if they were personally responsible for their funding. As former British prime minister Margaret Thatcher once said, "The problem with socialism is that eventually you run out of other people's money." Together with Milton Friedman's famous statement that "Nobody spends somebody else's money as carefully as they spend their own," it is clear that spending other people's money is much more fun than spending your own.

"Vocal advocates" of government are created that demand government expansion simply because expanded benefits are believed to be mostly funded by someone else. Citizens will have little interest in efficient government when it is funded by this tax system. The problem has been described as one where citizens act like shoppers who are no longer personally responsible for paying for every item placed in their grocery carts. Shopping carts would quickly become too small as shoppers figured out frugality reaped little individual reward. Many have experienced something similar when eating at an all-you-can-eat buffet. Diners eat and waste more food than when personally charged for each item placed on food trays.

Our tax system distorts choices in much the same way. Programs are bundled together without separate statements detailing costs of each program. It is impossible to compare costs with benefits attached to individual programs. Citizens have little incentive to scrutinize each and every program when they are bundled together into a huge blob labeled "government." They rationally focus on those programs where they experience such great values and ignore other programs because they see little connection to their tax bills. Little scrutiny of government efficiency is one symptom of this tax system. Government expansion of inefficient programs is another.

Growing progressivity of our tax system expands the ranks of "vocal advocates." In 2007, the top 1 percent of tax returns paid 40 percent of all federal individual income taxes.[15] These data do not include the roughly one-third of all tax returns that did not pay any income taxes thus making our tax system even more progressive.[16] Although "vocal advocates" enjoy receiving great deals from government, this is not efficient for society. They push for government expansion that few would accept if they were directly responsible for its payment. There are often much better uses of those same dollars either in the hands of citizens or other government programs.

Expanding numbers of citizens who pay income taxes is one means of informing more citizens about costs of government. One solution, as discussed below, is to introduce a flat tax that requires more citizens to pay income taxes and thus enables fuller disclosure of costs of government. Another solution, as discussed above, is to limit government size so that "vocal advocates" face greater competition from other "vocal advocates" for government programs. Other partial solutions include eliminating income tax withholding, having citizens cut a yearly check for their income tax bill, and sending citizens an annual statement detailing long-term unfunded liabilities of government.

ELIMINATE TAX PREFERENCES

Tax preferences reflect the very visible hand of government overturning efficient outcomes in markets. They give the public the false impression that government is smaller than it really is, push resources into inefficient activities, and are often directed toward those with political power. Tax preferences awarded to individuals and corporations of $3,480 per capita were granted in fiscal year 2011.[17]

The mortgage interest deduction is a tax preference that encourages citizens to overinvest in housing by lowering costs of purchasing homes. Citizens buy larger homes and take on more debt than otherwise. The many winners include home owners, lenders, and businesses selling furniture, paint, plumbing services, bookkeeping, yard supplies, and insurance. This tax preference provides "cover" for transferring income through government that is much less obvious than doling out checks. For example, with a 30-year fixed rate loan at 5.5 percent, a $250,000 mortgage allows tax reduction at the following tax rates: $3,416 (25%), $3,826 (28%), $4,510 (33%), and $4,783 (35%).[18] A $500,000 mortgage allows tax reduction of $6,833 (25%), $7,653 (28%), $9,020 (33%), and $9,566 (35%). Income transfers rise with income and size of mortgage.

Government pushes citizens to save less because it pushes more of their income toward servicing mortgage payments. Borrowers are also encouraged to take on more debt to maximize tax savings. Borrowers thus have less equity in their homes and they become more vulnerable to falling housing prices. Some home buyers would be better off saving more of their income, taking on smaller mortgages, owning fewer houses, renting rather than buying, investing in stock and bond markets, or simply paying down other debt such as on credit cards. This policy also harms citizens by sucking resources out of other activities even if they rarely receive explicit acknowledgment. Moreover, many poor individuals do not own houses and therefore cannot take advantage of this tax preference.

Even with the best of intentions, tax preferences promote inefficient outcomes because government lacks ability and motivation to guide resources toward efficient outcomes. Tax preferences also promote tax complexity that serves little purpose other than to create jobs in tax compliance and complicate assessment of tax equity. Skeptics might believe tax preferences promote fairness despite rewarding inefficiency. However, it remains unlikely that they are fair as long as their harm is underestimated or ignored. Again, thoughtful public debate on efficiency and fairness requires full disclosure of costs and benefits.

FLATTEN TAX RATES

Our income tax code taxes income at rates that rise with income and therefore incentives to hide income and lessen work rise with tax rates. This indicates that lowering tax rates raises economic incentives to work, save, and invest and lower incentives to hide income. Increases in after-tax income lead to more people wanting to work and for those who do work to work more.

It is also inefficient to tax corporations twice: first on income of corporations and then on income of owners. Our combined state and federal tax rate is 39 percent and is roughly 50 percent higher than most European countries.[19] Conventional wisdom is that corporations somehow bear its burdens, but only people can bear tax burdens and some will be poor. Owners shift the tax onto workers through reduced compensation and outsourcing simply because tax rates are lower in other countries. Customers bear burdens of higher prices and vendors see their payments reduced as well. Owners bear whatever they cannot shift.

A modified flat tax assigns one rate to all income—both corporate and noncorporate—above a threshold.[20] Despite conventional wisdom, a flat tax meets the vertical equity requirement that tax bills rise with income. Those making more income pay more taxes. Those making below the threshold pay no taxes. A flat tax also yields more efficient government if it causes more citizens to recognize true costs of providing government. As discussed in Chapter 10, our tax system has become increasingly progressive and a flat tax is one method that can be used to heighten awareness of citizens over the cost of government.

Unfortunately, many citizens continue to believe the rich pay the same taxes as the poor under flat taxation. Taxable income under a flat tax can be set at the threshold that defines poverty thus removing low-income citizens from tax rolls. Tax bills clearly rise with taxable income and it will be no secret that the rich pay more than those earning less. This tax system also allows for a more thoughtful discussion of how many dollars in taxes citizens should pay and should be welcomed by all those truly interested in promoting tax fairness.

One study suggests great confusion over flat taxation.[21] College students in accounting courses were asked, "Are progressive tax rates more or less fair than flat tax rates?" Students much preferred a progressive system by a margin of four to one when asked this question in the abstract. However, students chose, by the same margin, flat tax systems as fair when offered examples of tax bills and incomes for different taxpayers. Confusion is predictable given that many citizens have problems understanding our complex progressive income tax code.

A flat tax also lessens clutter associated with our current tax system that creates many jobs associated with tax complexity. These workers unwittingly waste resources and would contribute more to society by following jobs created when resources flow out of the tax compliance industry. The IRS has estimated that the tax compliance industry hires the equivalent of 3.8 million full-time workers—roughly six times larger than the automobile industry.[22] Resistance to tax simplification is understandable given how much their industry is likely to be destroyed by "ungluing" employment in tax compliance to create more productive employment in other industries.

Growing uncertainty is another symptom of today's tax code. While, in the late 1990s there were fewer than a dozen tax provisions subject to annual renewal, that number jumped to 141 in 2010.[23] These "temporary" tax changes subject to renewal include dozens of corporate tax preferences, capital gains tax rates, and the Alternative Minimum Tax. Uncertainty over tax policy is never good for hiring and investment because it discourages long-term planning. Again, our tax code picks favorites and, at the same time, losers under the ever-changing nature of our complex tax code.

Credibility is an essential ingredient to the success of the flat tax. Despite the fact that the 1986 Tax Reform Act flattened tax rates and eliminated various tax preferences, politicians quickly began raising rates, creating more tax brackets and introducing new tax preferences. There are valid concerns that a similar fate awaits a flat tax since Congress is apparently addicted to tinkering with the tax code. History demonstrates that Congress will believe it knows how to promote efficiency and fairness, despite evidence presented in this book. Meanwhile, unraveling of the flat tax will be tempting to those seeking more tax revenue through raising tax rates.

Flatter tax rates also create more job opportunities for citizens, including the poor, as the tax code promotes a larger more efficient economy. Punishing the rich through higher tax rates is not an effective means of reducing poverty because it shrinks the economy and creates fewer jobs. Recent analysis of dropping the federal corporate tax rate from 35 percent to 25 percent predicts job creation of 531,000 new private sector jobs in the private sector.[24] It is worth remembering that government efforts at helping the poor have been mostly driven by transferring income within a fixed pie and its record is mostly one of failure. It is time to shift focus toward rewarding efficiency and growing the economy rather than punishing highly productive citizens that encourages them to work less and spend more time hiding their income.

Notes

Chapter 1: Our Disappointment with Government

1. "Distrust, Discontent, Anger and Partisan Rancor. The People and Their Government," Pew Research Center, April 18, 2010, http://people-press.org/reports/pdf/606.pdf.
2. All data on federal, state, and local government expenditures are from the Office of Management and Budget (www.whitehouse.gov/omb) and the U.S. Census Bureau (www.census.gov).
3. Dana Blanton, "Fox News Poll: 62 Percent Think U.S. Is on the Decline," FoxNews.com, July 30, 2010. The national telephone poll was conducted for Fox News by Opinion Dynamics Corporation among 900 registered voters from July 27 to July 28. For the total sample, the poll has a margin of sampling error of plus or minus 3 percentage points, http://www.foxnews.com/us/2010/07/30/fox-news-poll-percent-think-decline/.
4. Bridget T. Long, "The Impact of Federal Tax Credits for Higher Education Expenses," in *College Choices: The Economics of Which College, When College, and How to Pay For It,* ed. Caroline Hoxby (Chicago: University of Chicago Press, 2004).
5. "Not Such a Bright Idea," *The Economist,* August 26, 2010.
6. Insurance Institute for Highway Safety, "Texting Bans Aren't Reducing Crashes in 4 States Where They've Been Enacted, Insurance Data Reveal," *Status Report* 45, no. 10 (September 28, 2010), http://www.iihs.org/research/topics/pdf/HLDI_Bulletin_27_11.pdf.

7. Robert Barro, "The Folly of Subsidizing Unemployment," *Wall Street Journal,* August 30, 2010.

8. Tom Coburn and John McCain, "Summertime Blues: 100 Stimulus Projects That Give Taxpayers the Blues," August 2010, http://coburn.senate.gov/public/index.cfm?a=Files.Serve&File_id=a7e82141–1a9e-4eec-b160–6a8e62427efb.

9. U.S. Department of Transportation, "Cash for Clunkers Wraps Up with Nearly 700,000 Car Sales and Increased Fuel Efficiency, U.S. Transportation Secretary LaHood Declares Program 'Wildly Successful,'" Press Release, August, 26, 2009, http://www.dot.gov/affairs/2009/dot13309.htm.

10. There is plenty of evidence that the "cash for clunkers" program drove up used car prices. See, for example, Jeff Jacoby, " 'Clunkers': A Classic Government Folly," *The Boston Globe,* September 1, 2010.

11. Christopher Knittel, "The Implied Cost of Carbon Dioxide under the Cash for Clunkers Program," Working Paper, University of California, Davis, August 2009, http://escholarship.org/uc/item/3g9504bb.

Chapter 2: What Markets Do Well

1. Adam Smith, *An Inquiry into the Nature and Causes of the Wealth of Nations,* 2 vols., ed. Edwin Cannan (London: Methuen, 1904). http://www.econlib.org/library/Smith/smWNCover.html.

2. Carl Bialik, "Online Polling, Once Easily Dismissed, Burnishes Its Image," *Wall Street Journal,* August 7, 2010.

3. U.S. Small Business Administration (Office of Advocacy), *Employer Firm Births and Deaths by Employment Size of Firm, 1989–2006,* http://www.sba.gov/advocacy.

4. David Dranove and Michael L. Millenson, "Medical Bankruptcy: Myth Versus Fact," *Health Affairs* 25 (2006): 74–83.

5. H. G. Parsa, John T. Self, David Njite, and Tiffany King, "Why Restaurants Fail," *Cornell Hotel and Restaurant Administration Quarterly* 46 (2005): 304–22.

6. Joseph A. Schumpeter, *Capitalism, Socialism, and Democracy,* 3d ed. (New York: Harper and Brothers, 1950).

7. "Taking Flight," *The Economist,* September 17, 2009.

8. Jessica E. Vascellaro and Sam Schechner, "Slow Fade-Out for Video Stores," *Wall Street Journal,* September 30, 2010.

9. Richard A. Epstein, "BP Doesn't Deserve a Liability Cap," *Wall Street Journal,* June 16, 2010.

10. Ann Zimmerman, "Rival Chains Secretly Fund Opposition to Wal-Mart," *Wall Street Journal,* June 7, 2010.

11. Julie Scharper, "Bill Requiring $10.59 'Living Wage' Dies in City Council Committee," *The Baltimore Sun,* July 22, 2010.

12. Andrea M. Dean and Russell S. Sobel, "Has Wal-Mart Buried Mom and Pop?" *Regulation* 31 (Spring 2008): 38–45, esp. 40.

13. Richard B. McKenzie, "In Defense of Monopoly," *Regulation* 32 (Winter 2009–2010): 16–19.

14. Smith, *An Inquiry into the Nature and Causes of the Wealth of Nations.*

15. Milton Friedman, "The Social Responsibility of Business Is to Increase Its Profits," *New York Times Magazine,* September 13, 1970.

16. Aneel Karnani, "The Case against Corporate Social Responsibility," *Wall Street Journal,* August 23, 2010.

17. Craig Barrett and James P. Moore Jr., "Outsourcing and the 21st-Century Economy," *Wall Street Journal,* September 30, 2010.

18. Matthew J. Slaughter, "Insourcing Jobs: Making the Global Economy Work for America," Research Report, Organization for International Investment, October 2004, http://mba.tuck.dartmouth.edu/pages/faculty/matthew.slaughter/pdf/insourcing_study_final.pdf.

19. Jonathan Weisman, "Stimulus Fight Hits the Trail," *Wall Street Journal,* August 17, 2010.

20. Editorial, "Uncle Sam, Venture Capitalist," *Wall Street Journal,* August 17, 2010.

Chapter 3: Theory Is Not Practice of Government

1. Of course, it is not a perfect guide because significant changes might take a few pages and insignificant changes might take many pages. http://www.gpoaccess.gov/fr/.

2. Clyde Wayne Crews Jr., *Ten Thousand Commandments. An Annual Snapshot of the Federal Regulatory State* (Washington, D.C.: Competitive Enterprise Institute, 2010), http://cei.org/studies-issue-analysis/ten-thousand-commandments-2010.

3. Even though auctioning pollution permits is more likely to promote efficiency than taxation, the public has shown little interest in having government pursue this approach.

4. Kelly D. Brownell and Thomas R. Frieden, "Ounces of Prevention—The Public Policy Case for Taxes on Sugared Beverages," *New England Journal of Medicine* 360 (April 30, 2009): 1805–9.

5. Michael L. Marlow and Alden F. Shiers, "Would Soda Taxes Really Yield Health Benefits?" *Regulation* 33 (Fall 2010): 34–38.

6. Fred Kuchler and Elise Golan, "Is There a Role for Government in Reducing the Prevalence of Overweight and Obesity?" *Choices* (Fall 2004): 41–45.

7. Padmaja Ayyagari, Partha Deb, Jason Fletcher, William T. Gallo, and Jody L. Sindelar, "Sin Taxes: Do Heterogeneous Responses Undercut Their Value?" NBER Working Paper No. 15124, July 2009.

8. Charles L. Baum and William F. Ford, "The Wage Effects of Obesity: A Longitudinal Study," *Health Economics* 13 (2004): 885–99.

9. K. McPherson, "Does Preventing Obesity Lead To Reduced Health-Care Costs?" *PLoS Medicine* 5 (2008): 183–84.

10. M. Stobbe, "Dieting for Dollars? More U.S. Employees Trying It," Associated Press, June 1, 2010.

11. C. Sayre, "A New Weight-Loss Plan: Getting Paid to Shed Pounds," *Time,* January 4, 2010.

12. Thom Shanker and Christopher Drew, "Pentagon Faces Growing Pressures to Trim Budget," *New York Times,* July 22, 2010.

13. Milton Friedman, "The Role of Government in Education," in *From Economics and the Public Interest,* ed. R. A. Solo (New Brunswick, N.J.: Rutgers University Press, 1995).

14. Michael L. Marlow, "The Influence of Private School Enrollment on Public School Performance," *Applied Economics* 42 (2010): 11–22.

15. Tom Coburn and John McCain, "Summertime Blues: 100 Stimulus Projects That Give Taxpayers the Blues," August 2010, http://coburn.senate.gov/public/index.cfm?a=Files.Serve&File_id=a7e82141–1a9e-4eec-b160–6a8e62427efb.

16. Editorial, "Stimulating Waste: How Politicians Use Tax Dollars for Self-Promotion," *Chicago Tribune,* July 18, 2010.

17. Ibid.

18. Robert J. Barro and Charles J. Redlick, "Macroeconomic Effects from Government Purchases and Taxes," NBER Working Paper No. 15369, September 2009.

19. Congressional Budget Office, "Federal Debt and the Risk of Fiscal Crisis," July 27, 2010, http://cbo.gov/doc.cfm?index=11659; and Olivier Blanchard and Roberto Perotti, "An Empirical Characterization of the Dynamic Effects of Changes in Government Spending and Taxes on Output," *Quarterly Journal of Economics* 117 (November 2002): 1329–68.

20. Andreas Bergh and Magnus Henrekson, *Government Size and Implications for Economic Growth* (Washington, D.C.: AEI Press, 2010).

21. Kate Andersen Brower and Nicholas Johnston, "Obama Says Auto Industry 'Growing Stronger,' Creating Jobs," *Bloomberg News,* July 30, 2010, http://www.bloomberg.com/news/2010–07–30/obama-tells-detroit-auto-workers-industry-creating-jobs-after-u-s-bailout.html.

22. Jim Malley and Thomas Moutos, "Does Government Employment 'Crowd-Out' Private Employment? Evidence from Sweden," *Scandinavian Journal of Economics* 98 (1996): 289–302.

23. Yann Algan, Pierre Cahuc, and André Zylberberg, "Public Employment and Labour Market Performance," *Economic Policy* 17 (2004): 7–66; and Horst Feldmann, "Government Size and Unemployment: Evidence from Industrial Countries," *Public Choice* 127 (2006): 443–59.

24. Lawrence B. Lindsey, "Did the Stimulus Stimulate?" *The Weekly Standard,* August 16, 2010.

25. Christina D. Romer and David H. Romer, "The Macroeconomic Effects of Tax Changes: Estimates Based on a New Measure of Fiscal Shocks," *American Economic Review* 100 (June 2010): 763–801.

26. Lauren Cohen, Joshua Coval, and Christopher Malloy, "Do Powerful Politicians Cause Corporate Downsizing?" Updated Version, Harvard Business School, March 16, 2010. http://www.people.hbs.edu/cmalloy/pdffiles/envaloy.pdf.

27. Ibid.

28. Richard H. Thaler and Cass R. Sunstein, *Nudge: Improving Decisions About Health, Wealth, and Happiness* (New Haven, Conn.: Yale University Press, 2008).

29. Thomas Sowell, *The Vision of the Anointed: Self-Congratulation as a Basis for Social* Policy (New York: Basic Books, 1995); and Thomas Sowell, *Intellectuals and Society* (New York: Basic Books), 2009.

Chapter 4: Government: The Last Place to Look for Efficiency

1. Business revenues obtained from *Fortune* magazine's rankings, http://money.cnn.com/magazines/fortune/fortune500/2010/full_list/index.html.

2. Jia Lynn Yang, Neil Irwin, and David S. Hilzenrath, "Fed Aid in Financial Crisis Went Beyond U.S. Banks to Industry, Foreign Firms," *Washington Post,* December 2, 2010.

3. This is not the first time Harley-Davidson has been subsidized. In April 1983, Harley-Davidson was on the brink of bankruptcy when President Ronald Reagan imposed a temporary tariff on imported Japanese motorcycles with engines larger than 700cc. The intended outcome

was to increase the cost of Japanese imports by 40 percent, decreasing to 10 percent over five years. This helped Harley-Davidson by raising prices of imported motorcycles. Of course, there were unintended consequences as well. The Japanese responded by downsizing their 750s into unique-to-America 700cc models thus shifting their production to reduce their harm from the tariffs. For more discussion, see Daniel Klein, "Taking America for a Ride: The Politics of Motorcycle Tariffs," *Cato Policy Analysis* 32 (January 12, 1984), http://www.cato.org/pub_display.php?pub_id=898.

4. Editorial, "Taxpayers Get Soaked," *Wall Street Journal,* May 24, 2006.
5. Ibid.
6. Ibid.
7. Ibid.
8. For an excellent discussion of reforms, see Eli Lehrer, "Reforming the National Flood Insurance Program after 35 Years of Failure," Issue Analysis No. 2, Competitive Enterprise Institute, 2008, http://cei.org/sites/default/files/Eli%20Lehrer%20-%20Reforming%20the%20National%20Flood%20Insurance%20Program.pdf.
9. J. Scott Holladay and Jason A Schwartz, "The Distributional Consequences of the NFIP," Policy Brief No. 7, Institute for Policy Integrity, New York University School of Law, April 2010, http://policyintegrity.org/documents/FloodingtheMarket.pdf.
10. William A. Niskanen Jr., *Bureaucracy and Representative Government* (Chicago: Aldine, 1971).
11. Chris Edwards, "Overpaid Federal Workers," Cato Institute Report, June 2010, http://www.downsizinggovernment.org/overpaid-federal-workers. Data from the U.S. Bureau of Economic Analysis indicate that federal civilian workers had an average wage of $79,197 in 2008. The average wage of the nation's 108 million private sector workers was $50,028.
12. Andrew G. Biggs, "Pampered Public Employees," *The Atlantic,* August 13, 2010.
13. Milton Friedman and Rose Friedman, *Tyranny of the Status Quo* (New York: Harcourt Brace Jovanovich, Publishers, 1983), 50.
14. It is illegal to compete against the U.S. Postal Service on first class mail. It also enjoys exclusive access to all letter boxes marked "U.S. Mail." It does, however, compete against private delivery services that are not allowed to use letter boxes and must leave deliveries by doors when no one answers the door.
15. Dennis C. Mueller, *Public Choice II* (Cambridge: Cambridge University Press, 1989). This section is based on pp. 261–66.

16. "America's Struggling Postal Service: Hoping For Deliverance," *The Economist,* April 15, 2010.

17. Government Accounting Office (GAO), "High-Risk Series: Restructuring the U.S. Postal Service to Achieve Sustainable Financial Viability," GAO-09–937SP, July 28, 2009, http://www.gao.gov/highrisk/risks/efficiency-effectiveness/restructuring_postal.php.

18. Matthew Philips, "Lost in the Mail," *Newsweek,* March 30, 2010.

19. Michael Barone, "Big Government Forgets How to Build Big Projects," *Washington Examiner,* August 18, 2010.

20. John Steele Gordon, "Incentives vs. Government Waste: What If Bureaucrats Could Benefit Financially from Finding Cost Savings?" *Wall Street Journal,* May 14, 2010.

21. For more on the SAVE Award, see http://www.whitehouse.gov/save-award.

22. John N. Friedman and Richard T. Holden, "The Rising Incumbent Reelection Rate: What's Gerrymandering Got to Do With It?" *The Journal of Politics* 71 (April 2009): 593–611.

23. Katherine Mangu-Ward, "Throwing the Bums Out Is Harder Than It Looks," *Reason,* September 15, 2010, http://reason.com/archives/2010/09/15/throwing-the-bums-out-is-harde.

24. Glenn R. Parker, "Competition in Congressional Elections," in *Studies of Congress,* ed. Glenn R. Parker (Washington, D.C.: Congressional Quarterly Press, 1985), 4.

25. Randall Fitzgerald and Gerald Lipson, *Pork Barrel: The Unexpurgated Grace Commission Story of Congressional Profligacy* (Washington, D.C.: The Cato Institute, 1984), xix.

26. Office of Management and Budget, *2003 Budget of the United States Government* (Washington, D.C.: OMB, 2001), http://www.gpoaccess.gov/usbudget/fy03/browse.html.

27. Citizens Against Government Waste, *2010 Congressional Pig Book* (Washington, D.C.: Citizens Against Government Waste, 2010), www.cagw.org.

28. James L. Payne, *The Culture of Spending: Why Congress Lives Beyond Our Means* (San Francisco: ICS Press, 1991).

Chapter 5: Government Rarely Promotes Fairness

1. Michael D. Tanner, "More Proof We Can't Stop Poverty By Making It More Comfortable," *Investor's Business Daily,* September 17, 2010.

2. Office of Management and Budget, *2011 Budget of the United States Government: Historical Tables,* http://www.gpoaccess.gov/usbudget/fy11/hist.html.

3. Ibid.

4. Arthur C. Brooks, "Happy Now?" *National Review Online,* June 2, 2010, http://www.nationalreview.com/articles/229872/happy-now/arthur-c-brooks.

5. Poverty thresholds (family size) in 2009 were defined as $10,830 (1), $14,570 (2), $18,310 (3), $22,050 (4), $25,790 (5), $29,530 (6), $33,270 (7), and $37,010 (8). See U.S. Bureau of the Census, Current Population Survey, Annual Social and Economic Supplements, Poverty and Health Statistics Branch/HHES Division, http://www.census.gov/cps/.

6. Even though one might be inclined to point out that poverty has been on the upswing since its low of 8.7 percent in 2000, this poverty metric has varied little over time. Its range of 8.7 percent to 12.3 percent mostly reflects the nature of our business cycle as it rises and falls with swings in unemployment.

7. Nicholas Eberstadt, "Poor Statistics," *Forbes,* March 2, 2009, http://www.aei.org/article/100073.

8. Council of Economic Advisors, *Economic Report of the President,* March 1992, http://fraser.stlouisfed.org/publications/erp/issue/1584/.

9. Gordon Tullock, *Welfare for the Well-to-Do* (Dallas: Fisher Institute, 1983). The Egg Marketing Board closed in 1971.

10. Tullock, *Welfare for the Well-to-Do,* 2.

11. United Auto Workers, "Who We Are," http://www.uaw.org/node/39.

12. General Accounting Office (GAO), "Low-Income Home Energy Assistance Program: Greater Fraud Prevention Controls Are Needed," GAO-10–621, June 2010, http://www.gao.gov/products/GAO-10–621.

13. GAO, "Hurricanes Katrina and Rita Disaster Relief: Improper and Potentially Fraudulent Individual Assistance Payments Estimated to Be between $600 Million and $1.4 Billion," GAO-06–844T, June 14, 2006, http://www.gao.gov/products/GAO-06–844T.

14. GAO, "Head Start: Undercover Testing Finds Fraud and Abuse at Selected Head Start Centers," GAO-10–733T, May 18, 2010, http://www.gao.gov/products/GAO-10–733T.

15. Daniel B. Klein and Stewart Dompe, "Reasons for Supporting the Minimum Wage: Asking Signatories of the 'Raise the Minimum Wage' Statement," *Econ Journal Watch* 4 (January 2007): 125–67,

http://econjwatch.org/articles/reasons-for-supporting-the-minimum-wage-asking-signatories-of-the-raise-the-minimum-wage-statement.

16. Bureau of Labor Statistics, "Characteristics of Minimum Wage Workers: 2008," U.S. Department of Labor, http://www.bls.gov/cps/minwage2008.htm.

17. Ralph E. Smith and Bruce Vavrichek, "The Wage Mobility of Minimum Wage Workers," *Industrial and Labor Relations Review* 46 (October 1992): 82–88.

18. Bureau of Labor Statistics, "Labor Force Statistics from the Current Population Survey," U.S. Department of Labor, http://www.bls.gov/cps/.

19. Editorial, "Morality and Charlie Rangel's Taxes," *Wall Street Journal,* July 27, 2009.

20. Rolfe Goetze, *Rent Control: Affordable Housing for the Privileged, Not the Poor: A Study of the Impact of Rent Control in Cambridge* (Cambridge, Mass.: GeoData Analysis, 1994).

21. For "Eye on the Bailout," see http://www.propublica.org/ion/bailout.

22. James Sherk, "UAW Workers Actually Cost the Big Three Automakers $70 an Hour," WebMemo No. 2162, Heritage Foundation, December 8, 2008, http://www.heritage.org/Research/Reports/2008/12/UAW-Workers-Actually-Cost-the-Big-Three-Automakers-70-an-Hour.

23. Tony Jackson, "GM Is Just a Hedge Fund in Disguise," *Financial Times,* August 22, 2010.

24. Darrell Issa and Jim Jordan, "Cleaning up the Mortgage Mess," *Wall Street Journal,* August 25, 2010.

25. In 1990, only 1 in 200 buyers had a down payment of less than or equal to 3 percent. By 2006, 30 percent put no money down. See Edward Pinto, "The Future of Housing Finance," *Wall Street Journal,* August 17, 2010.

26. The Federal Reserve System, aka the Fed, also played a major role in creating our financial mess. Created in 1913 by Congress, the Fed is the monopoly supplier of money and is responsible for keeping interest rates at historically low levels in recent years. Their role could easily fill another book and is a case study in the law of unintended consequences. Briefly, the Fed has flooded the economy with excess money in an attempt to spur economic growth. Unfortunately, economic growth often slows down eventually in response to past over-stimulus and so the Fed often counteracts with more money growth in what we have previously described as the vicious cycle of government policy. Meanwhile, excessive money growth and low interest rates

enable rapid investment in housing that contributes to price bubbles. Many dollars found their way into subprime mortgages as a result because lenders with so much liquidity found higher-risk borrowers another profit center. Again, it is tempting to blame markets for making such loans, but lenders were enabled by the Federal Reserve.

27. Peter Boettke and Steven Horwitz, *The House That Uncle Sam Built* (New York: Foundation for Economic Education, 2009), http://fee. org/doc/the-house-that-uncle-sam-built/.

28. Veronique de Rugy, "Is This What Deregulation Looks Like?" *The American,* September 17, 2009, http://www.american.com/archive/ 2009/september/is-this-what-deregulation-looks-like.

29. Lorraine Woellert and John Gittelsohn, "Fannie-Freddie Fix at $160 Billion with $1 Trillion Worst Case," *Bloomberg News,* June 13, 2010, http://www.bloomberg.com/news/print/2010–06–13/fannie-freddie-fix-expands-to-160-billion-with-worst-case-at-1-trillion.html.

30. Republican Commissioners on the Financial Crisis Inquiry Commission, "Financial Crisis Primer, Questions and Answers on the Causes of the Financial Crisis," Delivered as required by P.L. 111–21: The Fraud Enforcement and Recovery Act of 2009, December 15, 2010, http://keithhennessey.com/wp-content/uploads/2010/12/Financial-Crisis-Primer.pdf.

31. David, Streitfeld, "Biggest Defaulters on Mortgages Are the Rich," *New York Times,* July 9, 2010.

Chapter 6: Misconceptions of Tax Fairness

1. Congressional Budget Office (CBO), *An Analysis of the President's Budgetary Proposals for Fiscal Year 2011,* March 2010, http://www. cbo.gov/ftpdocs/112xx/doc11280/03–24-apb.pdf.

2. User fees on toll roads, bridges, museums, and campgrounds are approximations of the benefit principle. Tax-earmarking—for example, gasoline taxes earmarked for funding highways—also appears consistent with the benefit principle. But, these practices provide little revenue and are included in the "other" category of taxes mentioned above. Few of these programs are fully funded and so non-users or infrequent users subsidize users through higher taxes or reductions in programs from which they benefit.

3. Our tax system is much more complicated than shown here because there are many deductions and credits that are factored in. These complications are addressed in Chapter 8 on tax preferences.

4. Gerald Prante, "Summary of Latest Federal Individual Income Tax Data," Tax Foundation Fiscal Fact No. 183, Washington, D.C., July 2009, http://www.taxfoundation.org/news/show/250.html.

5. Scott A. Hodge, "Surge of 'Nonpayers' Will Be Part of Bush Tax Legacy," Tax Foundation Fiscal Fact No. 202, Washington, D.C., December 4, 2009, http://www.taxfoundation.org/publications/show/25586.html.

6. "Tax preferences" are policies that lower taxes and are fully explored in Chapter 8.

7. We ignore spending funded by public debt in this discussion.

8. "Federal Spending Received Per Dollar of Taxes Paid by State, 2005," Tax Foundation, http://www.taxfoundation.org/research/show/266.html.

9. David Albouy, "The Unequal Geographic Burden of Federal Taxation," *Journal of Political Economy* 117 (August 2009): 635–67.

10. Interview with Paul O'Neill, U.S. Secretary of the Treasury, *Financial Times,* May 21, 2001. This statement is his response to the question: "What are some of the areas you see need fixing?"

11. Michael J. Boskin, "Time to Junk the Corporate Tax," *Wall Street Journal,* May 6, 2010.

12. Eric Dash and Nelson D. Schwartz, "Banks Seek to Keep Profits as New Oversight Rules Loom," *New York Times,* July 16, 2010.

13. A related story is told in William F. Buckley Jr., "A Parable: The Tenth Man," *National Review,* April 27, 2001.

Chapter 7: Vocal Advocates Encourage Inefficient Government

1. This section follows Michael L. Marlow and William P. Orzechowski, "The Separation of Spending from Taxation: Implications for Collective Choices," *Constitutional Political Economy* 8 (1997): 151–63.

2. Citizens may move to other political jurisdictions to escape taxes they believe are too burdensome or unjust. They may also lobby for change or even run for office, but clearly this is not as easy as simply refusing to purchase products offered by sellers in markets.

3. Scott A. Hodge, "Tax Burden of Top 1% Now Exceeds That of Bottom 95%," Tax Foundation Policy Blog, July 29, 2009, http://www.taxfoundation.org/blog/show/24944.html.

4. Scott A. Hodge, "States Vary Widely in Number of Tax Filers with No Income Tax Liability," Tax Foundation Fiscal Fact No. 229, Washington, D.C., May 24, 2010, http://www.taxfoundation.org/research/show/26336.html.

5. Poll cited in Arthur C. Brooks, "'Spreading the Wealth' Isn't Fair: Surveys Show Americans Think Taxes Are Already too High, Even for the Rich," *Wall Street Journal,* April 1, 2010.

6. A constant flow of tax revenue also probably encourages government to live day-to-day rather than undergo longer-term planning of how to budget over the space of a year.

7. Michael Whalen, "Make Taxes Visible to Voters: 'Painless' Taxation Makes Big Government Possible," *Washington Times,* August 18, 2010.

8. James M. Buchanan and Richard E. Wagner, *Democracy in Deficit: The Political Legacy of Lord Keynes* (New York: Academic Press, 1977).

9. Michael A. Fletcher and Carol Morello, "Federal Spending Rises a Record 16%," *Washington Post,* September 1, 2010.

10. For this proposal, see http://www.treasurydirect.gov/NP/BPDLogin? application=np.

11. Veronique de Rugy, "Budgetary Three-Card Monte: War Spending Aside, Federal Budget Shenanigans Continue," *Reason,* May 2010, http://www.thefreelibrary.com/Reason/2010/April/8-p598.

12. Office of Management and Budget, Table 1.1: Summary of Receipts, Outlays, and Surpluses or Deficits: 1789–2015, in *2011 U.S. Budget of the United States,* http://www.whitehouse.gov/omb/budget/Historicals/.

13. Lorraine Woellert and John Gittelsohn, "Fannie-Freddie Fix at $160 Billion with $1 Trillion Worst Case," *Bloomberg News,* June 13, 2010, http://www.bloomberg.com/news/print/2010–06–13/fannie-freddie-fix-expands-to-160-billion-with-worst-case-at-1-trillion.html.

14. This model of voter behavior was developed by Charles Tiebout and is referred to as the Tiebout Model. See Charles M. Tiebout, "A Pure Theory of Local Expenditures," *Journal of Political Economy* 64 (October 1956): 416–24.

15. Arthur Laffer and Stephen Moore, "Soak the Rich, Lose the Rich," *Wall Street Journal,* May 18, 2009.

16. "LeBron Can Make More with Heat than Cavs," *Sports Biz with Darren Rovell,* CNBC Sports, July 8, 2010, http://www.cnbc.com/id/38146901.

17. Philip Shishkin, "Tax-Free Liquor Lures Buyers, Stirring Crossborder Tensions," *Wall Street Journal,* September 8, 2009.

18. Legislative Analyst's Office, "Analysis of the 2003–04 Budget Bill," California State Government, January 15, 2003, http://www.lao.ca.gov/analysis_2003/education/hied_08_6610_anl03.htm.

19. See, for example, Michael L. Marlow, "Fiscal Decentralization and Government Size," *Public Choice* 56 (1988): 259–69; and David

Joulfaian and Michael L. Marlow, "Government Size and Decentralization: Evidence from Disaggregated Data," *Southern Economic Journal* 56 (April 1990): 1094–1102.

Chapter 8: Tax Preferences: Government Playing Favorites

1. Government Accounting Office (GAO), "Tax Preferences Represent a Substantial Federal Commitment and Need to Be Reexamined," GAO-05–690, September 2005, http://www.gao.gov/new.items/d05690.pdf.
2. There is some controversy over whether tax preferences really represent revenue losses. Critics suggest this terminology implies they represent gifts from government to taxpayers in the form of lower tax bills. They believe that government does not have the right to tax all income sources and so taxpayers should not be thankful to government for tax preferences.
3. GAO, "Tax Preferences Represent a Substantial Federal Commitment and Need to Be Reexamined," 5.
4. Analytical Perspectives, *2011 Budget of the U.S. Government,* http://www.gpoaccess.gov/usbudget/fy11/index.html.
5. Scott A. Hodge, "Who Benefits Most from Targeted Corporate Tax Incentives?" Tax Foundation Fiscal Fact No. 236, July 27, 2010, http://www.taxfoundation.org/publications/show/26554.html.
6. GAO, "Tax Preferences Represent a Substantial Federal Commitment and Need to Be Reexamined."
7. A 401(k) retirement savings plan allows a worker to save for retirement and have the savings invested while deferring current income taxes on those dollars and earnings until withdrawal.
8. For census data, see http://www.census.gov/hhes/www/housing/hvs/qtr210/q210ind.html.
9. Editorial, "Candy Taxes Struggle to Define Candy," *Wall Street Journal,* May 17, 2010.
10. Janet Adamy, "Federal Tan Tax Burns Some Badly but Keeps Everybody in the Dark: Ultraviolet Light Sessions Mostly Subject To New Levy, but Spray-On Jobs Are Cool," *Wall Street Journal,* July 1, 2010.
11. Hodge, "Who Benefits Most from Targeted Corporate Tax Incentives?"
12. Janet Hook, "Senate Cuts to Recession Relief Bill Favor Special Interests," *Los Angeles Times,* June 23, 2010.
13. Randall Smith and Sharon Terlep, "GM Could Be Free of Taxes for Years," *Wall Street Journal,* November 3, 2010.
14. "Simpler Taxes: The Flat-Tax Revolution," *The Economist,* April 14, 2005.

15. Roberta Mann, "The (Not So) Little House on the Prairie: The Hidden Costs of the Home Mortgage Interest Deduction," *Arizona State Law Journal* 32 (Winter 2000): 1347–97; and William G. Gale, Jonathan Gruber, and Seth Stephens-Davidowitz, "Encouraging Homeownership through the Tax Code," *Tax Notes* (June 18, 2007): 1171–89.

16. Patrick Fleenor, "Tax Savings from Mortgage Interest Deduction Vary Significantly from State to State," Tax Foundation Fiscal Fact No. 230, May 25, 2010, http://www.taxfoundation.org/publications/show/26341.html.

17. Sanchi Gupta, "Characteristics of New Single Family Homes," In-Depth Analysis, National Association of Home Builders, September 11 2006, http://www.nahb.org/generic.aspx?sectionID=734&genericContentID=64030.

18. Richard K. Green and Patric H. Hendershott, "Home-Ownership and Unemployment in the U.S.," *Urban Studies* 38 (August 2001): 1509–20.

19. Ruth Simon and James R. Hagerty, "One in Four Borrowers Is Underwater," *Wall Street Journal,* November 24, 2009.

20. Final Report of the Federal Advisory Panel on Federal Tax Reform, Submitted to the U.S. Treasury, November 2005, http://govinfo.library.unt.edu/taxreformpanel/.

21. Peter J. Wallison, "How to Get Housing off Government's Juice," *Bloomberg News,* September 23, 2010.

22. Alan Zibel, "New-Home Sales Plunge 33 Pct with Tax Credits Gone," *Wall Street Journal,* June 23, 2010.

23. GAO, "Tax Preferences Represent a Substantial Federal Commitment and Need to Be Reexamined."

24. Final Report of the Federal Advisory Panel on Federal Tax Reform.

25. Ibid.

26. S. Mitra Kalita and Nick Timiraos, "Homeowner Perks Under Fire," *Wall Street Journal,* December 16, 2010.

27. Kelly Evans, "What a Drag: Mortgage-Refi 'Cash-Ins,'" *Wall Street Journal,* December 8, 2010.

28. "Simpler Taxes: The Flat-tax Revolution," *The Economist,* April 14, 2005.

Chapter 9: Unfunded Liabilities of Future Citizens

1. U.S. Treasury, Monthly Statement of the Public Debt of the United States, August 31, 2010, http://www.treasurydirect.gov/govt/reports/pd/mspd/mspd.htm.

2. Frank Newport, "Six in 10 Workers Hold No Hope of Receiving Social Security," *Gallup,* July 20, 2010, http://www.gallup.com/poll/141449/ Six-Workers-Hold-No-Hope-Receiving-Social-Security.aspx.

3. W. Mark Crain and Michael L. Marlow, "The Causal Relationship between Social Security and the Federal Budget," in *Social Security's Looming Surpluses: Prospects and Implications,* ed. Carolyn L. Weaver (Washington, D,C,: The AEI Press, 1990).

4. Congressional Budget Office (CBO), *The Long-Term Budget Outlook,* June 2010, http://www.cbo.gov/doc.cfm?index=11579.

5. A Summary of the 2010 Annual Reports, Social Security and Medicare Boards of Trustees, http://www.ssa.gov/OACT/TRSUM/index. html.

6. CBO, *Supplemental Data for the Congressional Budget Office's Long-Term Budget Outlook,* June 2010. Projections are for 2011–2015 and it is assumed no inflation takes place over those same years, http:// www.cbo.gov/doc.cfm?index=11579.

7. CBO, *The Long-Term Budget Outlook.*

8. Study discussed in *Economic Report of the President,* February 1992, 142, http://fraser.stlouisfed.org/publications/erp/issue/1584/.

9. Michael J. Boskin, Marcy Avrin, and Kenneth Cone, "Modelling Alternative Solutions to the Long-Run Social Security Funding Crisis," in *Behavioral Simulation Methods in Tax Policy Analysis,* ed. Martin Feldstein (Chicago: University of Chicago Press, 1983).

10. Data obtained from various issues of the *Statistical Abstract of the United States,* http://www.census.gov/compendia/statab/.

11. Dick Armey, "Opposing View on Retirement Income: Let's Upend Social Security," *USA Today,* August 9, 2010.

12. For example, see James M. Buchanan, "Social Insurance in a Growing Economy: A Proposal for Radical Reform," *National Tax Journal* 19 (December 1968): 386–95.

13. It should be understood, however, that government may decide to bail out failing private insurers thus undermining market regulation of bad business practices. Past bailouts of financial and automotive industries have rescued businesses that ordinarily would have been weeded out by competition. Business owners that operate with expectations of bailouts will be less likely to operate fully funded retirement and health insurance businesses.

14. CBO, *Supplemental Data for the Congressional Budget Office's Long-Term Budget Outlook.*

15. Office of Management Budget (OMB), *Budget Baselines, Historical Data, and Alternatives for the Future,* January 1993.

16. A rising ratio of budget deficits–to–GDP also indicates a rising ratio of national debt–to–GDP. Note, however, that rising deficits may lead to a falling ratio of national debt–to–GDP whenever the rate of GDP growth exceeds the rate of growth in the deficit.

17. Data obtained from the U.S. Treasury, http://www.treasurydirect.gov/govt/reports/pd/pd_accountrpt.htm.

18. CBO, *Supplemental Data for the Congressional Budget Office's Long-Term Budget Outlook*. Predictions are for what CBO calls its "alternative," and generally more realistic, scenario.

19. U.S. Treasury, Monthly Statement of the Public Debt of the United States.

20. Data from first quarter of 2009 obtained from *Economic Report of the President, 2010,* http://www.whitehouse.gov/administration/eop/cea/economic-report-of-the-President.

21. Net interest predictions obtained from CBO, *Supplemental Data for the Congressional Budget Office's Long-Term Budget Outlook.*

22. Ibid.

23. An accounting rule confounds our ability to assess budget deficits. Surpluses in Social Security and Medicare accounts lower, dollar-for-dollar, budget deficits of the federal government in the same year! Future unfunded liabilities therefore lower the difference between spending and tax revenues and make the budget deficit appear smaller than otherwise. But, recall that revenues associated with social insurance surpluses represent future unfunded liabilities. Unfortunately, this accounting rule distorts accounting of all liabilities incurred through today's budgetary policies thus confusing citizens about the true nature of their future liabilities.

24. James M. Buchanan, *Public Principles of Public Debt* (Homewood, Ill.: Irwin, 1958).

25. James M. Buchanan and Richard E. Wagner, *Democracy in Deficit: The Political Legacy of Lord Keynes* (New York: Academic Press, 1977).

26. Milton Friedman is often associated with this hypothesis. See, for example, Milton Friedman, *Tax Limitation, Inflation and the Role of Government* (Dallas, Tex.: Fisher Institute, 1978). This hypothesis is also called the "tax-spend hypothesis."

27. Friedman, *Tax Limitation, Inflation and the Role of Government,* 5.

28. Neela Manage and Michael L. Marlow, "The Causal Relation between Federal Expenditures and Receipts," *Southern Economic Journal* 7 (January 1986): 17–729; Paul R. Blackley, "Causality between Revenues

and Expenditures and the Size of the Federal Budget," *Public Finance Quarterly* 14 (April 1986): 139–56; and Rati Ram, "Additional Evidence on Causality between Government Revenue and Government Expenditure," *Southern Economic Journal* 54 (January 1988): 763–69.

29. Previous discussion showed that fewer income earners pay income taxes: the top 50 percent of income earners paid 97 percent of income taxes and one-third of all tax returns in 2007 owed no income taxes.

30. Sara Murray, "Obstacle to Deficit Cutting: A Nation on Entitlements," *Wall Street Journal,* September 15, 2010.

Chapter 10: More Efficient and Fairer Taxation

1. Congressional Budget Office, *An Analysis of the President's Budgetary Proposals for Fiscal Year 2011,* March 2010, http://www.cbo.gov/ftpdocs/112xx/doc11280/03–24-apb.pdf. Noncorporate business income is taxed under personal income. Recall that social insurance taxes are taxes on payroll.

2. The top rate is scheduled to rise to 39.6 percent in 2011.

3. Take-home pay is actually smaller once state and local income taxes are factored in.

4. Scott A. Hodge, "Tax Burden of Top 1% Now Exceeds That of Bottom 95%," Tax Foundation Policy Blog, July 29, 2009, http://www.taxfoundation.org/blog/show/24944.html.

5. Scott A. Hodge, "States Vary Widely in Number of Tax Filers with No Income Tax Liability," Tax Foundation Fiscal Fact No. 229, Washington, D.C., May 24, 2010, http://www.taxfoundation.org/research/show/26336.html.

6. Taxpayer Advocate Service, *The 2008 Annual Report to Congress—Volume One,* Internal Revenue Service. This section on complexity draws heavily from this publication, http://www.irs.gov/pub/irs-utl/08_tas_arc_intro_toc_msp.pdf.

7. "The Joy of Tax," *The Economist,* April 8, 2010.

8. Brookings Institution, *Aggregate AMT Projections and Recent History, 1970–2020,* Urban-Brookings Tax Policy Center Microsimulation Model (versions 0304–3, 1006–1, 0309–1, 0509–2), athttp://www.taxpolicycenter.org/numbers/Content/PDF/T09–0385.pdf.

9. The literature on flat taxes begins with Robert E. Hall and Alvin Rabushka, *The Flat Tax* (Stanford, Calif.: Hoover Institution Press, 1985).

10. In 1996 Steve Forbes proposed a flat tax of 17 percent on all personal and corporate earned income. Exemptions were allowed for unearned income such as capital gains, pensions, inheritance, and savings. Forbes also exempted income under $36,000 for a family of four from taxation. See Steve Forbes, *Flat Tax Revolution* (Washington, D.C.: Regnery Publishing, 2005).

11. "Dues and Don'ts," *The Economist,* August 12, 2010.

12. Internal Revenue Service, *IRS Updates Tax Gap Estimates,* IR-2006–028, February 14, 2006, http://www.irs.gov/newsroom/article/0,id= 154496,00.html.

13. Suzanne Daley, "Greek Wealth Is Everywhere but Tax Forms," *New York Times,* May 2, 2010.

14. Hodge, "Tax Burden of Top 1% Now Exceeds That of Bottom 95%."

15. Hodge, "States Vary Widely in Number of Tax Filers with No Income Tax Liability."

16. Federal Advisory Panel on Federal Tax Reform, "Simple, Fair, and Pro-Growth: Proposals to Fix America's Tax System," November 2005, http://govinfo.library.unt.edu/taxreformpanel/.

17. Editorial, "Europe's VAT Lessons," *Wall Street Journal,* April 15, 2010.

18. Michael L. Roberts, Cassie Bradley, and Peggy Hite, "Understanding Attitudes Toward Progressive Taxation," *Public Opinion Quarterly* 58 (1994): 165–90.

Chapter 11: Improving Government

1. Restricting the amount of scrutiny has also been enabled by creating entitlement status for Social Security, Medicare, and Medicaid programs that effectively "bake into the cake" their growth without annual budget deliberations.

2. "False Expectations. The Historic Infrastructure Investment That Wasn't," *The Economist,* October 21, 2010.

3. OECD, *Factbook 2010: Economic, Environmental and Social Statistics,* 2010, http://lbib.de/OECD-Factbook-2010-Economic-Environmental-and-Social-Statistics-66516.

4. W. Kurt Hauser, "The Tax and Revenue Equation," *Wall Street Journal,* March 25, 1993.

5. David Joulfaian and Michael L. Marlow, "The Relationship between On Budget and Off Budget Government," *Economics Letters* 35 (1991): 307–10.

6. Nicole V. Crain and W. Mark Crain, *"The Impact of Regulatory Costs on Small Firms,"* Office of Advocacy, U.S. Small Business Administration, 2010, http://www.sba.gov/sites/default/files/The_Impact_of%20_Regulatory_Costs_of_Small%20Firms.pdf. The regulatory cost per employee for small businesses (fewer than 20 employees) was $10,585, compared to $7,454 for medium firms (between 20 and 499 employees) and $7,755 for large firms. They partially blame the decline of small manufacturing on high regulatory costs since they are more likely to close or reallocate activity than larger businesses. Of course, all businesses seek to shift expenses of complying with regulatory requirements onto customers and workers too.

7. U.S. Department of Transportation, "Cash for Clunkers Wraps Up with Nearly 700,000 Car Sales and Increased Fuel Efficiency, U.S. Transportation Secretary LaHood Declares Program 'Wildly Successful,'" Press Release, August, 26, 2009, http://www.dot.gov/affairs/2009/dot13309.htm.

8. Robert J. Barro and Charles J. Redlick, "Macroeconomic Effects from Government Purchases and Taxes," NBER Working Paper No. 15369, September 2009.

9. Lawrence B. Lindsey, "Did the Stimulus Stimulate?" *The Weekly Standard,* August 16, 2010.

10. Kate Andersen Brower and Nicholas Johnston, "Obama Says Auto Industry 'Growing Stronger,' Creating Jobs," *Bloomberg,* July 30, 2010, http://www.bloomberg.com/news/2010–07–30/obama-tells-detroit-auto-workers-industry-creating-jobs-after-u-s-bailout.html.

11. Randall Smith and Sharon Terlep, "GM Could Be Free of Taxes for Years," *Wall Street Journal,* November 3, 2010.

12. Tony Jackson, "GM Is Just a Hedge Fund in Disguise," *Financial Times,* August 22, 2010.

13. Congressional Budget Office, *Supplemental Data for the Congressional Budget Office's Long-Term Budget Outlook,* June 2010. Projections are for 2011–2015 and it is assumed no inflation takes place over those same years, http://www.cbo.gov/doc.cfm?index=11579.

14. Ibid.

15. Gerald Prante, "Summary of Latest Federal Individual Income Tax Data," Tax Foundation Fiscal Fact No. 183, Washington, D.C., July 2009, http://www.taxfoundation.org/news/show/250.html.

16. Scott A. Hodge, "Surge of 'Nonpayers' Will Be Part of Bush Tax Legacy," Tax Foundation Fiscal Fact No. 202, Washington, D.C.,

December 4, 2009, http://www.taxfoundation.org/publications/show/25586.html.

17. *Analytical Perspectives Budget of the U.S. Government Office of Management and Budget, Fiscal Year 2011,* http://www.budget.gov.

18. S. Mitra Kalita and Nick Timiraos, "Homeowner Perks Under Fire," *Wall Street Journal,* December 16, 2010.

19. Michael J. Boskin, "Time to Junk the Corporate Tax," *Wall Street Journal,* May 6, 2010.

20. This would eliminate the corporation tax by simply taxing income once at the level of personal income.

21. Michael L. Roberts, Cassie Bradley, and Peggy Hite, "Understanding Attitudes Toward Progressive Taxation," *Public Opinion Quarterly* 58 (1994): 165–90.

22. "The Joy of Tax," *The Economist,* April 8, 2010.

23. John D. McKinnon, Gary Fields, and Laura Saunders, "'Temporary' Tax Code Puts Nation in a Lasting Bind," *Wall Street Journal,* December 14, 2010.

24. Karen A. Campbell and John L. Ligon, "The Economic Impact of a 25 Percent Corporate Income Tax Rate," WebMemo No. 3070, Heritage Foundation, December 2, 2010, http://www.heritage.org/Research/Reports/2010/12/The-Economic-Impact-of-a-25-Percent-Corporate-Income-Tax-Rate.

Index